Lecture Notes in Computer Science 10773

Commenced Publication in 1973
Founding and Former Series Editors:
Gerhard Goos, Juris Hartmanis, and Jan van Leeuwen

More information about this series at http://www.springer.com/series/7407

Dalibor Klusáček · Walfredo Cirne
Narayan Desai (Eds.)

Job Scheduling Strategies for Parallel Processing

21st International Workshop, JSSPP 2017
Orlando, FL, USA, June 2, 2017
Revised Selected Papers

 Springer

Editors
Dalibor Klusáček
CESNET
Prague
Czech Republic

Walfredo Cirne
Google
Mountain View, CA
USA

Narayan Desai
Google
Seattle, WA
USA

ISSN 0302-9743   ISSN 1611-3349 (electronic)
Lecture Notes in Computer Science
ISBN 978-3-319-77397-1   ISBN 978-3-319-77398-8 (eBook)
https://doi.org/10.1007/978-3-319-77398-8

Library of Congress Control Number: 2018934363

LNCS Sublibrary: SL1 – Theoretical Computer Science and General Issues

Printed on acid-free paper

This Springer imprint is published by the registered company Springer International Publishing AG part of Springer Nature
The registered company address is: Gewerbestrasse 11, 6330 Cham, Switzerland

Preface

This volume contains the papers presented at the 21st Workshop on Job Scheduling Strategies for Parallel Processing that was held in Orlando (FL), USA, on June 2, 2017, in conjunction with the 31st IEEE International Parallel and Distributed Processing Symposium (IPDPS 2017). The proceedings of previous workshops are also available from Springer as LNCS volumes 949, 1162, 1291, 1459, 1659, 1911, 2221, 2537, 2862, 3277, 3834, 4376, 4942, 5798, 6253, 7698, 8429, 8828, and 10353.

This year 20 papers were submitted to the workshop, of which we accepted ten. All submitted papers went through a complete review process, with the full version being read and evaluated by an average of four reviewers. We would like to especially thank our Program Committee members and additional reviewers for their willingness to participate in this effort and their excellent, detailed reviews.

From the very beginning, JSSPP has strived to balance practice and theory in its program. This combination has been repeatedly shown to provide a rich environment for technical debate about scheduling approaches. This year, building on this long tradition, JSSPP also welcomed papers providing descriptions of *open problems in large-scale scheduling*. A lack of real-world data often hampers the ability of the research community to engage with scheduling problems in a way that has real world impact. Our goal in this new venue was to build a bridge between the production and research worlds, in order to facilitate direct discussions, collaborations, and impact.

It was our pleasure that out of the ten accepted papers, two directly address the novel "open problems" track, sharing valuable insights into production systems, their workloads, usage patterns, and corresponding scheduling challenges. In their paper, Allcock et al. present details on job scheduling at the Argonne Leadership Computing Facility (ALCF). The paper described the specific scheduling goals and constraints, analyzed the workload traces from the petascale supercomputer Mira, and discussed the upcoming challenges at ALCF. Klusáček and Parák present a detailed analysis of a shared virtualized computing infrastructure that is used to provide grid and cloud computing services. In their work, they analyzed the differences between cloud and grid workloads and addressed some of the problems the infrastructure is facing, such as (un)fairness or problematic resource reclaiming.

In 1995, JSSPP was the venue where the seminal and widely used backfilling algorithm was presented for the first time. Now, 22 years after its introduction, many researchers are still focusing on improving its performance. This year we had two papers that directly focus on improving the performance of backfilling. Lelong, Reis, and Trystram propose a framework to evaluate the impact of reordering job queues using various policies in order to improve on average/maximum wait time. N'takpé and Suter evaluate a model where a part of the job workload is not sensitive to waiting as long as it is completed before a given deadline. This allowed them to perform some interesting optimizations for regular jobs in order to decrease the average wait time and slowdown.

Wang et al. focus on a somehow similar problem of supporting priority execution for high-priority real-time jobs while minimizing the delays for ordinary workloads in a classic batch scheduling scenario. Their solution investigated several techniques starting from a plain high-priority queue to somewhat more advanced approaches including pre-emption and application checkpointing. Friese et al. present a detailed methodology using a genetic algorithm for cost-efficient resource selection when scheduling complex scientific workflows with uncertainties in forecasted demands on distributed computing platforms such as "pay-per-use" public clouds.

Lohrmann et al. focus on optimizing the execution of complex I/O critical simulations that are performed using iterative workflows. To minimize I/O delays, in situ processing is commonly used to minimize the need for time-consuming disk operations. For this purpose the authors extended the Henson cooperative multi-tasking system that enables multiple distinct codes to run on the same node and share memory to speed up computations. Their major extension is a scheduler for Henson, which is used to schedule iterative trials of a complex simulation. Trials results are used as an input into a relaxed (computationally cheap) surrogate model that generates new, refined parameters for consecutive expensive trials. This iterative approach is used to increase the chance that the expensive simulation converges quickly.

While the majority of batch schedulers are based on job queues, there are few honorable mentions of pure planning systems, where each job is planned ahead upon its arrival, i.e., a complete schedule about the future resource usage is computed and made available to the users. In his paper, Axel Keller presents a detailed description of such a system called OpenCCS, focusing in detail on data structures and a heuristic that are used to plan and map arbitrary resources in complex combinations while applying time-dependent constraints.

Two papers focus on evaluating the system performance using newly proposed simulators and benchmarks, addressing the needs of current HPC systems, where both the workload and the infrastructure become more complex and heterogeneous, thus urgently requiring more advanced scheduling approaches. Rodrigo et al. propose a novel scheduler simulation framework (ScSF) that provides capabilities for workload modeling and generation, system simulation (using embedded Slurm simulator), comparative workload analysis, and experiment orchestration. This simulator is designed to be run over a distributed computing infrastructure facilitating large-scale tests. Lopez et al. present the Dynamic Job Scheduling Benchmark (DJSB), which is a novel tool allowing system administrators to evaluate the impact of dynamic resource (re)allocations between running jobs on the overall system performance. They use a set of experiments from the MareNostrum supercomputer to demonstrate how DJSB can be used to evaluate the impact of different dynamic resource management approaches on each job/application individually, as well as the overall dynamics of the system.

Enjoy the reading!

We hope you can join us at the next JSSPP workshop, this time in Vancouver, Canada, on May 25, 2018.

November 2017

Walfredo Cirne
Narayan Desai
Dalibor Klusáček

Organization

Workshop Organizers

Walfredo Cirne   Google, USA
Narayan Desai   Google, USA
Dalibor Klusáček   CESNET, Czech Republic

Program Committee

Henri Casanova   University of Hawaii at Manoa, USA
Julita Corbalan   Barcelona Supercomputing Center, Spain
Carlo Curino   Microsoft, USA
Hyeonsang Eom   Seoul National University, South Korea
Dick Epema   Delft University of Technology, The Netherlands
Dror Feitelson   Hebrew University, Israel
Liana Fong   IBM T. J. Watson Research Center, USA
Eitan Frachtenberg   Facebook, USA
Alfredo Goldman   University of Sao Paulo, USA
Allan Gottlieb   New York University, USA
Zhiling Lan   Illinois Institute of Technology, USA
Bill Nitzberg   Altair, USA
P-O Östberg   Umeå University, Sweden
Larry Rudolph   Two Sigma, USA
Uwe Schwiegelshohn   TU Dortmund University, Germany
Leonel Sousa   Universidade de Lisboa, Portugal
Mark Squillante   IBM, USA
Wei Tang   Google, USA
Ramin Yahyapour   University of Göttingen, Germany

Additional Reviewers

Helder Duarte
João F. D. Guerreiro
Diogo Marques
Jiaqi Yan
Xu Yang

Contents

Experience and Practice of Batch Scheduling on Leadership Supercomputers at Argonne

William Allcock[1], Paul Rich[1], Yuping Fan[2], and Zhiling Lan[2]($\boxtimes$)

[1] Argonne National Laboratory, Argonne, IL, USA
{allcock,richp}@anl.gov
[2] Illinois Institute of Technology, Chicago, IL, USA
yfan22@hawk.iit.edu, lan@iit.edu

Abstract. The mission of the DOE Argonne Leadership Computing Facility (ALCF) is to accelerate major scientific discoveries and engineering breakthroughs for humanity by designing and providing world-leading computing facilities in partnership with the computational science community. The ALCF operates supercomputers that are generally amongst the Top 5 fastest machines in the world. Specifically, ALCF is looking for the science that is either too big to run anywhere else, or it would take so long as to be impractical (i.e., "capability jobs"). At ALCF, batch scheduling plays a critical role for achieving a set of site goals within a set of constraints. While system utilization is an important goal at ALCF, its largest mission constraint is to enable extreme scale parallel jobs to take precedence. In this paper, we will describe the specific scheduling goals and constraints, analyze the workload traces collected in 2013–2017 from the 48-rack petascale supercomputer Mira, and discuss the upcoming scheduling challenges at ALCF.

1 Introduction

Argonne National Laboratory [1] is a U.S. Department of Energy (DOE) general research laboratory. Argonne performs research in a broad range of disciplines and operates several user facilities [2] that provide access to resources that are generally too large and expensive for universities or commercial companies to operate. One of those facilities is the Argonne Leadership Computing Facility [3] (ALCF). The ALCF fields supercomputers that are generally amongst the top 5 fastest machines in the world, as rated by the Top500 [4] site. From the ALCF web site:

> The Argonne Leadership Computing Facility's (ALCF) mission is to **accelerate major scientific discoveries and engineering breakthroughs** for humanity by designing and providing world-leading computing facilities in partnership with the computational science community.

Unlike most divisions at Argonne, the ALCF's primary focus is not on **doing** research, though we do some, but is on **enabling** research by operating a supercomputer facility for researchers around the world. Specifically, our mission is

© Springer International Publishing AG, part of Springer Nature 2018
D. Klusáček et al. (Eds.): JSSPP 2017, LNCS 10773, pp. 1–24, 2018.
https://doi.org/10.1007/978-3-319-77398-8_1

to enable the solution to the largest computational challenges, what we refer to as "capability jobs". We are looking for the science that is either too big to run anywhere else, or it would take so long as to be impractical. Access to ALCF resources is available via three different programs:

- Innovative and Novel Computational Impact on Theory and Experiment (INCITE) Program [5] (60% of the core-hours)
- Advanced Scientific Computing Research (ASCR) Leadership Computing Challenge (ALCC) Program [6] (30% of the core-hours)
- The Directors Discretionary (DD) program [7] (10% of the core-hours)

Note that these percentages are an allocation time constraint, but not a scheduling constraint. While they do generally end up split approximately along those lines simply because of the allocations, the scheduler does not track usage by program, nor does it use that to influence scheduling decisions.

The rest of this paper is organized as follows. We start by introducing Mira [14] and Cobalt at Argonne in Sect. 2. Section 3 describes the goals and constraints on scheduling at the ALCF. Section 4 describes the current scheduling algorithm used at ALCF. Section 5 presents our analysis on Mira log and our key observations. Section 6 describes the upcoming challenges at Argonne. Finally, we conclude the paper in Sect. 7.

2   Mira: The 48-Rack Blue Gene/Q

Mira is a is a 10-petaflops IBM Blue Gene/Q system [8] installed at Argonne National Laboratory. It is a 48-rack system, equipped with 786,432 cores and 768 TB of memory. Every 16 cores form a node and 512 nodes in a $4 \times 4 \times 4 \times 4 \times 2$ structure are grouped into a midplane. Each rack consists of two midplanes and the system has 48 racks. Mira was ranked ninth in the Top500 list in November 2017 [4]. It features 5D torus interconnection, which reduces the average number of hops and latency between compute nodes and thus achieves high efficient computation and saves the energy for transporting data across long distance. The smallest partition size on Mira is 512 nodes. Jobs smaller than the minimum partition run exclusively on one partition.

Mira logs record scheduling events of batch jobs on Mira including requested and utilized resources (i.e. requested time, used time, requested nodes count, used nodes count), timestamps of major scheduling events (i.e. submit time, start time, end time), and job execution environment (i.e. machine partitions). Table 1 shows the basic information about the Mira logs. There are 554 projects and 1054 users submitted jobs on Mira. 283,385 jobs were submitted during this period and approximately 70% of jobs exited system normally. Figure 1 shows the number of job submitted and core hours used per month.

The information in logs are useful for data analysis and new scheduler evaluation. Data analysis help administrators learn about machines' status and identify problems in a system. To evaluate a new scheduling policy, logs can be used

Table 1. Basic information of the job log

Period	April 9, 2013–January 31, 2017
Total number of jobs	283,385
Total number of projects	554
Total number of users	1,053
Percentage of jobs exit system normally	70.464915221342%

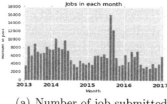

(a) Number of job submitted

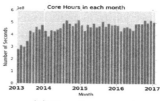

(b) Core hours used

Fig. 1. Number of jobs submitted and total core hours used in each month.

directly to generate the input workload for trace-based simulation. In simulations, jobs arrive according to timestamps in a trace. In order to schedule jobs, simulators require each job providing requested time and node.

3   ALCF Goals and Constraints

Schedulers and scheduling policies exist to achieve a set of goals within a set of constraints. Conceptually, that seems obvious, but enumerating them is not necessarily straightforward, accomplishing them is difficult, and because of the goal to enable capability jobs, the ALCFs are somewhat different than most.

The most obvious constraints are the metrics a facility is required to report on to its department, funding agency, etc. For the ALCF, the scheduling related items are:

- Total core hours delivered: This is based on theoretical hours (number of cores in the machine multiplied by the hours in a year) multiplied by factors for availability and utilization.
- Core hours delivered to the INCITE program as described above.
- Capability hours: A job is considered capability if it uses ≥20% of the nodes in the machine for a single scheduler job. Each year a minimum percentage of our jobs that have to be capability is agreed upon with our sponsors.
- Utilization: Utilization is reported, but there is no set minimum. Where many facilities will have utilization as the primary metric, the ALCF sacrifices some utilization in order to prioritize capability jobs.

Until recently, ALCF has been fielding IBM Blue Gene [8] machines, though the most recent machine is a Cray XC40 machine based on the Intel Knights

Landing many core processors. More than the processor, one could argue that what sets high-end supercomputers apart are their networks. They generally have proprietary, low latency, high bandwidth networks. The Blue Gene series runs an IBM proprietary torus network. The Blue Gene/P series had a 3D torus, the Blue Gene/Q series, including the ALCF's current production machine named Mira, has a 5D torus, and the new Cray has a dragonfly network topology.

This leads to our first constraint: The architecture of the machine itself. The Blue Gene is a very unique machine. Like all things, it has its advantages and disadvantages. The Blue Gene torus network is dynamically programmable enabling every job to have its own dedicated, electrically isolated network. This means practically zero performance jitter during communications, and while not a significant concern on an open science machine, zero chance for packet snooping for the security conscious. However, it does put constraints on node allocations. One of those constraints is that you cannot pick any random set of nodes for a given job. The nodes must be allocated in "partitions" which are controlled by the torus cabling. This generally means contiguous nodes, though 4K partitions can be built as 2K nodes, skip 2K nodes, and then the other 2K nodes. Nor can you allocate a single node. The Blue Gene has the concept of a pset, which is a set of compute nodes, and it its associated I/O node(s). On Mira, the ALCF's BG/Q, due to the I/O node configuration the pset size is 128 nodes, which is physically the smallest allocation possible. Additionally, due to the ALCF mission to run large jobs, by policy, as well as for resource isolation considerations, nothing smaller than a midplane, which is a contiguous group of 512 nodes, is allowed. See Fig. 2.

These constraints simplify the scheduling. They effectively reduce a 49,152 node BG/Q to a "96 allocation unit" system, where each "allocation unit" is a 512 node midplane. It also makes fragmentation much less of an issue. Due to the torus cabling design, only specific arrangements of midplanes are allowed to from larger partitions. Additionally, due to the network partitioning and isolation scheme, links are allocated to one and only one active partition at a time. To deal with this, the torus connections are considered a first class resource that needs to

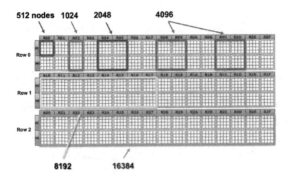

Fig. 2. Partitions on Mira.

be scheduled as well. To schedule a job, you not only needed the number of nodes, but those nodes needed to have the appropriate torus network connections.

Another hardware constraint that was different between the BG/P and the BG/Q was where the network hardware was at and how it could be managed. On the BG/P there is a separate link card that has all of the midplane to midplane network connectivity on it. The implication of this is that if a node failed, a node board (containing 32 nodes) could be taken offline to replace the node, and then brought back into production without affecting the network traffic of any other job. However, on the BG/Q, the torus optics are on the node boards and it has the concept of "pass through" such that a job not using the compute nodes on that particular node board could be using the network optics. This makes maintenance much more impactful. On the BG/P, when a node dies, the job dies, and the system automatically takes that node board offline. The scheduler would pick that up and automatically not schedule jobs on it, and the admin could immediately go replace the node if he chose. Similarly, on the BG/Q the node board is taken offline and the scheduler won't schedule on it, but the admin must wait for any job using pass through to finish before they can change a node. This lead to the addition of an extension to reservation support, such that you could choose to reserve only the compute nodes, or the compute nodes and the optics links. This avoids scheduling any future jobs that use the pass through links which could, theoretically, infinitely delay replacement of the compute nodes.

A second constraint came from the selection of projects that ran on our machines. We were supporting computer science projects doing operating systems research (Plan9 [9] and ZeptoOS [10]). This required us to be able to boot the Blue Gene into an alternate operating system. As an alternative OS could involve an IO node image as well [24], resource isolation to the IO node is also required.

These two constraints, the Blue Gene hardware and the need to boot alternate operating systems, drove the selection of scheduler software. ALCF uses an Argonne written and maintained scheduler called Cobalt. It's origins were from a DOE program called the "Scalable Systems Software Project" in the late 1990s, which later went on to become the SciDAC Scalable Systems Software ISIC [12]. When the ALCF was formed, the only scheduler that supported the Blue Gene was IBMs LoadLeveler, but it could not support alternate OSes. As a result, the ALCF decided to modify Cobalt [11] to support those two requirements.

3.1 Policy and Mission Constraints

For many facilities, utilization is the number one goal. While the ALCF considers utilization, its larger mission constraint of enabling extreme scale parallel jobs takes precedence. The ALCF prioritizes jobs that take up a significant fraction of the machine, up to and including jobs that consume the entire machine. In facilities that optimize purely for utilization, large jobs can be blocked for significant periods of time because smaller jobs monopolize the resources. In theory, if utilization were the only metric, a full machine job would never run unless it was the only job in the queue. Fair share algorithms help ameliorate "large job starvation" delays, but given that running the larger jobs is our primary mission, we needed a better way.

4 Description of the Current Cobalt Scheduling Algorithm

Cobalt does not attempt to construct a time-based schedule [23], nor does ALCF run a "fair share" algorithm. Instead, Cobalt periodically applies a scheduling "utility function" that calculates a priority increment for each job in the queue. The jobs are sorted into priority order and sets of resources, some of which may be in use at that point, are selected to run the highest priority jobs. Cobalt will then begin to "drain" those resources to make room for the jobs, backfilling jobs where it can. This draining obviously hurts utilization, but supports the mission to run large-scale "capability scale" jobs. When the facility first began production operations back in 2008 the utilization was at approximately 70%. Over time, scheduling algorithms have improved, ALCF has educated users and helped scale the computational algorithms, and policy adjustments have been made that have improved the utilization to approximately 90%.

Resource selection/allocation is based on network topology, heuristics based on what resources are in use, and when various resources are scheduled to be available. On the Blue Gene/P platform a static-partitioning scheme was required, using site-specified predefined partitions. On the Blue Gene/Q platform, a dynamic, on the fly, partition construction scheme could be used, or a more traditional static partitioning scheme could be used. The ALCF chose to use a hierarchical static partitioning scheme that utilized some features of the system wiring to its advantage. For instance, because of the unique Blue Gene Torus design, there can be a natural regular hierarchical structure to node partitions. A 32K node partition consists of two 16K node partitions, each of which consist of two 8K node partitions, and so forth. The implication of this is that once a small job, say a 1K node job, is started, it not only consumes those nodes, but it blocks all the larger partitions it is a member of. For that reason, Cobalt will preferentially select partitions that minimize the number of additional larger partitions that are blocked. Due to the constraints imposed by block-exclusive wiring, fragmentation of the torus is costly in terms of the impact on the throughput of larger jobs, which is compounded due to a need to favor workloads involving large jobs.

Generally, all jobs that are not part of user requested reservations are submitted to the default queue. These jobs are then run through a "job router" which applies scheduling policy to place them into one of three queues based on size and requested wall time:

- Prod-capability: Any job that requests $\geq 20\%$ of the nodes is routed to this queue up to the maximum run time of 24 h. This queue has access to all of the nodes on the machine. Ideally, every job would meet these criteria since these "capability" jobs are the ALCFs primary mission. Capability class core-hours is one of our reportable metrics.

- Prod-short: Any job that requests <20% of the nodes and has a requested wall time of ≤6 h is routed to this queue. This queue has access to all of the nodes on the machine. These are not capability jobs, but they are also relatively short so will block larger jobs for a shorter period of time.
- Prod-long: Any job that requests <20% of the nodes and has a requested wall time >6 h is routed to this queue. This queue only has access to 1/3 of the nodes on the machine. These jobs are small and long and so can block larger jobs for a significant length of time and thus are very disruptive our desired goal of running larger capability jobs. By restricting them to 1/3 of the machine, we guarantee that we have at least one 32K partition, and all of its sub-partitions, available to the prod-capability queue.

There are two corner cases that the Blue Gene architecture brings to this. First, the 20% limit for being considered capability was set when the ALCF had a Blue Gene/P, called Intrepid [13]. Intrepid was a 40K node machine and 20% of that was 8K nodes, which was the size of one of the torus partitions. However, when the ALCF installed Mira, a Blue Gene/Q, it was 48 racks and 20% of that was 9.6K, which was not a supported partition size. To deal with this, a "split" capability metric was developed. A metric for both 8K nodes and 16K nodes was set and the weighted average of the two is 20%. The second corner case deals with jobs that request irregular size partitions. The partition sizes are generally powers of two with the exceptions of 12K (25% of the machine) and 24K (50% of the machine) partitions. In Fig. 3, a pictorial depiction of the queues, prod-capability appears to be at 4096 rather than 8192. The line is at 4097, because if a job were to request 4097 nodes, Cobalt would have to allocate an 8K partition in order to accommodate it. For purposes of queue routing, a 4097 node job will get routed to the prod capability queue, but for purposes of the capability metric, only jobs that request ≥8K nodes qualify.

While the job is being routed to its queue, a site-specific "filter" script sets an initial score for the job. This is based on the project that the job belongs to, with INCITE and ALCC projects getting a more favorable initial score, and

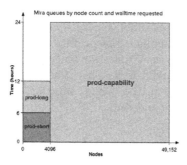

Fig. 3. Mira queues by node count and walltime requested.

the project's allocation status. Projects that have exceeded their allocation, in addition to being routed to backfill, are given a starting score that diminishes proportionally to how much time they have used beyond their initial allocation. Jobs in the backfill queue have their score capped to below that of any production queue job. After that, during each "scheduling iteration", which is currently 15 s, a "utility function" is executed for each job. This utility function calculates a priority increment that is added to the current job priority. The jobs are then ordered based on priority, and resource allocations are made to run the highest priority job first. The heart of the current utility function in use is:

$$\frac{(queued\_time - hold\_time)^2}{score\_wall\_time^3} * \frac{size}{MAX\_SIZE} * project\_weight \qquad (1)$$

Where

- $(queued\_time - hold\_time)$ is referred to as the eligible time; The length of the time that job has been in the queue and it was eligible to be considered to run.
- $score\_wall\_time$ is the requested wall time normalized to be a minimum of one hour and a maximum of 12 h.
- $size$ is the number of nodes requested.
- MAX_SIZE is the total number of nodes in the machine (48K or 49152 for Mira).
- $project\_weight$ is an arbitrary value that is based on the project/account being charged that defaults to 1.0, but which the facility can adjust if there is a reason to prefer or retard the score increment for that project.

  The general concepts behind this algorithm are as follows:

- The fraction of the machine $size/MAX\_SIZE$ is a multiplier, so larger jobs will gain priority faster and will tend toward the top of the priority which meets the goal of enabling large jobs to run. This dominates the early part of score accrual and "stratifies" jobs.
- The longer the requested wall time, the longer the user should be willing to wait for it to run. This is handled in the first term of the equation:

$$\frac{(queued\_time - hold\_time)^2}{score\_wall\_time^3} \qquad (2)$$

Once the jobs eligible wait time ($queued\_time - hold\_time$) squared exceeds the requested wall time cubed, the priority growth increases rapidly. The assumption about longer wait times for longer wall times is psychology and arbitrary, but it has worked well. This time factor also provides an anti-starvation factor for jobs in the queue, ensuring that a job will eventually reach the front of the line and run.

4.1   Negative Accounts and Overburn

ALCF has a variety of policies regarding what to do when an allocation reaches zero. For Director's Discretionary accounts, they are blocked from running.

If they want to continue running they must request another allocation. INCITE and ALCC projects may continue to run, but only in backfill. There is an exception referred to as "overburn". During the third quarter of the allocation year (INCITE is on the calendar year; ALCC is July 1st to June 30th), ALCF allows accounts to run in the prod-capability queue at up to 200% of their allocation before all of their jobs are forced to backfill. Jobs that would go to prod-short or prod-long still get routed to backfill under this policy, even in an overburn period.

Overburn helps to smooth out the delivery time. We were finding that users were "hoarding" their allocations, causing them to wait until later in the year to perform their runs. As INCITE and ALCC allocations are "use or lose" at the end of their term, this would result in a rush at the end of the year and significant increases in user wait times. This policy incentivizes both earlier running, as users that have not used their allocations do not benefit from the policy, as well as the use of capability size jobs. Part of this incentive is that these capability runs get normal capability priority, in this case. We disable overburn during the fourth quarter of an allocation cycle so that projects that were late to start or otherwise have large percentages of their allocations remaining do not have to compete for priority against projects that have completed their allocations.

4.2   Big Run Mondays

The ALCF typically engages in preventative maintenance on its resources once every two weeks on Monday. During these periods no jobs run due to highly disruptive work that may be occurring on the resource itself, or on supporting infrastructure of the facility. As this necessitates draining the full machine's resources at the beginning of maintenance, we effectively open the machine for a full-machine job for "free". Before the machine is released back to normal operation, a set of capability-sized non-backfill, non-overburn jobs is selected and has their scores altered to be at the front of the queue. Scores are set such that the largest of the capability jobs run first, making the best use of this "free" drain of the system's resources.

4.3   Interactions with User Behavior

In some sense, scheduling algorithm and policy development are an ongoing "arms race" with the users of the system. Facilities are constantly receiving feedback from the users on issues they are seeing, new needs they might have, etc. This feedback may be direct via surveys or trouble tickets, or it may be indirect in how they interact with the scheduler. Everyone wants their results as fast as possible, and some users get extremely creative when trying to achieve that. Below we describe some of the user behaviors and how they were addressed.

4.3.1   Eligible Time vs. Queued Time

Originally the first term of the utility function was just $queued\_time^2$. However, we found that users were submitting dummy jobs and putting them on hold to let them accrue priority until they were ready to run the jobs. They would have all the right parameters, so the qalter fix above wouldn't discourage this, as exiting a hold does not cause a job to be requeued. The solution to that was to subtract the hold time so that we were using what we now refer to as eligible time in the first term.

4.3.2   Dependency Chaining

To actually complete the science, most science teams require many millions of core hours. To allow all projects to make incremental progress, maximum run times are established and the users must make their runs in pieces, writing out restart files, usually referred to as "check points", that the next job can use to pick up where the previous job left off.

Another common queue parameter is the "max queued" parameter. Even if thousands of jobs are required to complete an overall computation, only so many can be in the queue at once. This keeps the size of the queue manageable, but also prevents a science team from queuing up an entire years worth of work and having them all gaining priority, which would effectively allow them to monopolize the queue. Sometimes the jobs are independent and can run in parallel and one job failure has no impact on the other jobs, but other times, the jobs are steps in an overall workflow and they must proceed in sequence and the next one can only proceed if the previous one completes successfully. For the latter situation, we provide "dependency chaining". When you submit a job, you can specify another job ID that it depends on which places that job in a "dep hold" state. The scheduler will ensure they run in sequence and if a job fails, the scheduler will place the dependent job into a "dep fail" state until the user can fix the problem and re-run the failed job. A scheduling issue for this is that because subsequent jobs are in a hold state, they cannot accrue priority and it extends the total time to solution. To ameliorate this problem, Cobalt assigns the starting score of a dependent job to a facility configurable percentage (currently 50%) of the priority that the preceding job had when it started running. For instance, if job B depends on job A, and Job A had a priority of 200 when it started running, when it completes, the starting priority of Job B will be set to 100 (50% of 200). An exception to this is that should the jobs current priority be higher than the newly calculated dependency priority, the current priority is maintained.

4.3.3   Using Qalter to Game the System

Early on, some users would submit a job so as to maximize its score function and accrue priority as rapidly as possible, and then qalter it to the real job parameters. For instance, they might submit a full machine job maximizing the $size/MAX\_SIZE$ term. Additionally, they might set a wall time of 5 min which means that the priority would begin to grow superlinearly (quadratically) after only 11.2 min (square root of $5^3 = 11.2$; see the first term of the utility function described above). Then, just before it was ready to run, they would use the qalter command and modify the job parameters to what they really were, perhaps a 512 node job for 12 h. To discourage this type of behavior, we modified Cobalt so that any qalter command that would result in a change of queue (for instance, from prod-capability to prod-long in the example above) results in the jobs priority being reset to the starting default as if it were a new job submission.

4.3.4 Adding a Floor and Ceiling on the Wall Time Parameters in the Utility Function

In general, the behavior achieved with the current utility function accomplishes ALCF goals and usually behaves predictably. However, there were corner cases early on that required adjustments. One of them was regarding the *score_wall_time* parameter. The algorithm had been running stably, but utilization had dropped and ALCF began to get user complaints that the jobs start times were not behaving as expected. Investigation into this determined that mathematically, things were working as they should, but a recent change in max wall time from 12 to 24 h for capability jobs had an impact we had not anticipated. This resulted in situations where a preferred capability job would accrue score unusually slowly due to the very large denominator of the wait-time factor of the score function. Placing the 12 h ceiling allowed for a good turnaround on these longer jobs without unduly favoring them. The one-hour floor was placed due to very similar scenarios where a large, short job would get to the front of the queue very rapidly. In instances where a user may be debugging at scale or running some other high node count, but short duration workload we would end up in a pattern where a user would submit a short job, run the job, and then submit another soon after the job ended, resulting in a very unfavorable "sawtooth" drain pattern, causing a severe impact to utilization. The ceiling and the floor corrected these two issues.

4.3.5 Risks of High Initial Scores

Very early in the life of Mira, there was a need to significantly increase the throughput of some projects that had trouble initially getting started on the new platform. A policy change was implemented such that a job's initial score would depend not only on the queue, but the number of core hours left in the allocation. This would result in a very high initial score for any job in an "underburned" project. The following scenario would then happen:

1. A large, long job is the top priority and a set of resources is selected and begins to drain. This is hurting utilization, but that is expected and normal so far.
2. A small job is submitted from an unburned, favored, project.
3. After several hours of draining the machine for the large job, the small job enters ahead of, or soon passes the large job and becomes the top priority job. Because it is small and the scheduler had been draining, there is very likely an open resource, so the scheduler immediately starts the new top priority job (the small job). Once the small job is started, the large job is once again top priority, but now the partition is blocked by the small job, so a different partition is selected and it begins to drain.

This resulted in a loss of utilization, which, at the time was considered acceptable in light of the INCITE time delivery goal of the ALCF. This, however, had the side effect of making large, capability-sized jobs, very unfavorable on the system, in addition to user complaints of very unexpected scheduling behavior. Due to these negative effects, this initial score policy was reverted after the end of the INCITE year.

5   Mira Log Analysis and Key Observations

This section presents the results of our analysis on Mira logs from April 9, 2013 to January 31, 2017. We conduct our analysis on Mira logs from several aspects, such as queues, users, exit codes, modes, co-analysis with RAS logs, cycles, and account. Particularly, we provide job distribution on queues, exit codes, modes. We find two frequent users in Mira logs and examine the effect of their behavior on Mira. Next, we look for the correlations between exit codes and modes. Further, we analyze the Mira job logs with RAS logs. We provide users' weekly and daily submission cycles. Finally, we show statistics of overburn per month.

5.1   Queues

In this subsection, we explore jobs in prod-short, backfill, prod-capability, prod-long, and prod-1024-torus queues. We make the following observations.

Observation 1. *In Table 2, the number of jobs in prod-short queue is much more than other queues. The total core hours consumed by jobs in prod-capability is more than half of the core hours used by all jobs. On average, jobs in prod-long queue ran longest time (24907 s), while jobs in prod-capability queue used the most number of nodes (13530 nodes). In addition, jobs in prod-capability on average consume large core hours (656480).*

Observation 2. *In Table 2, jobs in prod-short queue have higher priority than jobs in backfill queue. Although jobs in backfill queue on average used less core hours than jobs in prod-short queue, the average wait time of the jobs in backfill queue is much higher than that of jobs in prod-short queue.*

Observation 3. *In Table 2, jobs in prod-capability queue have higher priority than jobs in prod-long queue. Jobs in prod-capability queue on average used more core hours than jobs in prod-long queue, their mean wait times are almost the same.*

Observation 4. *In Fig. 4, the total number of jobs submitted in each year decreases, whereas the total core hours used in each year increases. From Sep. 15, 2013 to Sep. 15, 2014, we observe that a large decrease in the submission of short jobs, while the number of jobs in backfill queue increases.*

Table 2. Statistic of queues

	Prod-short	Backfill	Prod-capability	Prod-long	Prod-1024-torus
Mean used nodes	1080	1043	13530	1253	1024
Mean wait seconds	45243	61279	278510	276839	17338
Mean walltime seconds	6754	4118	20151	39734	3499
Mean runtime seconds	4361	2789	12544	24907	14652
Mean used core hours	23082	16794	656480	137328	66687
Mean requested core hours	22406	16663	651597	33966	66687
Total used core hours	4289056697	883159087	13126325662	2221830694	149446510

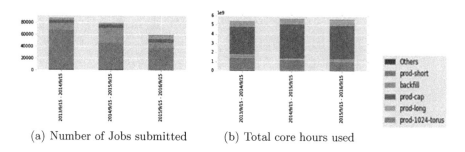

(a) Number of Jobs submitted   (b) Total core hours used

Fig. 4. Number of jobs and total core hours used by queues in each year.

5.2 Users

In this subsection, we analyze the Mira logs based on users. We analyze two frequent users on Mira.

5.2.1 User 15303315089691

Observation 5. *User 15303315089691 submitted most jobs in Mira. In Fig. 5, we can see from Aug. to Oct. in 2015, this user submitted more than 20,000 jobs in Mira. All the jobs submitted in this period of time queued in backfill queue and the job size is 512. In Fig. 6(a), the submissions of user 15303315089691 lead to large increase in the total number of jobs submitted to Mira during that period. However, because these jobs are small jobs ran short times, they did not affect the total core hours used in Mira too much as shown in Fig. 6(b).*

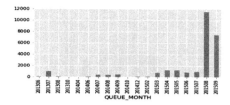

Fig. 5. Number of jobs submitted by user 15303315089691 in each month.

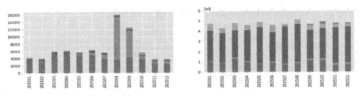

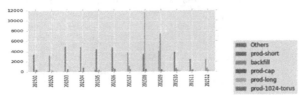

(a) Number of jobs submitted in each queue in each month

(b) Core hours used in each queue in each month

(c) Average wait time of jobs in each queue in each month

Fig. 6. The correlation between runtime, used nodes and queues.

Observation 6. *In Fig. 6(c), we can see that large increase in the number of jobs submitted to backfill queue only affect the average wait time of jobs in backfill queue. The average wait time of jobs in backfill queue increases significantly, but there is no evidence showing that other queues were affected by the surge.*

5.2.2 User 32764951387776

Observation 7. *In Fig. 7, user 32764951387776 submitted 48 capability jobs in April 2016. As shown in Figs. 8 and 9, the large submission by this user leads to less total number of jobs submitted in April 2016, but the total core hours used in that month increases. Therefore, large jobs can boost system utilization.*

Observation 8. *In Fig. 10, increasing number of jobs queued in prod-capability increases the average wait time of jobs in prod-capability, backfill, and prod-long queues. The increases in the average wait time of jobs in prod-long and backfill are more obvious. Therefore, job wait time of jobs in prod-long and backfill is prone to be affected by the number of job submissions in prod-capability queue.*

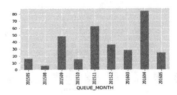

Fig. 7. Number of jobs submitted by User 32764951387776 in each month.

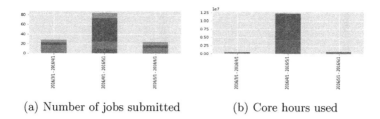

(a) Number of jobs submitted (b) Core hours used

Fig. 8. Number of jobs submitted and core hours used by User 32764951387776 in each month during March 1. 2016 to June 1. 2016.

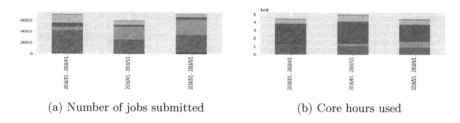

(a) Number of jobs submitted (b) Core hours used

Fig. 9. Number of jobs submitted and core hours used by all users in each month during March 1. 2016 to June 1. 2016.

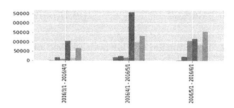

Fig. 10. Average job wait time of jobs in different queues in each month during March 1. 2016 to June 1. 2016.

5.3 Exit Codes

The exit codes in Mira logs follow the standard exit codes in Linux. For example, 0 means a job exits Mira normally. 1 means general errors caused by users. In this subsection, we analyze the distribution of exit codes. Figure 11 presents the distribution of exit codes.

Observation 9. *In Fig. 12, Jobs in prod-short, backfill, and prod-torus queues have the higher probability of exiting system normally.*

Observation 10. *In Fig. 13, users have different distributions of exit codes. For example, 90% of jobs of user 8445397395848 exit system normally, whereas more than half of jobs of user 41675626785343 exit system with code 143.*

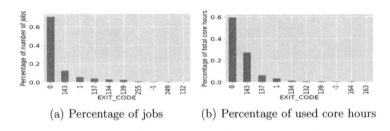

(a) Percentage of jobs   (b) Percentage of used core hours

Fig. 11. Distribution of exit codes.

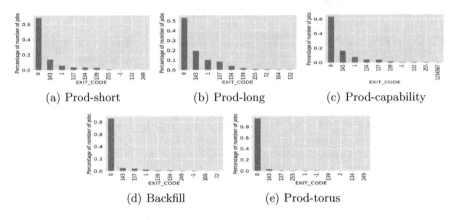

(a) Prod-short   (b) Prod-long   (c) Prod-capability

(d) Backfill   (e) Prod-torus

Fig. 12. Distribution of exit codes based on queues.

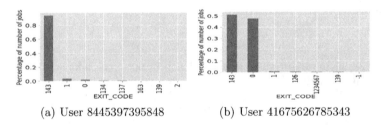

(a) User 8445397395848   (b) User 41675626785343

Fig. 13. Distribution of exit codes based on users.

5.4 Modes

Mira support three types of job submission: basic job submission, script submission, and interactive job submission. Basic job submission allows users to submit an executable. Basic job submissions are further divided into several modes (i.e. c1, c2, c4, c8, c32, and c64) based on the number of ranks per nodes. For example, c2 means 2 ranks per node. Script submission enables users submit a single Cobalt job script and conduct multiple runs within a script, if jobs in a script all require the same size partition. The script mode is more flexible and a user need to wait only once to run all jobs in a script. Interactive submission allocates

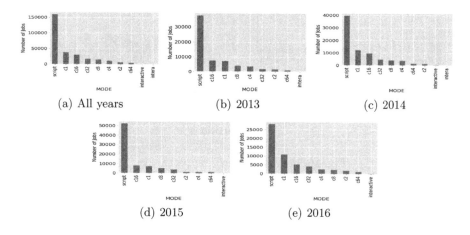

(a) All years   (b) 2013   (c) 2014

(d) 2015   (e) 2016

Fig. 14. Mode distribution

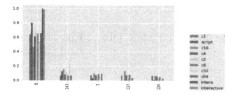

Fig. 15. Percentage of jobs in Combination of Exit codes and Modes.

partitions and gives a user a shell prompt when the interactive session start. Users can submit jobs and debug jobs in interactive mode.

Observation 11. *In Fig. 14, script is the most popular mode in all years. In addition, there is a trend towards using c1 mode. A node in Mira can run at most 64 MPI ranks. The probable reason for not fully use 64 ranks is some resources in a node are not sufficient to run a job. For example, memory may not be sufficient to share between 64 MPI ranks, hence users may request to use less ranks in one node.*

Observation 12. *In Fig. 15, jobs in script modes have higher probability of exiting system normally. 80% of jobs in script mode exit system normally, whereas less than 50% of jobs in c16 mode exit system normally. 22% of jobs in c32 mode exit system with code 143.*

5.5 Co-analysis on RAS and Job Logs

Reliability, Availability, and Serviceability (RAS) logs are the primary source of information that a system administrator can use to understand failures [20]. Co-analysis on RAS and job logs can reveal the job related failures.

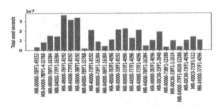

(a) Number of Failures of Top 25 partitions (b) Number of seconds used on different partitions

Fig. 16. Failures and jobs on partitions.

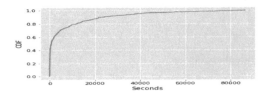
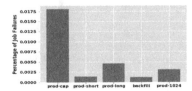

Fig. 17. CDF of Failure happened after jobs started.

Fig. 18. Percentage of jobs having fatal failures in different queues.

Observation 13. *From Fig. 16, we can see bigger jobs and partitions have the higher failure probability. Jobs using all the nodes have the highest failure counts. In addition, the total failure counts (Fig. 16(a)) is related to total used node hours of the partitions (Fig. 16(b)).*

Observation 14. *From Fig. 17, we can see that more than half of the failures happened at the very beginning of job execution.*

Observation 15. *From Fig. 18, jobs in prod-capability have the highest probability of failures. This is probably because of jobs in this queue are bigger than jobs in other queues, hence, they have higher probability of failure.*

5.6 Cycles

In this subsection, we focus on analyzing user behavior and their submission cycles.

Observation 16. *From Figs. 19 and 20, more jobs were submitted on Wednesday and Thursday. More jobs were submitted in May and August. Users have their own submission pattern. Some users are more active on weekdays, while others are more active on weekends.*

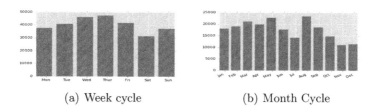

(a) Week cycle   (b) Month Cycle

Fig. 19. Job submission cycles

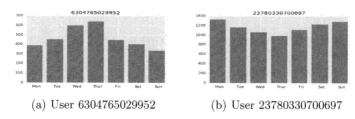

(a) User 6304765029952   (b) User 23780330700697

Fig. 20. Users week cycle

5.7   Account

In this subsection, we analyze INCITE and ALCC accounts and the overburn effects of these accounts.

Observation 17. *Overburn jobs consists of 13% of the total jobs. Approximately 20% of core hours are overburn. In Fig. 21, overburn is highly utilized from July to September.*

Observation 18. *In Fig. 22, project 902672531503 is the largest project in Mira. The analysis on overburn shows that in July and August, approximate 57% of jobs of this project were overburn, which makes up 80% of total core hours used by this project.*

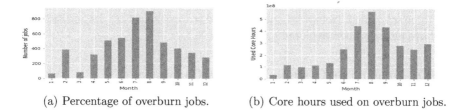

(a) Percentage of overburn jobs.   (b) Core hours used on overburn jobs.

Fig. 21. Distribution of overburn jobs per month.

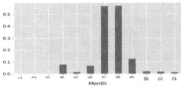
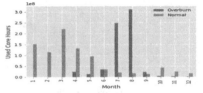

(a) Percentage of overburn jobs.   (b) Core hours used on overburn jobs.

Fig. 22. Distribution of overburn jobs per month of project 902672531503.

6   Upcoming Challenges at Argonne

For many years DOE facilities have been on the bleeding edge of parallel computing and managing large volumes of data. For somewhere on the order of 30 years, the basic workload has been massively parallel jobs, batch scheduled, with relatively long run times and few jobs.

While that workload will continue to be a major part of the mission for the foreseeable future, the science teams and DOE are asking the DOE facilities to support a broader range of workloads which are going to raise challenges across the board including scheduling. Here is a brief description of the workloads and the potential scheduling challenges associated with them.

6.1   Multi-scheduling

Changes in architecture are requiring multiple resources to be considered "first class citizens" from a scheduling perspective. One that is already appearing is power management [21,22]. Power consumption of the largest machines may exceed what the data center has available and the scheduler will need to consider job power consumption to avoid exceeding power limits. Some architectures can also gain performance improvements if the power is managed on the node. Another that is already here is the "burst buffer" [25]. This is a very fast, generally very close, storage cache. In the future we will need to also consider space available in the burst buffer. Similarly, Argonne has a research project to investigate making RAM a manageable, allocable network resource, which would also need to be scheduled. Network bandwidth and storage space are also possibilities that have already been explored.

6.2   On-Demand or Deadline Sensitive Computing

Many of the experimental "instruments" such as light sources like the Argonne Advanced Photon Source [15], or fusion tokamaks like the current DIII-D [16] or the future ITER [17] require, or at the very least could greatly benefit by having, computational capabilities that could be available on demand (as soon as a data acquisition is complete) that can complete in a short period of time so that the results can be used to adjust parameters for the next run. This is almost in direct conflict with the traditional workload where a single job can consume the entire machine for long (12–24 h) periods of time. How can both demands be accommodated? Here are some potential solutions:

- A fraction of the machine is reserved during periods when the instruments are running, assuming they are fairly regular and scheduled. This hurts utilization since the reserved nodes sit idle while the run is in progress.
- Pre-emption: With the right job mix and the right machine characteristics this is a potentially very good solution. However, some machines, the Blue Gene in particular, are not very amenable to this. The Blue Gene reboots the nodes between every job, and for a full machine job that could take 5 min. It also takes time to kill a job and do appropriate cleanup. If the total allowable time is 15 min, a number often suggested for the fusion community, the overhead to do pre-emption is approaching 50%. There is also the loss of science from the last check point till the job was killed. This can easily be several hours and that is a non-trivial loss on a very important and expensive resource.
- What if... we could design a hardware/system software system that enabled rapid, efficient, and low cost "task switches", resembling more what an operating system does on a multi-core processor? This would enable us to then simply "suspend" the job running, task switch to the time constrained job, possibly backfilling if the size of the suspended job is much bigger than the needs of the time-constrained job. How would you schedule this? How would you do the accounting for it?

6.3   High Throughput Computing (HTC) Workloads

HTC workloads tend to be the polar opposite of big parallel jobs. They tend to require little or no communication between them. They tend to be small, often single core, or single node. They tend to be short, a few minutes, or even a few seconds. There tend to be many of them, potentially tens of thousands or even millions. Typical batch scheduler may not scale well for that number of jobs, and the startup and shutdown of some large supercomputers would fail under that sort of load. For instance, the Blue Gene records every hardware event that occurs in a DB2 relational database. The kind of job thrashing that an HTC workload brings could run the database out of resources and crash the machine. We had it happen early on until we built throttles in to prevent it, but that means the HTC workloads cannot practically run. From a pure architecture point of view, HTC jobs don't fit on a big parallel machine. They have no need of the very expensive, generally proprietary interconnect, and they are a perfect fit for distributed computing, which is what the High Energy Physics Community has been doing for years. So why the push for HTC jobs on supercomputers? They represent a very sizeable investment. They can potentially provide better time to solution.

- Deal with queue depths of millions
- Possibly batch job starter (ala Condor)

6.4   Complex Domain Specific Software Stacks

Typically, the environment on a batch compute cluster is a "take it or leave it" affair. There is a single base OS and a set of supported packages. Your application must either be able to run in that environment or you must be able to build any required ancillary packages yourself in that environment. At the very least, this can require significant effort on the part of the application scientists/developers to build and support multiple environments. In the worst case, they simply cannot make use of the resource because their software stack can't run in the environment. Perhaps there are libraries they don't control that can't build, or there are vetted algorithms that cannot be altered or wont run. Perhaps you could build your software, but it requires root access, something most facilities are not willing to provide.

Virtual machines and particularly containerization are offering a paradigm that can potentially support these complex software stacks. The applications scientist can build complete end-to-end images of their software stack and execute those on the system. There are projects like Shifter [18] and Singularity [19] that are attempting to enable root access inside the container while ameliorating the security concerns that come along with that for the facility.

6.5   Coordinated Services and Access to Remote Data

Another paradigm that is becoming more common are computational tasks that either require the compute nodes to have internet access and/or they require another application/service to be up and running while the computational job is running. Many facilities, ours included, put the compute nodes on an internal non-routable network. This is primarily done as a security measure, but it can also have a cost factor. If there are other services required to run, there are several options:

- Provide resources for "always on" long running services; But this brings several issues: who installs and maintains it? If the user, what about root access? Who deals with the issues if it goes down? What about differing hardware and software requirements? For instance, if this service is a local database it might require very substantial core, RAM, and I/O resources.
- Provide resources that can be co-scheduled and used "on-demand" and spin the services up and down with the job. A virtual machine facility either internal or something like Amazon Web Services could be used for this, but those can take several minutes to spin up. How do you avoid your computational resource from sitting idle while that happens?

6.6   Workflows

The work required to achieve scientific output is much more than just running the computational jobs. Much of that work is repetitive and mundane, particularly when the science involves multiple facilities, which is becoming the norm rather than the exception. You have to sequence the jobs in the right order to satisfy data dependencies (the output of one job is the input to another), you may have to move data from one facility to another, archive/backup results, etc. Many science projects are moving towards using automated workflow tools to manage this complexity. This brings at least two issues to the facility:

- Remote job launch: You may no longer have a user sitting on your login node submitting jobs, so how do you enable your scheduler to support this and do so in a way that avoids the application developers from having to support a different mechanism at every facility?
- Security: Not only is the user not logged into the system, a user can't be sitting by ready to type their password when the workflow system decides to submit a batch of jobs at 3AM on Sunday morning. How do we balance supporting the science workflows with securing our facilities so we don't end up on the front page of the New York Times because our supercomputer launched a Denial-Of-Service attack against the White House?
- Impacts of having the WAN as a critical component: If the data is distributed and needs to be moved, as opposed to moving the compute to the data, scheduling becomes much more difficult because WAN transfer times are notoriously difficult to predict, and if the data movement is happening while the job is running there is a high probability that the compute resources will go idle while waiting for data due to WAN performance variability.

7   Conclusions

In summary, we have described the specific batch scheduling goals and constraints at ALCF. We have also analyzed workload traces collected from the production petascale supercomputer Mira and made eighteen key observations at various perspectives. Finally, we have discussed the upcoming scheduling challenges at Argonne and potential solutions to some of the challenges.

Acknowledgement. This research used resources of the Argonne Leadership Computing Facility, which is a DOE Office of Science User Facility supported under Contract DE-AC02-06CH11357. Zhiling Lan is supported in part by US National Science Foundation grants CNS-1320125 and CCF-1422009.

References

1. Argonne National Laboratory. http://www.anl.gov/
2. Argonne National Laboratory User Facilities. http://www.anl.gov/user-facilities
3. Argonne Leadership Computing Facility. http://www.alcf.anl.gov/
4. Top500. https://www.top500.org/
5. Innovative and Novel Computational Impact on Theory and Experiment (INCITE) Program. http://www.doeleadershipcomputing.org/incite-program/
6. Advanced Scientific Computing Research (ASCR) Leadership Computing Challenge (ALCC) Program. https://science.energy.gov/ascr/facilities/accessing-ascr-facilities/alcc/

7. The Directors Discretionary (DD) program. https://www.alcf.anl.gov/dd-program
8. IBM Blue Gene. https://en.wikipedia.org/wiki/Blue_Gene
9. Plan9. https://en.wikipedia.org/wiki/Plan_9_from_Bell_Labs
10. ZeptoOS. http://www.mcs.anl.gov/research/projects/zeptoos/
11. Cobalt. http://trac.mcs.anl.gov/projects/cobalt/
12. SciDAC Scalable Systems Software ISIC. http://www.scidac.gov/ASCR/ASCR_SSS.html
13. Intrepid. https://www.alcf.anl.gov/intrepid
14. Mira. https://www.alcf.anl.gov/mira
15. Argonne Advanced Photon Source. https://www1.aps.anl.gov/
16. DIII-D. https://en.wikipedia.org/wiki/DIII-D_(fusion_reactor)
17. ITER. https://www.iter.org/
18. Shifter. https://github.com/NERSC/shifter
19. Singularity. http://singularity.lbl.gov/
20. Zheng, Z., Yu, L., Tang, W., Lan, Z.: Co-analysis of RAS log and job log on Blue Gene/P. In: Proceedings of IPDPS (2011)
21. Yang, X., Zhou, Z., Wallace, S., Lan, Z., Tang, W., Coghlan, S., Papka, M.: Integrating dynamic pricing of electricity into energy aware scheduling for HPC systems. In: Proceedings of the International Conference for High Performance Computing, Networking, Storage and Analysis (SC) (2013)
22. Wallace, S., Yang, X., Vishwanath, V., Allcock, W., Coghlan, S., Papka, M., Lan, Z.: A data driven scheduling approach for power management on HPC systems. In: Proceedings of the International Conference for High Performance Computing, Networking, Storage and Analysis (SC) (2016)
23. Zhou, Z., Yang, X., Lan, Z., Rich, P., Tang, W., Morozov, V., Desai, N.: Improving batch scheduling on Blue Gene/Q by relaxing 5D torus network allocation constraints. In: Proceedings of IEEE IPDPS (2015)
24. Zhou, Z., Yang, X., Zhao, D., Rich, P., Tang, W., Wang, J., Lan, Z.: I/O-aware batch scheduling for petascale computing systems. In: Proceedings of IEEE Cluster (2015)
25. Yan, J., Yang, X., Jin, D., Lan, Z.: Cerberus: a three-phase burst-buffer-aware batch scheduler for high performance computing. In: Proceedings of the International Conference for High Performance Computing, Networking, Storage and Analysis (SC), Poster Session (2016)

Analysis of Mixed Workloads
from Shared Cloud Infrastructure

Dalibor Klusáček$^{(\boxtimes)}$ and Boris Parák

CESNET a.l.e., Brno, Czech Republic
{klusacek,parak}@cesnet.cz

Abstract. Modern computing environments such as clouds, grids or HPC clusters are both complex and costly installations. Therefore, it has always been a major challenge to utilize them properly. Workload scheduling is a critical process in every production system with an unwanted potential to hamper overall performance if the given scheduler is not adequate or properly configured. Therefore, researchers as well as system administrators are frequently using historic workload traces to model/analyze the behavior of real systems in order to improve existing scheduling approaches. In this work we provide such real-life workload traces from the CERIT-SC system. Importantly, our traces describe a "mixed" workload consisting of both cloud VMs and grid jobs executed over a shared computing infrastructure. Provided workloads represent an interesting scheduling problem. First, these mixed workloads involving both "grid jobs" and cloud VMs increase the complexity of required (co)scheduling necessary to efficiently use the underlying physical infrastructure. Second, we also provide a detailed description of the setup of the system, its operational constraints and unresolved issues, putting the observed workloads into a broader context. Last but not least, the workloads are made freely available to the scientific community allowing for further independent research and analysis.

Keywords: Cloud · Grid · Workloads · Scheduling · Simulation

1 Introduction

Workload traces from various real-life systems have been used by researchers for decades. Notable examples represent the Parallel Workloads Archive [4] and the Grid Workloads Archive [7] that contains plethora of historic workloads, mainly from HPC-like systems. Similarly, there are several publicly available traces[1] from large cloud/hadoop/cluster installations including, e.g., Eucalyptus IaaS cloud workload [25], Facebook Hadoop traces [24] or Google cluster workload [22].

The increasing popularity of resource virtualization introduces new scheduling problems. For example, different types of applications/frameworks can now

---

[1] Nice overview can be found at: http://bit.ly/2kLf44d.

© Springer International Publishing AG, part of Springer Nature 2018
D. Klusáček et al. (Eds.): JSSPP 2017, LNCS 10773, pp. 25–42, 2018.
https://doi.org/10.1007/978-3-319-77398-8_2

be hosted simultaneously in a shared physical infrastructure. This was not a usual scenario 15 years ago. Today, applications and services can be relatively easily encapsulated as, e.g., VMs or containers and run in an isolated fashion within a data-center. Therefore, it is very important to collect information about such installments, where different computing paradigms meet in a single infrastructure in order to understand the nature and influence of such co-existence and its potential impact on existing scheduling approaches, both local (e.g., batch scheduling system) and global (e.g., Mesos-like inter-application scheduling [6]).

The traces presented in this paper come from the Czech *CERIT Scientific Cloud (CERIT-SC)* installation [2] and represent such mixed workloads. Simply put, they capture a mixture of two different types of applications — standard computational jobs and cloud VMs — that each use their own resource manager and scheduling approaches to handle their jobs and VMs, respectively. Both of them use the same fully virtualized infrastructure to execute the workloads. Moreover, we present detailed information about system configuration and its usage policies, maintenance periods and operational constraints, including details concerning applied scheduling approaches and system performance objectives. We also discuss current problems with existing system setup and provide several examples of future research and development. Of course, these workload traces are freely available to other researchers [12].

This paper is organized as follows. Section 2 describes the shared computing environment of CERIT-SC, giving details about the hardware, middleware and system constraints including its scheduling policies. Next, the workload traces are presented in Sect. 3 and their major characteristics are discussed and compared. Section 4 describes the optimization criteria that the CERIT-SC uses when optimizing its performance. Existing open problems are discussed in Sect. 5 where several unresolved issues with the current system configuration are presented. Finally, Sect. 6 describes the formats of our workload traces, introduces some available workload parsers and concludes the paper.

2   System Description

Workload traces described in this paper were collected during the year 2016 and come from the CERIT-SC site, which is the largest partition of the Czech national grid and cloud infrastructure *MetaCentrum* [18]. MetaCentrum has some 13,288 CPU cores out of which 5,224 belong to the CERIT-SC partition. Within CERIT-SC, 3,912 CPU cores (75%) are fully virtualized using OpenNebula framework [19] and can be used by various applications, while the remaining 1,312 CPU cores are not virtualized and are exclusively used for "bare metal" grid-like computations. In this paper, we will only concentrate on the mixed workloads coming from the shared and fully virtualized partition.

The shared partition is managed by OpenNebula and allows for simultaneous execution of two major classes of workloads. The first type is represented by classic virtual machines (VM) that are submitted by the users of the system and serve for various purposes, e.g., they host a database or a web server, or they encapsulate some "exotic" software or operating system (OS) which cannot be executed on the "bare metal" nodes that all use Debian 8 OS. Second, there is a special type of VM which we call a "grid worker" VM. Once deployed and started, this VM behaves as a "normal" node of the grid infrastructure, i.e., computational jobs from the CERIT-SC's batch resource manager (RM) can be executed within such VMs. The scheme of the current system configuration is shown in Fig. 1.

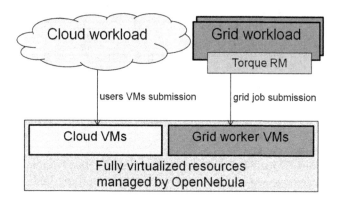

Fig. 1. The scheme of the shared virtualized infrastructure in CERIT-SC.

The biggest advantage of this mechanism is that the actual amount of resources available either to the grid or to the cloud can be easily and dynamically adapted, simply by changing the number of running grid worker VMs. This allows for greater flexibility and better distribution of resources compared to the standard situation where resources are statically allocated either to the cloud or to the grid and cannot be easily reallocated.

2.1   Physical Clusters

The physical infrastructure of CERIT-SC's virtualized environment consists of six major clusters that vary heavily by means of their size and per-node parameters. The largest cluster is *zapat* (1760 CPU cores, 16 cores and 128 GB RAM per node), followed by *zebra* (960 CPU cores, 40 cores and 256 GB RAM per node), *zegox* (576 CPU cores, 12 cores and 90 GB RAM per node), *zefron* (320 CPU cores, 40 cores and 1 TB RAM per node), *zigur* (256 CPU cores, 8 cores and 128 GB RAM per node) and *zorg* (40 CPU cores, 40 cores and 512 GB RAM per node). The availability of nodes and clusters varied slightly during 2016 as shows Fig. 2.

2.2   Resource Managers

CERIT-SC is using two independent resource managers within its shared infrastructure. First, it is the OpenNebula software stack [19] which is responsible for

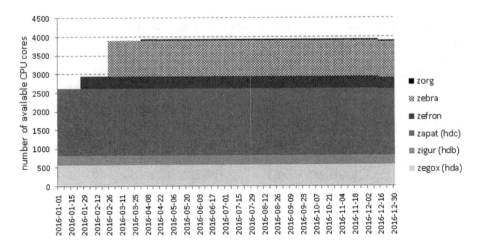

Fig. 2. The number of CPU cores available in CERIT-SC during 2016.

virtualization and VM life-cycle management. Using OpenNebula, both regular users' VMs are deployed as well as those special "grid worker" VMs that serve for running computational batch jobs from our grid-like batch system. For this purpose, we use the Torque resource manager [1] with a custom built advanced job scheduler that has been throughly described at JSSPP 2016 [13]. While every user of our system can run a regular VM, only the system administrator can manipulate with those "grid worker" VMs.

2.3 Operational Constraints and Policies

In our system, most operational constraints are related to the batch scheduling system, i.e., the Torque resource manager. This system is heavily optimized with quite a complex set of system policies and usage constraints. For example, jobs are automatically assigned into system queues, the amount of resources available to a given queue or user is carefully selected while a complex job scheduling approach based on conservative backfilling [20] is used in order to efficiently use the available infrastructure as well as to meet several user-oriented criteria [13]. Importantly, job scheduling is subject to an advanced multi-resource aware fair-sharing mechanism that guarantees that resources are used in a fair fashion with respect to system users. Beside that, additional metrics like expected job slowdown and wait time are also used when prioritizing users' jobs. More details about the system configuration and applied constraints can be found in [13,15].

In contrast to the batch system, the cloud-operating OpenNebula framework represents a rather simple environment. We use the default VM scheduler in OpenNebula (mm_sched), which uses a simple VM-matching approach. No advanced methods like VM prioritization, fair-sharing or automatic VM migrations/re-scheduling are applied because they are not currently supported.

The exact amount of physical resources that are delegated to the grid-like computations using "grid worker" VMs is selected by the system administrator, i.e., there is no automatic load-balancing feature applied in the system.

3 Workload Description

In this section we describe the main characteristics of the mixed workloads collected during 2016 in CERIT-SC. During this one year period there were 11,382 running VMs. Out of these 11,147 represented normal user cloud VMs while 235 represented "grid worker" VMs. Concerning the grid workload from the Torque resource manager, there were 472,328 jobs computed inside those 235 grid worker VMs during 2016.

3.1 Main Characteristics of Cloud VMs and Grid Jobs

We now proceed to the analysis of the cloud and grid workload in CERIT-SC, starting with some major characteristics of cloud VMs and grid jobs. Figure 3 shows scatter plots of all cloud VMs (left) and grid jobs (right). A "dot" represents one job/VM and its x and y coordinates represent the number of requested CPU cores and RAM in GB, respectively. Therefore, Fig. 3 allows us to see the differences among those two workloads by means of their resource requirements.

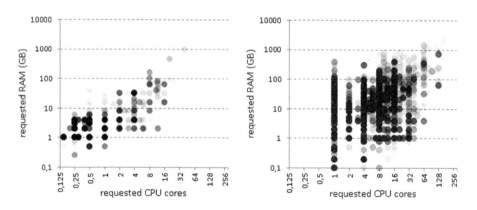

Fig. 3. CPU and RAM requirements for cloud VMs (left) and grid jobs (right).

Clearly, there are large differences among the two workloads. Generally speaking, the grid workload is much more variable, with lots of jobs that request more CPUs and/or larger chunks of RAM. In fact, a large amount of grid jobs is using only few CPUs but lots of available RAM. On the other hand, cloud workloads are less CPU and RAM demanding. Also, VMs frequently request only a fraction of one physical CPU which never happens in the grid. When a VM is submitted in OpenNebula, its owner can specify the amount of both physical and virtual

CPUs (vCPUs). While the minimal vCPU value is 1.0, i.e., the guest OS inside a VM always "sees" at least 1 CPU, the user or the system administrator can specify that this virtual CPU(s) corresponds to a fraction of physical CPU(s), allowing for explicit *CPU overcommitting*.

Figure 4 shows the actual impact of such overcommitting by comparing the number of allocated CPUs and vCPUs during 2016. Although the average over-commitment of a VM[2] was 3.6, physical CPUs in CERIT-SC were — on average — overcommitted only by the factor of 1.42 during 2016. The latter value is lower since the dominant part of infrastructure's physical CPUs has been utilized by VMs having relatively low vCPUs to CPUs ratio.

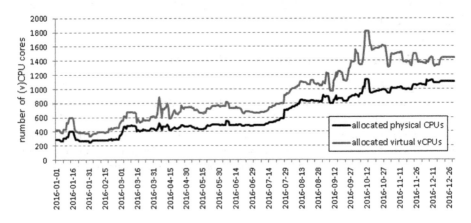

Fig. 4. The level of overcommitment (allocated CPUs vs. corresponding vCPUs).

Another important parameter of the workload is the VM's and job's execution time (duration) and their wait times, i.e., the time before a VM or a job is actually started. For this purpose, we present cumulative distribution functions (CDF) of VM and job durations and wait times. These CDFs are shown in Fig. 5, where the duration is on the left and the wait time is on the right. In the CDF, the y-axis represents the fraction of jobs that have duration less than or equal to a given duration/wait time, which is shown on the x-axis.

Not surprisingly, there are significant differences between the cloud and grid workloads. Concerning execution time, all grid jobs have some upper bound on their maximum execution time, which is specified either by a user or by a default queue limit. This is not the case for cloud VMs whose maximum runtime is unbounded and unknown in general. In CERIT-SC, the maximum allowed runtime for grid jobs is 2 months. In grid, jobs are terminated once reaching their maximum execution time. This causes the "staircase-like" shape of the CDF for grid jobs, where several such "stairs" can be observed (e.g., at 2, 4 and 24 h) which correlate to the most popular user-provided runtime estimates.

---

[2] VM overcommitment factor is computed as vCPUs/CPUs.

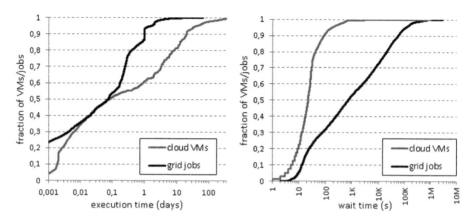

Fig. 5. The CDFs of VM/job execution time (left) and wait time (right).

In cloud, the runtime is not bounded and (as can be seen in the CDF) there are VMs that ran throughout the whole one year period (i.e., the CDF reaches maximum as x approaches 365 days). Figure 5 (left) also reveals that several cloud VMs and quite a few grid jobs actually terminated right after their start, most probably due to a misconfiguration or some form of failure.

The CDFs of wait times are shown in Fig. 5 (right) and show major differences between the workloads. In the cloud, 70% of VMs start within 30 s and 99% of all VMs are running no later than 10 min after their submission. This is natural as cloud is used for more interactive work and system administrators periodically check that there are free resources available for the newly coming VMs. On the other hand, grid job wait times are more spread with many jobs waiting more than 10 min (52% of jobs). The nature of batch computations is different from the cloud, as user-to-job interactions are not very common, i.e., it is natural to have a significant backlog of waiting jobs in the system. Therefore, job wait times may be as high as two weeks in extreme cases ($\approx$1.2 M seconds).

3.2 Infrastructure Utilization by Cloud and Grid Workloads

Let us briefly describe how the system resources were used by these two workloads (cloud VMs vs. "grid worker" VMs). Figure 6 shows the distribution of available CPU cores to the cloud and grid, respectively. It reveals that the amount of resources available for each particular framework was changing throughout time. Especially, the continuous increase of cloud VMs is nicely visible. While in January 2016 the cloud VMs only required 284 CPUs, by the end of the year their total allocation was over 1,100 CPUs. This was only possible by reducing the allocation for "grid worker" VMs, as shown in Fig. 6.

The figure also reveals some minor inconsistencies — the number of available CPUs is sometimes smaller than the number of allocated CPUs. These anomalies are caused by the imperfect accounting of OpenNebula, which only stores timestamps when a VM was running in the past, but it does not record the

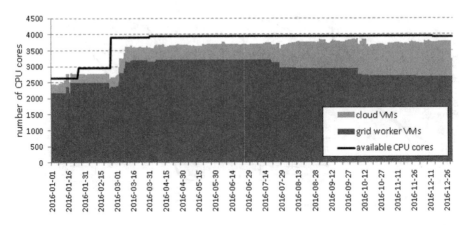

Fig. 6. The number of CPU cores allocated to the cloud VMs and "grid worker" VMs.

actual amount of resources used during the VM's "offline" periods. It is therefore impossible to accurately measure the real system resource usage. Unlike a common grid job which has a well defined start and completion time, a VM can be launched and paused repeatedly while (sometimes) still blocking resources during its "offline" period. This is the case for VMs in "suspend/power-off" states while VMs that are "undeployed" or "shutdown" do not consume any resources [21]. Since this VM state-related information is not available, we have approximated the real resource consumption as if all VMs used their resource allocations during their "offline" periods, which leads to the observed minor inconsistencies.

The allocation of free CPU cores by the cloud VMs varies in time and is 72% on average[3]. For better visibility, the actual allocation of "grid worker" VMs by the grid jobs from the Torque batch system is shown in separate Fig. 7, both for CPU (top) and RAM (bottom). As can be seen, the allocation levels vary from high to rather low, which is quite common behavior in grid-like system and relates to several factors including limited job runtime and daily/weekly cycles of user submissions. The average CPU utilization in CERIT-SC's grid partition is 77%. Frequently, CPUs/RAM cannot be used to their full capacity due to the fragmentation of system resources. Simply put, although the overall (theoretical) capacity is sufficient to accommodate further workload, job requirements (e.g., its user-defined topology) cannot be satisfied with the current placement of already running jobs. Figure 7 also reveals that in CERIT-SC's grid workload the most constraining resource is usually the CPU, while plenty of free RAM is generally available most of the time.

Unfortunately, the lack of accounting data both in the OpenNebula and the Torque does not allow us to construct similar charts of actual CPU/RAM load

---

[3] As discussed in Sect. 2.2, "grid worker" VMs are started/stopped by the system administrator, so the 72% utilization of cloud VMs is computed with respect to the remaining (i.e., available) capacity in the system (see Fig. 6).

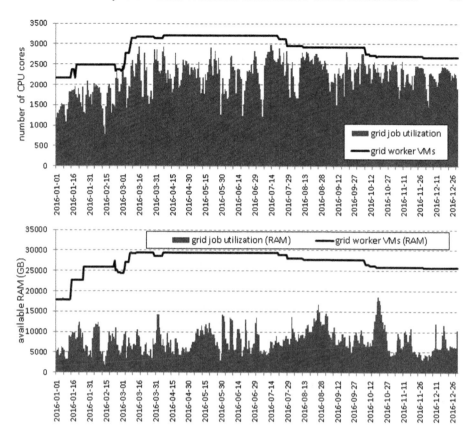

Fig. 7. The allocation of "grid worker" VMs by jobs from the Torque batch system showing CPU (top) and RAM (bottom) allocations.

neither for the cloud VMs nor the grid jobs. Therefore, we do not know exactly to what extent the resources allocated for cloud VMs and/or grid jobs were actually used throughout the time. For grid jobs, we only know the average CPU load per job. Using this data, we see that the CPU load is usually quite high (78% on average). We have no accounting data concerning real CPU/RAM load for cloud VMs in CERIT-SC system. Fortunately, we have such data from a separate cluster that is fully dedicated for cloud VMs[4]. Figure 8 shows the actual CPU load in this cluster, suggesting that the CPU load of cloud VMs is typically much smaller than for grid jobs, being only 5–30% in most cases. Although this data come from a different cluster, we expect analogous behavior in CERIT-SC, given the same user-base and similar workload.

---

[4] It is the *dukan* cluster which is not part of the CERIT-SC infrastructure but it executes similar workloads from the same user-base.

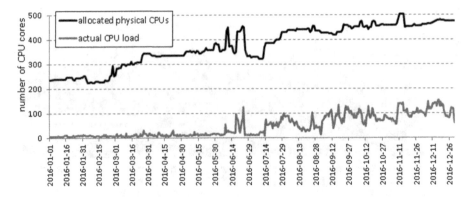

Fig. 8. The actual load of allocated CPUs by cloud VMs in *dukan* cluster during 2016.

3.3 User-Oriented View of the Workloads

So far, the major differences among the workloads have been discussed by focusing on the characteristics of individual VMs and/or jobs. In the following text, we provide another complementary view of the workload, which analyzes the workload on a per-user level. For this purpose, we have prepared stacked charts in Fig. 9 that show the amount of allocated CPU cores per-user during 2016, both for cloud VMs (top) and grid jobs (bottom).

Figure 9 complements our previous observations concerning typical VM and job durations in Sect. 3.1. In the cloud environment, the majority of CPU cores is consumed by ~15 users with long running (continuous) workloads. In the grid, the situation is exactly opposite. Most CPU cores are consumed by many different users that execute rather time-constrained workloads, which is natural since every grid job has a firm runtime limit. This strict limitation combined with typical day-to-day and weekly cycles makes the overall utilization curve of the grid workload much more "noisy".

3.4 Maintenance Periods

The final part of this section focuses on maintenance periods in CERIT-SC system. It is fair to say that the following description and presented data is not based on some advanced monitoring tool, instead we only rely on the system administrator's log of planned upgrades/repairs. Minor offline periods and minor unplanned failures may not be captured here, however all major interventions and downtimes are likely documented in this log[5].

Using this data we were able to reconstruct major system upgrades and maintenance periods that are shown in Fig. 10. As the chart shows, the overall number of offline CPUs is quite low during the year (~1.3% of available CPUs), except for one event at the beginning of May, where a total of 416 CPUs (28 nodes) was switched off for a week due to the planned HDD firmware upgrade.

---

[5] This log is available at: https://github.com/CERIT-SC/cerit-maintenance.

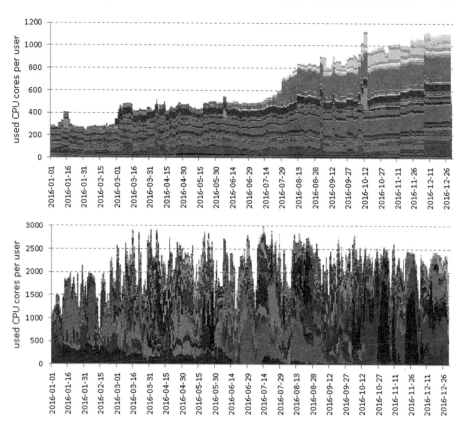

Fig. 9. Users' CPU usage over the time for cloud VMs (top) and grid jobs (bottom).

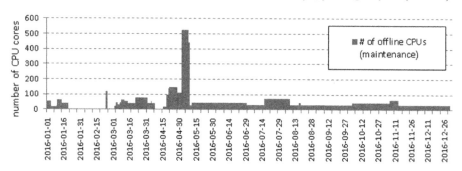

Fig. 10. Number of offline CPUs undergoing maintenance during 2016.

This was the only case, when the total number of offline CPUs exceeded 500, causing 13.3% of the infrastructure being unusable for a week.

4   Optimization Criteria Used in the System

Those two systems operating over the CERIT-SC infrastructure have different goals, i.e., different sets of optimization criteria. In both the cloud and the grid partition, these goals are only enforced in a "best-effort" manner, i.e., no formal Service Level Agreements are established, although there are various Service Level Indicators/Objectives [10] that are optimized/targeted.

We now describe these major goals (i.e., objectives and their indicators) in order to allow other researchers to use our workloads to analyze new/existing scheduling approaches using realistic optimization goals. We would like to emphasize that it is not a good idea to compare simulation-based results with those of the original workload, since there are many unknown constraints that influence the quality of the original schedule (as seen in the original workload). Typically, simulation-based results tend to show much better results than those original (real) schedulers. In reality, real schedulers employ various considerations that limit their options, and lead to sub-optimal scheduling [16].

Sadly, many of these "considerations" cannot be reconstructed as they are not recorded anywhere[6]. For more details please refer to [14,16]. Let us start with the grid-related criteria system before proceeding to the cloud-related and global criteria.

4.1   Grid Optimization Criteria

The grid partition is subject to four major optimization criteria, which we describe in the following text.

First, we aim to minimize the *avg. wait time* [3] which is the mean time that jobs spend waiting before their executions start. Second, the *avg. bounded slowdown* [5] is minimized, which is the mean of jobs bounded slowdowns. The bounded slowdown is the ratio of the actual response time of the job (the time from its submission to its termination) to the response time if executed without any waiting. To avoid huge slowdowns of extremely short jobs, the minimal job runtime is bounded by some predefined time constant (e.g., 10 s), sometimes called a "threshold of interactivity" [5].

We also focus on *resource utilization*, i.e., the goal is to minimize the number of idle CPUs throughout the time. The system does not use any "green goals", i.e., no methods to reduce the carbon footprint/energy consumption are used or even planned to be used in the future.

Last but not least, *user-to-user fairness* is considered as one of the most important goals in CERIT-SC grid partition and is managed by a fair-sharing approach that uses so-called *Normalized User Wait Time (NUWT)* metric [13]. For a given user, NUWT is the total user wait time divided by the amount

---

[6] For example, real schedulers must limit the number of concurrently running licensed applications (jobs using licensed SW) with respect to the number of available software licenses, i.e., even if resources are free some jobs must wait until a license is available. Such information is not usually recorded in the workload.

of previously consumed system resources by that user. Then, the user-to-user fairness is optimized by minimizing the mean and the standard deviation of all NUWT values. It follows the classical fair-share principles, i.e., a user with lower resource usage and/or higher total wait time gets higher priority over more active users and vice versa [8]. The calculation of NUWT reflects consumptions of multiple resources (CPU and RAM utilization), representing a solution suitable for systems having heterogeneous workloads and/or infrastructures.

4.2   Cloud Optimization Criteria

Just like in the grid, there are no "green" objectives and no formal SLAs and the service is provided in a best-effort fashion. While the grid partition have quite robust optimization goals, the cloud partition (currently) uses only two simple objectives and further criteria are likely to be included/developed in the future.

First, the goal is to *minimize the wait time* of (newly submitted) pending VMs, thus maximizing the number of concurrently running VMs. In other words, the goal is to *minimize the number of VMs that have to wait* for their deployment. This two criteria (number of waiting VMs and their wait time) are currently used by the system administrators when (de)allocating physical nodes for the cloud partition. The "algorithm" is to keep a decent part of the cloud nodes free for newly arriving VMs. The utilization criterion is used as an auxiliary indicator, i.e., low utilization implies that some nodes should be returned to the grid and vice versa. No further indicators/objectives are currently (actively) measured and optimized/enforced.

A notable difference with respect to the grid partition is the (current) absence of any fairness-related objective and/or technique to enforce fair use of resources which is becoming an apparent problem. This is a general problem in those private clouds that do not use the "pay-per-use" model (or some other equivalent of money/credit). Further details are provided in the following Sect. 5 which discusses open scheduling problems in CERIT-SC.

4.3   Global Criteria

Except for the overall CPU utilization (total allocated CPUs throughout the time), there are currently no global criteria used to measure the performance of the whole system, i.e., how well the cloud and grid partitions co-exist together.

5   Open Problems

Although the CERIT-SC system is production-grade and currently operates without any major problems, there are still several unresolved (scheduling) problems that must be addressed in the (near) future. In the following text we summarize these problems and their origins.

5.1   Advanced VM-Packing and Adaptive Re-scheduling

In the cloud environment, we would like to improve the quality of VM scheduling. Especially, we want to investigate whether VMs can be efficiently "packed" on the physical nodes such that their combined resource requests (e.g., CPU, RAM, disk space, disk I/O and network I/O) are reasonably balanced *throughout the time*. Here we are facing the limits of the current VM scheduler used in the Open-Nebula framework which does not provide any intelligent VM (re)scheduling heuristic that would adapt VMs allocations in time. By default, it only schedules VMs upon their deployment based on their predefined resource requests. No further optimization — based on an actual performance of a running VM — is done during a VM lifetime.

Clearly, this leaves an open space for improvements as currently some nodes may be occupied by idle VMs (resource wasting) while other nodes may be overloaded with VMs competing for resources such as CPUs, I/O, etc. As was demonstrated in Fig. 8, there seem to be many opportunities how to improve, e.g., the CPU load. For example, the scheduler should be able to dynamically reschedule idle VMs, possibly migrating them to heavily overbooked nodes, thus freeing their original hosts for more demanding or new (pending) VMs. Similarly, when a node becomes overloaded by its VMs, some of them should be rescheduled/migrated to decrease the host's contention.

In order to actually enable such functionality one must however not only develop a new advanced scheduler but also invest in the underlying infrastructure to allow such live VM migrations. In this case, a dedicated distributed storage facility (e.g., the *Ceph* [23]) is needed to allow for live migrations, which is not currently fully operational in CERIT-SC.

5.2   Resource Reclaiming

As discussed in Sect. 2, the major benefit of resource virtualization in CERIT-SC is that the actual amount of resources available either to the grid or to the cloud can be easily and dynamically adapted, simply by changing the number of running "grid worker" VMs. In practice however, this mechanism does not work that easily due to the nature of our cloud workload. In fact, it works flawlessly when more resources are required for the cloud VMs. In that case, several "grid worker" nodes are first drained, i.e., all grid jobs running inside the worker are completed and new jobs are not allowed to start there. Then the given "grid worker" VM is terminated and its host becomes available to the classic cloud VMs. The problem is that the same mechanism does not work so easily in the opposite direction, i.e., it is not always easy to drain a host that is hosting running cloud VMs. As discussed in Sect. 3.1, in CERIT-SC the runtime of a VM is unbounded and unknown, in general. Therefore it is impossible to drain a node by the same mechanism that works in the grid. Theoretically, VMs that execute on a node can be migrated, but this may not be always possible, e.g., when the cloud infrastructure is already saturated by running VMs.

This is currently our major threat, since the cloud allocations in our system are increasing very quickly (see Fig. 9 (top)), yet we do not have any "automated" resource-reclaiming mechanism. Another problem is that CERIT-SC *provides its resources for free* to anyone who is affiliated with the scientific/academia community in the Czech Republic (university students/teachers, academic researchers, etc.). Therefore, it does not use some form of the "pay-per-use" model which is otherwise very suitable to motivate users to stop their VMs once they are not needed anymore. At the same time, CERIT-SC's budget is fixed, i.e., we cannot just buy another cluster whenever the demand is approaching the available capacity.

5.3   Fair-Sharing in Cloud

The absence of the "pay-per-use" model together with the rather poor resource-reclaiming in our cloud brings another problem — the resources are allocated to the users without considering some overall fairness. This is in great contrast with the grid installation, where fairness is one of the major optimization goals and is managed by the fair-sharing approach [13]. As was shown in Fig. 9 (top), the majority of cloud resources is consumed by few users over a long time period, yet there is no automated mechanism that would force them to decrease their allocations, letting other users to use the system.

Apparently, we should adopt some analogy of the fair-sharing in our cloud installation. Perhaps a good starting point would be to prioritize users (based on their resource usage) and automatically decrease allocations for long running VMs of low priority users (i.e., increase VMs overcommitment factor). Solving this problem will however require major changes in the current, rather naive, scheduler used in the OpenNebula framework.

5.4   Load-Balancing

Upon solving the problems mentioned in Sects. 5.1–5.3 we start to focus on the global scheduling problems such as load-balancing among the applications/frameworks. Certainly, our workloads indicate that there are many opportunities to use temporarily idle resources. For example, short jobs from the grid can probably "steal the cycles" when cloud VMs are idle, because the average load of allocated CPU cores in the cloud is currently bellow 30% in most cases. For this purpose a "sleeping grid worker" VM could be launched on every host with a huge overcommitment factor during its idle phase. Then, upon the request of the batch system, such a sleeping grid worker VM can be woken up by increasing its resource allocations and used for (short) grid jobs. In this way, many short and/or narrow grid jobs can use even very time-limited opportunities, e.g., when cloud VMs are idle during the night.

The question is to how to actually implement such an inter-application scheduling. One way is to try to build upon existing frameworks like Apache Mesos [6], or use some form of a module in the existing underlying platform — in this case inside the OpenNebula SW stack. The decision process is further complicated by the fact that new frameworks like OpenStack [9] and/or Docker [17] are currently tested and will be probably offered in the near future to our users. Therefore we must not only focus on the "optimal result" but also keep in mind that our development team has a limited capacity. Thus, every new framework and/or functionality then brings not only opportunities but problems too.

6   Workload Formatting and Conclusion

In this paper we have provided a detailed analysis of the mixed workload traces from the CERIT-SC system. Presented workloads can be freely obtained at the JSSPP's public workload archive [12]. Since the workload logs come from two different systems, they are provided in two different formats.

The grid-based workload is formatted according to the well-know Standard Workload Format (SWF) which is adopted in the Parallel Workloads Archive [4]. SWF formatting rules are described at the Parallel Workloads Archive's website[7]. Additional information that are not supported by the original SWF format but may be useful for some simulations are added at the end of each job entry (i.e., at the end of a line) into newly defined fields and are separated by whitespaces. These additional fields include the specifications of used computing node(s) (i.e., hostname(s)), human-readable name of the queue, so-called "node-spec" (i.e., detailed job description taken from the qsub command, including per-node specified number of requested resources) and the number of requested GPUs.

The cloud-based workload describing all VMs is formatted in a JSON (JavaScript Object Notation) format [11]. Unlike the jobs in the grid workload that are non-preemptible, cloud VMs can be executed repeatedly and thus require more complex data structure to describe their (repeated) executions. For this purpose the array feature of JSON is very suitable.

Although there are many SWF and JSON parsers available [4,11], we provide a set of simple java parsers that can be used to parse the aforementioned workload traces. Moreover, they calculate and print several statistics that were used in this paper. These parsers are provided along with the workloads at the JSSPP's workload archive [12].

Acknowledgments. We kindly acknowledge the support and computational resources provided by the MetaCentrum under the program LM2015042 and the CERIT Scientific Cloud under the program LM2015085, provided under the programme "Projects of Large Infrastructure for Research, Development, and Innovations" and the project Reg. No. CZ.02.1.01/0.0/0.0/16_013/0001797 co-funded by the Ministry of Education, Youth and Sports of the Czech Republic. We also highly appreciate the access to CERIT Scientific Cloud workload traces.

---

[7] SWF format: http://www.cs.huji.ac.il/labs/parallel/workload/swf.html.

References

1. Adaptive Computing Enterprises, Inc.: Torque 6.1.0 Administrator Guide, February 2017. http://docs.adaptivecomputing.com
2. CERIT Scientific Cloud, February 2017. http://www.cerit-sc.cz
3. Ernemann, C., Hamscher, V., Yahyapour, R.: Benefits of global Grid computing for job scheduling. In: Proceedings of the 5th IEEE/ACM International Workshop on Grid Computing, GRID 2004, pp. 374–379. IEEE (2004)
4. Feitelson, D.G.: Parallel workloads archive, February 2017. http://www.cs.huji.ac.il/labs/parallel/workload/
5. Feitelson, D.G., Rudolph, L., Schwiegelshohn, U., Sevcik, K.C., Wong, P.: Theory and practice in parallel job scheduling. In: Feitelson, D.G., Rudolph, L. (eds.) JSSPP 1997. LNCS, vol. 1291, pp. 1–34. Springer, Heidelberg (1997). https://doi.org/10.1007/3-540-63574-2_14
6. Hindman, B., Konwinski, A., Zaharia, M., Ghodsi, A., Joseph, A.D., Katz, R., Shenker, S., Stoica, I.: Mesos: a platform for fine-grained resource sharing in the data center. In: Proceedings of the 8th USENIX Conference on Networked Systems Design and Implementation, NSDI 2011, pp. 295–308, Berkeley, CA, USA. USENIX Association (2011)
7. Iosup, A., Li, H., Jan, M., Anoep, S., Dumitrescu, C., Wolters, L., Epema, D.H.J.: The Grid workloads archive. Future Gener. Comput. Syst. **24**(7), 672–686 (2008)
8. Jackson, D., Snell, Q., Clement, M.: Core algorithms of the Maui scheduler. In: Feitelson, D.G., Rudolph, L. (eds.) JSSPP 2001. LNCS, vol. 2221, pp. 87–102. Springer, Heidelberg (2001). https://doi.org/10.1007/3-540-45540-X_6
9. Jackson, K.: OpenStack Cloud Computing Cookbook. Packt Publishing, Birmingham (2012)
10. Jones, C., Wilkes, J., Murphy, N., Smith, C., Beyer, B.: Service level objectives. In: Beyer, B., Jones, C., Petoff, J., Murphy, N. (eds.), Site Reliability Engineering: How Google Runs Production Systems, Chap. 4. O'Reilly Media (2016). https://landing.google.com/sre/book.html
11. Introducing JSON, February 2017. http://www.json.org/
12. Klusáček, D.: Workload traces from CERIT Scientific Cloud, February 2017. http://jsspp.org/workload/
13. Klusáček, D., Chlumský, V.: Planning and metaheuristic optimization in production job scheduler. In: Desai, N., Cirne, W. (eds.) JSSPP 2015-2016. LNCS, vol. 10353, pp. 198–216. Springer, Cham (2017). https://doi.org/10.1007/978-3-319-61756-5_11
14. Klusáček, D., Tóth, Š.: On interactions among scheduling policies: finding efficient queue setup using high-resolution simulations. In: Silva, F., Dutra, I., Santos Costa, V. (eds.) Euro-Par 2014. LNCS, vol. 8632, pp. 138–149. Springer, Cham (2014). https://doi.org/10.1007/978-3-319-09873-9_12
15. Klusáček, D., Tóth, Š., Podolníková, G.: Real-life experience with major reconfiguration of job scheduling system. In: Desai, N., Cirne, W. (eds.) JSSPP 2015-2016. LNCS, vol. 10353, pp. 83–101. Springer, Cham (2017). https://doi.org/10.1007/978-3-319-61756-5_5
16. Krakov, D., Feitelson, D.G.: High-resolution analysis of parallel job workloads. In: Cirne, W., Desai, N., Frachtenberg, E., Schwiegelshohn, U. (eds.) JSSPP 2012. LNCS, vol. 7698, pp. 178–195. Springer, Heidelberg (2013). https://doi.org/10.1007/978-3-642-35867-8_10

17. Merkel, D.: Docker: lightweight Linux containers for consistent development and deployment. Linux J. **2014**(239), 2 (2014)
18. MetaCentrum, February 2017. http://www.metacentrum.cz/
19. Montero, R.S., Llorente, I.M., Miloji, D.: OpenNebula: a cloud management tool. IEEE Internet Comput. **15**(2), 11–14 (2011)
20. Mu'alem, A.W., Feitelson, D.G.: Utilization, predictability, workloads, and user runtime estimates in scheduling the IBM SP2 with backfilling. IEEE Trans. Parallel Distrib.Syst. **12**(6), 529–543 (2001)
21. Managing virtual machines, February 2017. https://archives.opennebula.org/documentation:rel4.4:vm_guide_2
22. Reiss, C., Wilkes, J., Hellerstein, J.L.: Google cluster-usage traces: format+schema. Technical report, Google Inc., Mountain View, CA, USA, November 2011. Version 2.1. Posted at https://github.com/google/cluster-data. Accessed 17 Nov 2014
23. Singh, K.: Ceph Cookbook. Packt Publishing, Birmingham (2016)
24. SWIM workload repository, February 2017. https://github.com/SWIMProjectUCB/SWIM/wiki/Workloads-repository
25. Wolski, R., Brevik, J.: Using parametric models to represent private cloud workloads. IEEE Trans. Serv. Comput. **7**(4), 714–725 (2014)

Tuning EASY-Backfilling Queues

Jérôme Lelong, Valentin Reis$^{(\boxtimes)}$, and Denis Trystram

Univ. Grenoble Alpes, CNRS, Inria, LIG, LJK, Grenoble, France
{jerome.lelong,valentin.reis,denis.trystram}@imag.fr

Abstract. EASY-Backfilling is a popular scheduling heuristic for allocating jobs in large scale High Performance Computing platforms. While its aggressive reservation mechanism is fast and prevents job starvation, it does not try to optimize any scheduling objective *per se*. We consider in this work the problem of tuning EASY using queue reordering policies. More precisely, we propose to tune the reordering using a simulation-based methodology. For a given system, we choose the policy in order to minimize the average waiting time. This methodology departs from the First-Come, First-Serve rule and introduces a risk on the maximum values of the waiting time, which we control using a queue thresholding mechanism. This new approach is evaluated through a comprehensive experimental campaign on five production logs. In particular, we show that the behavior of the systems under study is stable enough to learn a heuristic that generalizes in a *train/test* fashion. Indeed, the average waiting time can be reduced consistently (between 11% to 42% for the logs used) compared to EASY, with almost no increase in maximum waiting times. This work departs from previous learning-based approaches and shows that scheduling heuristics for HPC can be learned directly in a policy space.

1 Introduction

The main challenge of the High Performance Computing community (HPC) is to build extreme scale platforms that can be efficiently exploited. The number of processors on such platforms will drastically increase and more processing capabilities will obviously lead to more data produced [10]. Moreover, new computing systems are expected to run more flexible workloads. Seldom supported by the existing managing resource systems, the future schedulers should take advantage of this flexibility to optimize the performance of the system. The extreme scale generates a huge amount of data at run-time. Collecting relevant information is a prerequisite for determining efficient allocations.

The resources of such platforms are usually subject to competition by many users submitting their jobs. Parallel job scheduling is a crucial problem to address for a better use of the resources. Efficient scheduling of parallel jobs is a challenging task which promises great improvements in various directions, including improved machine utilization, energy efficiency, throughput and response time. The scheduling problems are not only computationally hard, but in practice they are also plagued with uncertainty as many parameters of the problem

© Springer International Publishing AG, part of Springer Nature 2018
D. Klusáček et al. (Eds.): JSSPP 2017, LNCS 10773, pp. 43–61, 2018.
https://doi.org/10.1007/978-3-319-77398-8_3

are unknown while taking decisions. As a consequence, the actual production platforms currently rely on very basic heuristics based on queues of submitted jobs ordered in various ways. The most used heuristic is the well-known EASY-backfilling policy [20,24]. While EASY is simple, fast to execute and prevents starvation, it does not fare especially well with respect to cumulative cost metrics such as the average waiting time of the jobs. Therefore, many HPC code developers and system administrators intend to tune this heuristic by reordering either the *primary* queue or the *backfilling* queue. Since such reordering of job queues may introduce starvation in the scheduling, this results in a dilemma between the average and maximal costs. In order to solve this dilemma, we introduce a thresholding mechanism that can effectively manage the risk of reaching too large objective values. This issue is further complicated by the dependency of the relative scheduling performances on system characteristics and workload profiles. We propose in this work to use simulations in order to choose queue reordering policies. Finally, we study the empirical generalization and stability of this methodology and open the door for further learning-based approaches.

The rest of the paper is organized as follows: Sect. 2 reviews existing resource management approaches from the literature. Section 3 describes the context and states the problem. Section 4 describes an experimental setup that is essential to the discussion. Section 5 introduce our approach, illustrating the discussion with results from the KTH-SP2 trace. Section 6 describes the thresholding mechanism used. Section 7 validates this approach using a comprehensive experimental campaign on 5 logs from the Parallel Workload Archive [14].

2   Related Works

This section presents current solutions to the scheduling problem and the current direction taken by the field.

2.1   Scheduling Heuristics in HPC Platforms

While parallel job scheduling is a well studied theoretical problem [19], the practical ramifications, varying hypotheses, and inherent uncertainty of the problem in HPC have driven practitioners and researchers alike to use and study simple heuristics. The two most popular heuristics for HPC platforms are EASY [24] and Conservative [21] Backfilling.

While Conservative Backfilling offers many advantages [25], it has a significant computational overhead, perhaps explaining why most of the machines of the top500 ranking [3] still use at the time of this publication a variant of EASY Backfilling.

2.2   EASY

There is a large body of work seeking to improve EASY. Indeed, while the heuristic is used by various resource and job management softwares (most notably SLURM [2]), this is rarely done without fine tunings by system administrators.

Several works explore how to tune EASY by reordering waiting and/or back-filling queues [29], sometimes even in a randomized manner [23], as well as some implementations [17]. However, as successful as they may be, these works do not address the dependency [5] of scheduling metrics on the workload. Indeed these studies most often report *post-hoc* performance since they compare algorithms after the workload is known.

The dynP scheduler [27] proposes a systematic method to tuning these queues, although it requires simulated scheduling runs at decision time and therefore costs much more than the natural execution of EASY.

2.3   Data-Aware Resource Management

There is a recent focus on leveraging the high amount of data available in large scale computing systems in order to improve their behavior. Some works use collaborative filtering to colocate tasks in clouds by estimating application interference [30]. Others are closer to the application level and use binary classification to distinguish benign memory faults from application errors in order to execute recovery algorithms (see [31] for instance).

Several works use this method in the context of HPC, in particular [16,29], hoping that better job runtime estimations should improve the scheduling [9]. Some algorithms estimate runtime distributions model and choose jobs using probabilistic integration procedures [22].

However, these works do not address the duality between the cumulative and maximal scheduling costs, as mentioned in [16].

While these previous works intend to estimate uncertain parameters, we consider in this paper a more pragmatic approach, which is to directly learn a good scheduling policy from a given policy space.

3   Problem Setting

This section describes the generic platform model used in this paper. It recalls the EASY heuristic and defines two scheduling cost metrics to be minimized. Finally, it motivates and introduces the problem statement of this paper.

3.1   System Description

The problem addressed in this paper is the one faced by Resource and Job Management Systems (RJMS) such as SLURM [2], PBS [1] and OAR [7] and more recently by Flux [4].

The crucial part of these softwares is the scheduling algorithm that determines where and when the submitted jobs are executed. The process is as follows: jobs are submitted by end-users and queued until the scheduler selects one of them for running. Each job has a provided bound on the execution time and some resource requirements (number and type of processing units). Then, the

RJMS drives the search for the resources required to execute this job. Finally, the tasks of the job are assigned to the chosen nodes.

In the classical case, these softwares need to execute a set of concurrent parallel jobs with rigid (known and fixed) resource requirements on a HPC platform represented by a pool of m identical resources. This is an on-line problem since the jobs are submitted over time and their characteristics are only known when they are released. Below is the description and the notations of the characteristics of job j:

- Submission date r_j (also called *release date*)
- Resource requirement q_j (number of processors)
- Actual running time p_j (sometimes called *processing time*)
- Requested running time $\widetilde{p}_j$ (sometimes called *walltime*), which is an upper bound of p_j.

The resource requirement q_j of job j is known when the job is submitted at time r_j, while the requested running time $\widetilde{p}_j$ is given by the user as an estimate. Its actual value p_j is only known *a posteriori* when the job really completes. Moreover, the users have incentive to over-estimate the actual values, since jobs may be "killed" if they surpass the provided value.

3.2 EASY Backfilling

The selection of the job to run is performed according to a scheduling policy that establishes the order in which the jobs are executed. EASY-Backfilling is the most widely used policy due to its simple and robust implementation and known benefits such as high system utilization [24]. This strategy has no worst case guarantee beyond the absence of starvation (i.e. every job will be scheduled at some moment).

The EASY heuristic uses a job queue to perform job starting/reservation (the *primary* queue) and job *backfilling* (the *backfilling* queue). These queues can be dissociated and the heuristic can be parametrized via both a primary policy and a backfilling policy. This is typically done by ordering both queues in an identical manner using job attributes. In the following, we denote by EASY-P_R-P_B the scheduling policy that starts jobs and does the reservation according to policy P_R and backfills according to policy P_B. For the sake of completeness, Algorithm 1 describes the EASY-P_R-P_B heuristic.

This paper makes use of 7 classical queue reordering policies that are presented below:

- FCFS: First-Come First-Serve, which is the widely used default policy [24].
- LCFS: Last-Come First-Serve.
- LPF: Longest estimated Processing time $\widetilde{p}_j$ First.
- SPF: Smallest estimated Processing time $\widetilde{p}_j$ First [25].
- LQF: Largest resource requirement q_j First.
- SQF: Smallest resource requirement q_j First.

Algorithm 1. EASY-P_R-P_B policy

Input: Queue Q of waiting jobs.
Output: None (calls to $Start()$)
    Starting jobs in the P_R order
 1: Sort Q according to P_R
 2: **for** job j **do**
 3:    Pop j from Q
 4:    **if** j can be started given the current system use. **then**
 5:      $Start(j)$
 6:    **else**
 7:      Reserve j at the earliest time possible according to the estimated running times of the currently running jobs.
       Backfill jobs in the P_B order
 8:      $L \leftarrow Q$
 9:      Sort L according to P_B
10:      **for** job j' in L **do**
11:        **if** j' can be started without delaying the reservation on j. **then**
12:          $Start(j')$
13:        **end if**
14:      **end for**
15:      **break**
16:    **end if**
17: **end for**

- EXP: Largest Expansion Factor First [25], where the expansion factor is defined as follows:

$$\frac{wait_j + \widetilde{p}_j}{\widetilde{p}_j} \tag{1}$$

where $wait_j$ is the waiting time until now of job j.

This search set is taken to maximize semantic diversity, without passing judgement on which policy should be the best for a particular objective.

3.3   Scheduling Metric

A system administrator may use one or multiple cost metric(s). Our study of scheduling performance relies on the waiting times of the jobs, which is one of the more commonly used reference.

$$\textbf{Wait}_j = start_j - r_j \tag{2}$$

Like other cost metrics, the waiting time is usually considered in its *cumulative* version, which means that one seeks to minimize the average waiting time (**AvgWait**). In the following, we will also use the maximal version of this cost metric which we denote by **MaxWait**, a.k.a the maximal value of the waiting time of all the jobs from a scheduling run.

3.4   Problem Description

There are in the authors' view two main difficulties when effectively tuning the EASY heuristic. Each of these two issues are illustrated below by a dedicated scheduling experiment.

First, the relative performance of EASY policies is sensitive to the context [5, 25]. Table 1 illustrates this effect by comparing the AvgWait of two different queue ordering policies on the logs of two different workloads from the Parallel Workload Archive. The results suggest that there is no "one size fits all" choice of primary and backfilling queue policies. In such a situation, tuning EASY must be done locally for each HPC system. This can be done via simulation, taking care that the results *generalize* to the future.

Second, starvation may occur when changing the EASY queue policy away from FCFS. This issue concerns the method used to measure the objective. Most systems use a variant of the EASY- FCFS-FCFS policy, where the FCFS policy is used both for primary and backfilling queues. The main advantage of this choice is that it controls the *starvation risk* by greedily minimizing the maximum values of the job waiting times. Indeed, a job might be indefinitely delayed when not starting jobs in the FCFS order. This effect was pointed out in some related works [16, 29] that optimize the average cost by removing the FCFS constraint. Table 2 illustrates this effect by reporting the AvgWait and MaxWait of the EASY-SPF-SPF and EASY-FCFS-FCFS strategies on the CTC-SP2 trace.

In this paper, we would like to study the following question: **How to leverage workload data in order to improve cumulative cost metrics while controlling their maximum values?**

In order to answer this question, we investigate the use of simulation to tune EASY-P_R-P_B by reordering its two queues. The first conclusion is that reordering the primary queue is more beneficial than simply reordering the backfilling queue. However, this introduces a risk on the maximum values of the objective,

Table 1. AvgWait performance of EASY-EXP-EXP and EASY-SQF-SQF on the original CTC-SP2 and SDSC-SP2 traces, in seconds.

	CTC-SP2	SDSC-SP2
EASY-EXP-EXP	3074	6765
EASY-SQF-SQF	2090	11234

Table 2. AvgWait and MaxWait performance of EASY-SPF-SPF and EASY-FCFS-FCFS on the original CTC-SP2 trace, in seconds.

	EASY-SPF-SPF	EASY-FCFS-FCFS
AvgWait	2784	3974
MaxWait	661280	176090

which we control by hybridizing FCFS and the reordering policy via a thresholding mechanism. Finally, we show that the experimental performance of the thresholded heuristics generalizes well to unseen data.

4   Experimental Protocol

This section motivates the statistical approach used to measure performance and describes the simulation method.

4.1   Statistical Approach

The experimental approach used in this paper is statistical by nature. Figure 1 shows how the AvgWaits of the 7 primary policies used along with FCFS backfilling evolves during the first 150 weeks of the "cleaned"[1] KTH-SP2 trace from the Parallel Workloads Archive. The variability [5,15] of cost metrics and their sensitivity to small changes in the workload logs [28] have been thoroughly studied in the literature. Our approach to measuring performance without reporting noise from workload flurries [28] is to aggregate the cost metric on a large number of generated logs. In this way, we can report the variability along with the average values. The trace generation approach of this paper follows in part the methodology of [12]: We design a trace resampler in order to generate weeklong workload logs from an original dataset. The resampling technique used is simplistic in nature: for each system user, a random week of job submissions

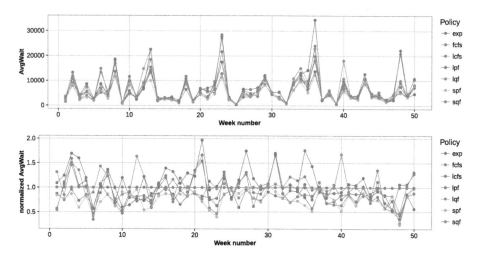

Fig. 1. AvgWait obtained for the 7 main queue policies with **FCFS** backfilling for 150 generated weeks on the KTH-SP2 trace. First, in absolute value, and then normalized with respect to EASY-FCFS-FCFS.

---

[1] See the Parallel Workloads Archive [14] for details.

from the original trace is used. This approach is combinatorially sufficient to generate infinitely many logs while preserving the natural dependency of the workload on the weekly period and the variability in load. On the downside, the seasonal effect and the dependency between users are lost. Moreover, there is no user model or other feedback loop in the simulations. In all experiments, the performance of every policy is evaluated by averaging the cost values over 250 generated weeks.

4.2 Simulation Method and Testbed

While high quality simulators like SimGrid [8] are available in practice, this paper focuses on backfilling behavior and does not need to use such advanced tools. This is motivated by the fact that one needs to use a high-performance approach to simulation in order to perform the high number of scheduling runs necessary for this study (the total number of week-long simulations in this paper is of the order of 10^6). Therefore, experiments are run with a specially written lightweight backfilling scheduler. Since there is a need for both speed of execution and generality of application, our scheduler simulator discards all topological information from the original machines. Using this simulator, a week of EASY backfilling can be replayed in under a tenth of a second for the KTH-SP2 machine, the I/O operations (reading and writing a swf file) included. All simulations are performed on a Dell PowerEdge T630 machine with 2x Intel(R) Xeon(R) CPU E5-2697 v3 @ 2.60 GHz/14 cores (28 cores/node), and 260 GB of RAM. We use a minimalistic approach to reproducible research [26] and provide a snapshot of the work that includes a build system that runs the experiments using the *zymake* [6] minimalistic workflow system. The archive includes our simulator and a nix [11] file that describes the dependencies.

5 Primary and Backfilling Queues

This section presents a dedicated experimental campaign that uses the KTH-SP2 trace in order to illustrate the contradictory effect of average and maximum cost.

5.1 Maximum and Average Cost

Figures 2 and 3 show a bi-objective view of the *post-hoc* optimization problem of choosing a primary and backfilling policy among all 49 possible combinations (7 policies for the primary queue and 7 for the backfilling queue). The two objectives are the cumulative and maximal costs. In order to obtain a truthful overview of the variability, we use a sample size of 250 weeks and all values are recentered on the performance of EASY-FCFS-FCFS for that particular week. Figures 2 and 3 vary in terms of y axis. In Fig. 2, the y axis is the maximum MaxWait over simulated week, i.e. the highest waiting time of any job on all the simulated weeks. In Fig. 3, the y axis is the average MaxWait over the 250 weeks.

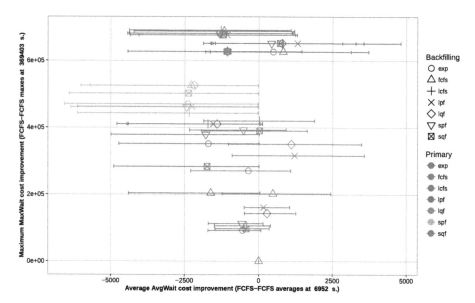

Fig. 2. Maximum and average waiting time cost of the 49 heuristics generated by using the 7 possible policies as primary and backfilling ordering averaged over 250 resampled weeks. All values are relative to the value obtained by the **EASY** primary queue policy with **EASY** backfilling. The maximum MaxWait value reported is the maximum waiting time of all jobs in the 250 weeks. The average AvgWait value is the mean of the weekly waiting time averages, and the range indicates the first and last decile of the samples.

The average value reported is the mean average cost over individual weeks, which allows for displaying deciles in both directions. Note that Fig. 2 is a more aggressive way of reporting this value. There are two main observations.

First, it seems possible to improve the AvgWait on this machine as far as to reduce it of 30% *in hindsight* compared to the EASY-FCFS-FCFS baseline. However, such AvgWait improvements seem to entail an increase in MaxWait. Expectedly, the EASY-FCFS-FCFS heuristic has a good MaxWait behavior.

Second, there seems to be regularities in the performance's behavior: The main factor certainly come from the primary queue policy, while the importance of the backfilling policy varies depending on the primary policy. It appears that some policies such as SQF do not lead to many backfilling decisions, while others like LQF encourage frequent backfilling. Additionally, there are some backfilling policies, such as SPF and ExpFact that systematically outperform the others.

5.2   Comparing Backfilling Policies

It is an interesting question to ask whether some backfilling policies are consistently better than others regardless of primary scheduling policies. As Fig. 4 shows, the AvgWait performance of all backfilling policies relative to

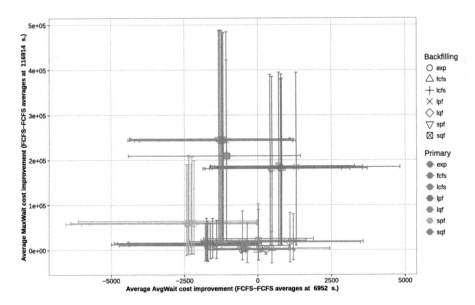

Fig. 3. Maximum and average waiting time cost of the 49 heuristics generated by using the 7 possible policies as primary and backfilling ordering averaged over 250 resampled weeks. All values are relative to the value obtained by the **EASY** primary queue policy with **EASY** backfilling. The average MaxWait value reported is the average of the maximum waiting time over 250 weeks. The average AvgWait value is as in Fig. 2 the mean of the weekly waiting time averages, and the range indicates the first and last decile of the samples, both in x and y scale.

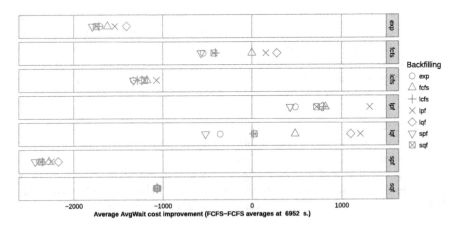

Fig. 4. Performance improvement over EASY-FCFS-FCFS of the 7 Backfilling policies conditioned on Primary policy.

EASY-FCFS-FCFS presents roughly the same relative performance for each primary queue policy. Namely, for this machine the SPF backfilling policy was always the best from our search space in hindsight. We do not elaborate on this aspect here. In the next section, we focus on the maximal costs incurred by the tuned heuristic.

6 Queue Threshold

This section introduces control over the maximal costs using a thresholding mechanism.

6.1 Thresholding and Risk

The future costs Wait_j of a waiting job j are lower-bounded at any time t by the value of the waiting time so far, $t - r_j$.[2] A simple way to introduce robustness

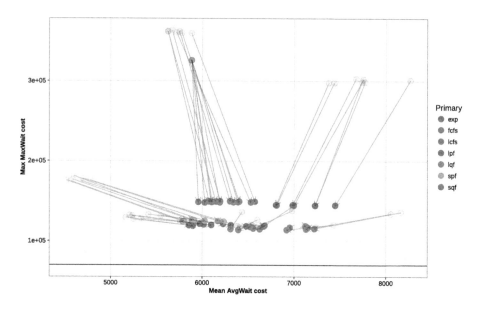

Fig. 5. Maximum and average waiting time cost of the 7 heuristics generated by using the 7 possible thresholded primary policies with SPF backfilling averaged over 250 resampled weeks. The threshold T is chosen at a value of 20 h. All values are relative to the value obtained by the **EASY** primary queue policy with **EASY** backfilling. The average MaxWait value reported is the maximum waiting time of all jobs in the 250 weeks. The average AvgWait value is as in Fig. 2 the mean of the weekly waiting time averages. Semi-transparent points represent the performance of the un-thresholded policies.

---

[2] Note that this is also valid for the more refined Average Bounded Slowdown [13] metric.

into the heuristic is therefore to force jobs with unusually high values of $t - r_j$ ahead of the primary queue. One way to do this is to introduce a threshold parameter T and push jobs with $t - r_j > T$ immediately ahead of the primary queue after the primary queue sorting step (line 1 of Algorithm 1). If more than one job is in this situation, these jobs are ordered by submission time r_j at the head of the queue.

Figure 5 illustrates the effect on 7 possible heuristics on the KTH-SP2 system with $T = 20\,h$. The heuristics search space is diminished by fixing the backfilling policy to SPF (see Subsect. 5.2) for pure visual reasons and exhaustive treatment is delayed to Sect. 7. The threshold is reported as a horizontal line on the figure. The MaxWait is greatly reduced, while all AvgWait values are (perhaps expectedly) moved towards EASY-FCFS-FCFS. This mechanism seems to be a hopeful candidate for tuning the queue policies while controlling the waiting time of rogue jobs.

The next section gives a glimpse of the behavior of generalization in this framework.

7 Experimental Validation

This section presents a systematic study of EASY-P_R-P_B tuning.

7.1 Generalization Protocol

The goal of the experimental campaign is to study how the performance of different heuristics generalize empirically. That is to say, can EASY Backfilling be tuned on specific workload data? We follow the most simple protocol for assessing learnability:

The initial workload is split at temporal midpoint in two parts, the *training* and *testing* logs. Each of these are used to resample weeks. For each HPC log from the Parallel Workload archive used in the experiment, this process results in two databases of 250 weeks each. The experimental campaign will consist in running simulations on the training weeks, selecting the best performing policy (tuning the heuristic), and evaluating the performance of this policy on the testing weeks. The search space for EASY-P_R-P_B will be the set of dimension 49 composed by the choice of 7 policies as Primary reordering policy and 7 policies as Backfilling reordering policy.

This simple approach to measuring performance generalization corresponds to the situation where a system administrator having retained usage logs from a HPC center must choose a scheduling policy for the next period.

7.2 Workload Logs

Table 3 outlines the five workload logs from the Parallel Workloads Archive [14] used in the experiments. These logs cover both older and more recent machines

Table 3. Workload logs used in the simulations.

Name	Year	# CPUs	# Jobs	Duration
KTH-SP2	1996	100	28k	11 months
CTC-SP2	1996	338	77k	11 months
SDSC-SP2	2000	128	59k	24 months
SDSC-BLUE	2003	1, 152	243k	32 months
CEA-Curie	2012	80, 640	312k	3 months

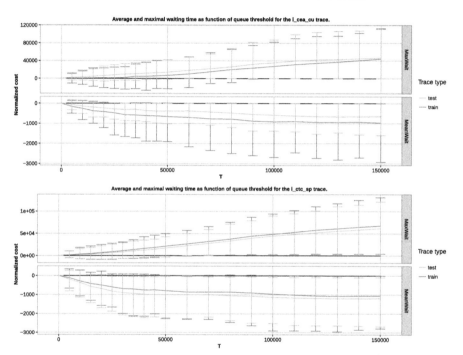

Fig. 6. AvgWait and MaxWait generalization of thresholded policies as affected by the queue threshold. The Value reported as "train" is that of the least costly heuristic among the 49 possible policy parametrizations averaged on the *training* logs. The Value reported as "test" is the averaged cost of the same heuristic on the *testing* logs. This figure is continued as Fig. 7.

of varying size and length. The logs are subject to pre-filtering. The filtering step excludes jobs with $\widetilde{p}_j < p_j$ and jobs whose "requested_cores" and "allocated_cores" fields exceed the size of the machine.

7.3   Empirical Generalization Results

Figure 7 summarizes the behavior of the empirical generalization and risk of the waiting time with respect to the value of the threshold T. There is a fortunate

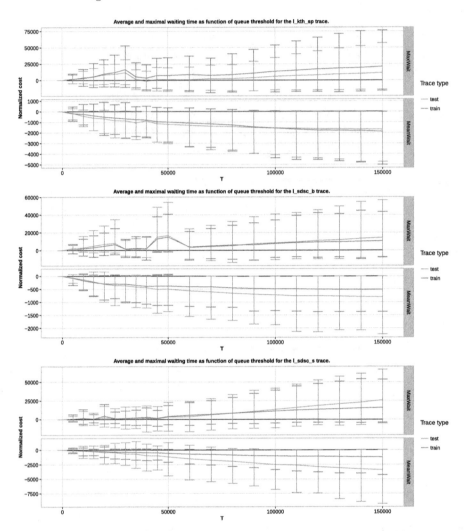

Fig. 7. Follow-up from Fig. 7.

effect in that the values from the lower parts of the graphs (the *AvgWait* cost) seem to decrease faster than values from the upper part (the *MaxWait* cost), which increases linearly with T.

By using an aggressive approach (no threshold), the AvgWait can be reduced until 80% to 65% compared to the EASY-FCFS-FCFS baseline. However, in that case the values of the MaxWait can jump as high as 250% that of the baseline.

By using a conservative approach (thresholding at 20 h), the AvgWait can be reduced until 90% to 70% in expectation, while keeping the MaxWait increase under 175% of the baseline in all cases.

Figure 8 shows how the AvgWait of the 49 combination of queue and back-filling policies evolve from the training to the testing logs when we use this conservative threshold of 20 h, with a higher sample size that was not permitted by the previous experiment. This confirms the previous values and gives

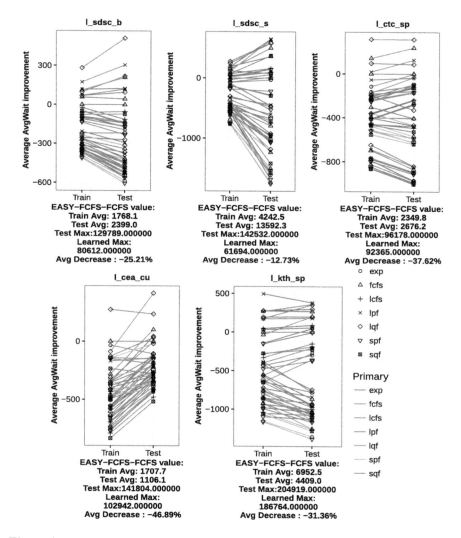

Fig. 8. AvgWait generalization of thresholded policies obtained by using a threshold value of 20 h. Note that each plot has a different vertical y axis. The reported AvgWait and MaxWait values are averaged over 250 resampled weeks from the training or testing original logs, and we report the difference with the cost of EASY-FCFS-FCFS. The average of the baseline EASY-FCFS-FCFS is reported under the figure, along with the average MaxWait obtained by the best training policy on the testing logs (the "learned" policy).

visual insight into the stability of the performance. Finally, we state the fact that while simplicity of exposure forces us to only deal with the waiting time, the results presented in this work are also valid for the more refined Average Bounded Slowdown [13].

7.4 Generalization with $T = 20\,h$

The final step is to study how the performance thresholded queue policies generalizes. Figure 8 shows how the performance of all various queue and backfilling policies evolve from *training* to *testing* logs when the threshold is set to an example value of 20 h. While the values change from *training* to *testing* logs, the relative order of policies seems to be roughly conserved. This leaves hope for generalization. Moreover, it is possible from this figure to measure the improvement resulting from our methodology. We obtain AvgWait average diminutions of 21%, 11%, 36%, 42% and 29% respectively for the SDSC-BLUE, SDSC-SP2, CTC-SP2, CEA-CURIE, and KTH-SP2 machines. The approach does keep the average MaxWait in a reasonable range, and in fact the average testing AvgWait of the learned policy only surpasses that of EASY-FCFS-FCFS on the CEA-Curie trace, with a minor increase, the learned strategy's average MaxWait is of 88747 compared to a value of 86680 for the baseline.

8 Conclusion

This work leverages the fact that the performance of scheduling heuristics depends on the workload profile of the system. More precisely, we investigated the use of simulation to tune the EASY-Backfilling heuristic by reordering its two queues. The first conclusion is that reordering the primary queue is more beneficial than simply reordering the backfilling queue. However, this introduces a risk on the maximum values of the objective, which we control by hybridizing FCFS and the reordering policy via a thresholding mechanism. Finally, we showed that the experimental performance of the thresholded heuristics generalizes well. Therefore, this framework allows a system administrator to tune EASY using a simulator. Moreover, the attitude torwards risk in maximum values can be adapted via the threshold value. With a low threshold value, the increase in maximal cost is small but the learned policy does not take too much risk. It is possible to gain more by increasing the threshold, but this comes with an increase in the maximal cost. Two questions concerning the learning of EASY policies arise from this work.

First, the stability of other EASY heuristic classes remains unknown. The "simple" class of composed of 7 primary policies and 7 backfilling policies (cardinality 49) can generalize using thresholding. It is natural to ask whether it could be possible to learn using a larger set heuristics, such as parametrized queue policies or mixtures of reordering criterias. One could for instance consider the class of mixed policies that choose a job based on a linear combination of the 7 criteria. A more ambitious endeavor is to ask whether it is possible to learn a contextual job ranking model [18] that performs well.

Acknowledgements. Authors are listed in alphabetical order. We warmly thank Eric Gaussier and Frederic Wagner for discussions as well as Pierre Neyron and Bruno Breznik for their invaluable help with experiments. We gracefully thank the contributors of the Parallel Workloads Archive, Victor Hazlewood (SDSC SP2), Travis Earheart and Nancy Wilkins-Diehr (SDSC Blue), Lars Malinowsky (KTH SP2), Dan Dwyer and Steve Hotovy (CTC SP2), Joseph Emeras (CEA Curie), and of course Dror Feitelson. This work has been partially supported by the LabEx PERSYVAL-Lab (ANR-11-LABX-0025-01) funded by the French program Investissement d'avenir. Experiments presented in this paper were carried out using the Digitalis platform (http://digitalis.imag.fr) of the Grid'5000 testbed. Grid'5000 is supported by a scientific interest group hosted by Inria and including CNRS, RENATER and several Universities as well as other organizations (https://www.grid5000.fr).

References

1. PBS Pro 13.0 administrator's guide. http://www.pbsworks.com/pdfs/PBSAdminGuide13.0.pdf
2. SLURM online documentation. http://slurm.schedmd.com/sched_config.html
3. TOP500 online ranking. https://www.top500.org/
4. Ahn, D.H., Garlick, J., Grondona, M., Lipari, D., Springmeyer, B., Schulz, M.: Flux: a next-generation resource management framework for large HPC centers. In: 2014 43rd International Conference on Parallel Processing Workshops, pp. 9–17, September 2014
5. Aida, K.: Effect of job size characteristics on job scheduling performance. In: Feitelson, D.G., Rudolph, L. (eds.) JSSPP 2000. LNCS, vol. 1911, pp. 1–17. Springer, Heidelberg (2000). https://doi.org/10.1007/3-540-39997-6_1. http://dl.acm.org/citation.cfm?id=646381.689680
6. Breck, E.: zymake: a computational workflow system for machine learning and natural language processing. In: Software Engineering, Testing, and Quality Assurance for Natural Language Processing, pp. 5–13. Association for Computational Linguistics (2008)
7. Capit, N., Da Costa, G., Georgiou, Y., Huard, G., Martin, C., Mounié, G., Neyron, P., Richard, O.: A batch scheduler with high level components. In: IEEE International Symposium on Cluster Computing and the Grid, CCGrid 2005, vol. 2, pp. 776–783. IEEE (2005)
8. Casanova, H., Giersch, A., Legrand, A., Quinson, M., Suter, F.: Versatile, scalable, and accurate simulation of distributed applications and platforms. J. Parallel Distrib. Comput. **74**(10), 2899–2917 (2014). http://hal.inria.fr/hal-01017319
9. Chiang, S.-H., Arpaci-Dusseau, A., Vernon, M.K.: The impact of more accurate requested runtimes on production job scheduling performance. In: Feitelson, D.G., Rudolph, L., Schwiegelshohn, U. (eds.) JSSPP 2002. LNCS, vol. 2537, pp. 103–127. Springer, Heidelberg (2002). https://doi.org/10.1007/3-540-36180-4_7
10. DOE ASCAC Report: Synergistic challenges in data-intensive science and exascale computing (2013)

11. Dolstra, E., Visser, E., de Jonge, M.: Imposing a memory management discipline on software deployment. In: Proceedings of the 26th International Conference on Software Engineering, ICSE 2004, pp. 583–592. IEEE (2004)

12. Feitelson, D.G.: Resampling with feedback — a new paradigm of using workload data for performance evaluation. In: Dutot, P.-F., Trystram, D. (eds.) Euro-Par 2016. LNCS, vol. 9833, pp. 3–21. Springer, Cham (2016). https://doi.org/10.1007/978-3-319-43659-3_1

13. Feitelson, D.G., Rudolph, L.: Metrics and benchmarking for parallel job scheduling. In: Feitelson, D.G., Rudolph, L. (eds.) JSSPP 1998. LNCS, vol. 1459, pp. 1–24. Springer, Heidelberg (1998). https://doi.org/10.1007/BFb0053978

14. Feitelson, D.G., Tsafrir, D., Krakov, D.: Experience with using the parallel workloads archive. J. Parallel Distrib. Comput. **74**(10), 2967–2982 (2014). http://www.sciencedirect.com/science/article/pii/S0743731514001154

15. Frachtenberg, E., Feitelson, D.G.: Pitfalls in parallel job scheduling evaluation. In: Feitelson, D., Frachtenberg, E., Rudolph, L., Schwiegelshohn, U. (eds.) JSSPP 2005. LNCS, vol. 3834, pp. 257–282. Springer, Heidelberg (2005). https://doi.org/10.1007/11605300_13

16. Gaussier, E., Glesser, D., Reis, V., Trystram, D.: Improving backfilling by using machine learning to predict running times. In: Proceedings of the International Conference for High Performance Computing, Networking, Storage and Analysis, SC 2015, pp. 641–6410. ACM, New York (2015)

17. Jackson, D., Snell, Q., Clement, M.: Core algorithms of the Maui scheduler. In: Feitelson, D.G., Rudolph, L. (eds.) JSSPP 2001. LNCS, vol. 2221, pp. 87–102. Springer, Heidelberg (2001). https://doi.org/10.1007/3-540-45540-X_6

18. Joachims, T.: Optimizing search engines using clickthrough data. In: Proceedings of the Eighth ACM SIGKDD International Conference on Knowledge Discovery and Data Mining, pp. 133–142. ACM (2002)

19. Leung, J.Y.: Handbook of Scheduling: Algorithms, Models, and Performance Analysis. CRC Press, Boca Raton (2004)

20. Lifka, D.A.: The ANL/IBM SP scheduling system. In: Feitelson, D.G., Rudolph, L. (eds.) JSSPP 1995. LNCS, vol. 949, pp. 295–303. Springer, Heidelberg (1995). https://doi.org/10.1007/3-540-60153-8_35

21. Mu'alem, A.W., Feitelson, D.G.: Utilization, predictability, workloads, and user runtime estimates in scheduling the ibm sp2 with backfilling. IEEE Trans. Parallel Distrib. Syst. **12**(6), 529–543 (2001). https://doi.org/10.1109/71.932708

22. Nissimov, A., Feitelson, D.G.: Probabilistic backfilling. In: Frachtenberg, E., Schwiegelshohn, U. (eds.) JSSPP 2007. LNCS, vol. 4942, pp. 102–115. Springer, Heidelberg (2008). https://doi.org/10.1007/978-3-540-78699-3_6

23. Perkovic, D., Keleher, P.J.: Randomization, speculation, and adaptation in batch schedulers. In: 2000 ACM/IEEE Conference on Supercomputing, p. 7, November 2000

24. Skovira, J., Chan, W., Zhou, H., Lifka, D.: The EASY — LoadLeveler API project. In: Feitelson, D.G., Rudolph, L. (eds.) JSSPP 1996. LNCS, vol. 1162, pp. 41–47. Springer, Heidelberg (1996). https://doi.org/10.1007/BFb0022286. http://dl.acm.org/citation.cfm?id=646377.689506

25. Srinivasan, S., Kettimuthu, R., Subramani, V., Sadayappan, P.: Characterization of backfilling strategies for parallel job scheduling. In: Proceedings of the International Conference on Parallel Processing Workshops, pp. 514–519. IEEE (2002)

26. Stodden, V., Leisch, F., Peng, R.D.: Implementing Reproducible Research. CRC Press, Boca Raton (2014)

27. Streit, A.: The self-tuning dynP job-scheduler. In: Abstracts and CD-ROM Proceedings of International Parallel and Distributed Processing Symposium, IPDPS 2002, April 2002
28. Tsafrir, D., Feitelson, D.G.: Instability in parallel job scheduling simulation: the role of workload flurries. In: Proceedings 20th IEEE International Parallel Distributed Processing Symposium, 10 pp., April 2006
29. Tsafrir, D., Etsion, Y., Feitelson, D.G.: Backfilling using runtime predictions rather than user estimates. Technical report TR 5, School of Computer Science and Engineering, Hebrew University of Jerusalem (2005)
30. Ukidave, Y., Li, X., Kaeli, D.: Mystic: predictive scheduling for GPU based cloud servers using machine learning. In: 2016 IEEE International Parallel and Distributed Processing Symposium (IPDPS), pp. 353–362, May 2016
31. Vishnu, A., van Dam, H., Tallent, N.R., Kerbyson, D.J., Hoisie, A.: Fault modeling of extreme scale applications using machine learning. In: 2016 IEEE International Parallel and Distributed Processing Symposium (IPDPS), pp. 222–231, May 2016

Don't Hurry Be Happy:
A Deadline-Based Backfilling Approach

Tchimou N'takpé[1] and Frédéric Suter[2,3(✉)]

[1] Université Nangui Abrogoua, Abidjan, Côte d'Ivoire
`tchimou.ntakpe@gmail.com`, `ntakpeeul_sfa@una.edu.ci`
[2] Centre de Calcul de l'IN2P3/CNRS, Lyon, Villeurbanne, France
`frederic.suter@cc.in2p3.fr`
[3] Inria, Lyon, France

Abstract. Computing resources in data centers are usually managed by a Resource and Job Management System whose main objective is to complete submitted jobs as soon as possible while maximizing resource usage and ensuring fairness among users. However, some users might not be as hurried as the job scheduler but only interested in their jobs to complete before a given deadline.

In this paper, we derive from this initial hypothesis a low-complexity scheduling algorithm, called Deadline-Based Backfilling (DBF), that distinguishes regular jobs that have to complete as early as possible from deadline-driven jobs that come with a deadline before when they have to finish. We also investigate a scenario in which deadline-driven jobs are submitted and evaluate the impact of the proposed algorithm on classical performance metrics with regard to state-of-the-art scheduling algorithms. Experiments conducted on four different workloads show that the proposed algorithm significantly reduces the average wait time and average stretch when compared to Conservative Backfilling.

1 Introduction

To ensure a fair access to resources among users while maximizing resource utilization, most data-centers rely on a *Resource and Job and Management System* (RJMS). Many different systems exist, be they commercial or Open Source, in the High Performance Computing (HPC) [1–3] or Big Data [4–6] worlds. However, they all follow some common principles while the specifics of the managed workloads differ. For instance, they rely on simple yet efficient scheduling algorithms to ensure scalability. Most schedulers in HPC thus adopt a *First-Come-First-Served* (FCFS) policy [7], usually combined with some *backfilling* techniques to minimize resource idle times. This choice to keep the complexity of the scheduling algorithm as low as possible implies that managing fairness and optimizing the resource utilization are usually done through external mechanisms such as quotas, priorities, or queues. Finally, the common goal of most

---

Work partially supported by the MOEBUS ANR project (13-ANR-INFR- 01).

D. Klusáček et al. (Eds.): JSSPP 2017, LNCS 10773, pp. 62–82, 2018.
https://doi.org/10.1007/978-3-319-77398-8_4

resource and job management systems is to serve, and thus complete, the submitted jobs as soon as possible. This allow them to increase both the system throughput and the users' satisfaction.

In this paper, we aim at studying the impact of a simple assumption on the management of a given workload by a resource and job management system: *"what if some users were not interested in their jobs to complete as soon as possible, but only before a given deadline?"*. For instance, some users may not need their results before the next day. Some periodic jobs may also exist that are important but not urgent, the only constraint being to execute them within the defined period. Then, it makes no difference whether such jobs complete as soon as possible, from the resource management system point of view, or just before when the user said s/he would need his/her results. The same reasoning can even be applied to longer time periods. Such a choice would obviously depend on some voluntary users, but we believe that this slack given by some users for the execution of their jobs could offer an extra degree of freedom to the scheduler. Delaying such deadline-driven jobs would give space to more urgent jobs that would thus start and complete earlier. Note that urgency does not necessarily implies importance. In this work, we only consider the urgency, or absence of, of a job as an optimization lever.

Following this initial hypothesis, we design a low-complexity scheduling algorithm, called *Deadline-Based Backfilling (DBF)*, that distinguishes *regular jobs* that have to complete as early as possible from *deadline-driven jobs* that come with an ultimate deadline before when they have to finish. We also propose a generic scenario in which various proportions of deadline-driven jobs are submitted to assess the impact of the proposed strategy on the scheduling of more urgent jobs. Experiments, conducted on four different workloads from the *Parallel Workloads Archive* (PWA) [8] show that DBF significantly reduces the average wait time and stretch when compared to Conservative Backfilling [9,10].

The remainder of this paper is organized as follows. In Sect. 2 we recall the principle of the most popular algorithms used in RJMS. Then in Sect. 3 we describe the workloads and platforms used for our evaluation and how we prepared data for our study. Section 4 details the principle of the proposed Deadline-Based Backfilling scheduling algorithm. In Sect. 5, we explain how we do select deadline-driven jobs and assign them deadlines. We evaluate the impact of the proposed algorithm on classical performance metrics and compare it to state-of-the-art scheduling algorithms in Sect. 6. Finally, we discuss related work in Sect. 7 before concluding this paper in Sect. 8.

2   Background on Job Scheduling

The scheduling algorithm is not the only component of a RJMS that influences resource utilization. Ordering policies, or priorities, are defined according to the characteristics of the jobs, their resource requirements, or the previous usages of the users submitting them. Another important component are queues that define a set of constraints on jobs, resources, or user profiles, e.g., job lasting between a day and a week, requesting up to 16 nodes, and belonging to users from a certain scientific collaboration. Queues can also be configured to only have access to a certain pool of resources. The combination of ordering policies and queues defines the final order in which jobs are presented to the scheduler. A common setting is to a apply one or more ordering policies within each queue and then define the browsing order of these queues. While these two components of a RJMS can be key to performance [11], in this work we focus on the scheduling algorithm and assume that the list of jobs has already been formed.

Most of the scheduling algorithms underlying RJMS handle jobs following a FCFS policy. However, the different requests for resources of the jobs usually lead to resource fragmentation and idle times. To increase resource usage this basic policy is often completed by a *backfilling* mechanism. Backfilling consists in moving jobs forward in the queue in order to fill "holes" in the schedule.

The Extensible Argonne Scheduling sYstem (EASY) [12] algorithm has been designed for the IBM SP2 supercomputer and is a popular variant of backfilling. In this algorithm, only the first waiting job is considered for allocation, with a guaranteed starting time. When this first job cannot start right away because its requested number of processors is not available, the algorithm browses the list of waiting jobs to find candidates for backfilling. These candidates are jobs that can start immediately, but without delaying the first job of the list.

Conservative Backfilling (CBF) is a less aggressive alternative to EASY with similar performance. It determines an allocation for each job when it enters the system. Then a job can be a candidate to backfilling if and only if it can begin its execution immediately without delaying *any* of the other pre-allocated jobs.

These two backfilling approaches increase the utilization of the resources and decrease the average waiting time of jobs with regard to FCFS alone, but the order in which jobs are scheduled may differ from the submission order. These dynamic modifications of the schedule prevent the more aggressive EASY algorithm to provide users with some guaranteed upper bound on the starting (and thus estimated completion) time of a given job. By design, the more conservative CBF algorithm gives such an upper bound right after the submission of a job, as backfilling can only make jobs start earlier than initially planned.

3   Workloads and Platforms

In this study, we consider different workload logs, i.e., traces of job submissions, extracted from the *Parallel Workloads Archive* (PWA). More precisely, we selected four workloads whose characteristics in terms of distributions of allocations, i.e., the number of processors used to execute a given job, and execution times per job cover a broad and representative range. Unfortunately, none of these publicly available workloads comprises information on the respective urgency of the submitted jobs. These workloads are:

SDSC-BLUE (http://www.cs.huji.ac.il/labs/parallel/workload/l_sdsc_blue/), in its cleaned 4.2 version, contains information on the submission of 250,440 jobs from April 2000 to January 2003 on the IBM SP Blue Horizon of the San Diego Supercomputer Center, that is made of 144 8-way nodes.

SDSC-DS (http://www.cs.huji.ac.il/labs/parallel/workload/l_sdsc_ds/) covers a year of activity from March 2004 through March 2005 on the DataStar cluster of the San Diego Supercomputer Center. It is composed of 96,089 jobs executed on 184 nodes. This cluster is made of two kinds of nodes, 176 8-way and 8 32-way SMP nodes for a total of 1,664 processors. We used the cleaned version of the log as recommended by the maintainers of the PWA.

HPC2N (http://www.cs.huji.ac.il/labs/parallel/workload/l_hpc2n/) covers three and a half years of activity from July 2002 through January 2006 on the Seth Cluster of the High-Performance Computing Center North in Sweden. This cluster is composed of 120 dual processor nodes. The original log comprised 527,371 jobs but 324,500 jobs from a burst submission by a single user were removed, leaving 202,871 jobs in the cleaned log.

ANL-Intrepid (http://www.cs.huji.ac.il/labs/parallel/workload/l_anl_int/) accounts for the submission of 68,936 jobs on the IBM Blue Gene/P Intrepid of the Argonne Leadership Computing Facility at Argonne National Laboratory from January 2009 to September 2009. This machine has 40 racks of 1,024 quad-cores nodes for a total of 163,840 cores. However, due to the specificity of the Blue Gene/P system, nodes are grouped into partitions. Eight racks are partitioned in groups of 64 nodes (or 256 cores) while the remaining racks group nodes by 512 (or 2,048 cores). Note that the number of processors requested by jobs are rounded up to the closest multiple of the partition size.

In this work, we only use a subset of the fields that describe a job in the Standard Workload Format (SWF) as we only aim at scheduling jobs and not optimizing their execution with regard to their memory or network usage. Then a job can be only modeled by its *submission time*, the *requested number of processors*, and the *requested time* or walltime. The selected workloads all comprise a certain number of anomalies that were detected and documented by the maintainers of the PWA during their conversion to the SWF format. Table 1 summarizes the anomalies we consider relevant for our study.

The first two columns correspond to invalid entries in the workloads as the corresponding jobs either logged a negative execution time or were allocated a negative number of processors. Such jobs usually have a "canceled" status in the logs.

Table 1. Summary of anomalies in workloads from the Parallel Workloads Archive.

Workload	Runtime < 0	CPU < 0	Used CPU > Req. CPU	Runtime > Walltime	Runtime > Walltime + 1'
SDSC-BLUE	10,770	19,516	458	23,434	8,115
SDSC-DS	11,176	0	0	10,658	1,043
HPC2N	0	0	729	14,817	6,170
ANL-Intrepid	0	0	30,948	12,241	9,096

In the experiments presented in Sect. 6, we decided to discard these jobs for all the considered algorithms.

The third column shows that, in most workloads, there are jobs that got more processors than requested. This is especially true for ANL-Intrepid where requests are rounded up to fit the partition requirements. In this workload, the number of cores allocated to jobs are rounded up to multiples of either 256 or 2,048. We adapted the descriptions of the clusters accordingly to represent a set of the smallest allocable number of cores. We also make a simplifying yet not impacting assumption about the platforms. We consider the clusters, or partitions, to be fully homogeneous. This means that a job requesting four nodes can indifferently be allocated a contiguous set of nodes (e.g., $\{p_1, p_2, p_3, p_4\}$) or a disjoint set of nodes (e.g., $\{p_1, p_6, p_8, p_{22}\}$).

Finally the last two columns indicate that a fair amount of jobs report an execution time longer than the expressed walltime. For most of them, the extra time is less than a minute and can be explained by the time needed by the system to kill a job when it reaches its walltime. However, the last column shows that many jobs continue their execution despite the expiration of their walltime. For all these jobs, we chose to stop them when the walltime is reached.

The SDSC-DS and SDSC-BLUE workloads comprise a non-negligible number of interactive jobs. Such jobs correspond to submissions from users who need a direct and immediate access to the machine. This access mode is thus orthogonal to the idea of letting the scheduler delay jobs. Moreover these jobs are usually scheduled on a limited and distinct subset of the available resources. Consequently, we decided to remove these jobs from the original traces.

All these alterations of the original logs prevent us to compare simulation results to their contents. However, in this study we compare the results of our proposal to those achieved by state-of-the-art algorithms. As long as we use the same input workloads for all scheduling algorithms, results remain comparable.

4 A Deadline-Based Backfilling Algorithm

Scheduling a job J_i amounts to find its place in the resource usage profile, i.e., a list of sets of available resources at a given time, maintained by the scheduler. Selecting a specific slot for a job determines the starting date $start_i$ of its execution. The exact set of resources used for the execution of a job is only determined when the job is about to start. In our deadline-based scheduling proposal, we consider two types of jobs. A regular job is a job that once submitted, at time $submit_i$, will be definitely scheduled in a way to minimize its completion date $completion_i$. Conversely, a deadline-driven job is associated to a $deadline$ d_i such that the job can be scheduled at any time as long as its execution within a walltime $walltime_i$ can be completed before the deadline expires. Such jobs can be scheduled as regular jobs but their tentative allocations can be reconsidered if new regular jobs enter the system.

Our algorithm is an *online* scheduling algorithm, as CBF or EASY are. As these algorithms do we privilege a low-complexity in our design to ensure the

Algorithm 1. Determination of a definitive allocation for a regular job J_r.

```
1:  for all J_i ∈ L_1 do
2:      Cancel current allocation of J_i
3:  end for
4:  L_tmp ← J_r
5:  Get_Allocation(J_r)
6:  for all J_i ∈ L_1 do
7:      Get_Allocation(J_i)
8:  end for
9:  while ∃ J_i ∈ L_1 | ct_i > d_i do
10:     L_tmp ← L_tmp ∪ J_i
11:     L_1 ← L_1 \ J_i
12:     for all J_i ∈ L_tmp ∪ L_1 do
13:         Cancel current allocation of J_i
14:     end for
15:     for all J_tmp ∈ L_tmp do
16:         Get_Allocation(J_tmp)
17:     end for
18:     for all J_j ∈ L_1 do
19:         Get_Allocation(J_j)
20:     end for
21: end while
22: if {J_i ∈ L_tmp | ct_i > d_i} ≠ ∅ then
23:     S_max ← max(submit_j|J_j ∈ L_tmp ∧ ct_j > d_j)
24:     L_tmp ← L_tmp ∪ {J_j ∈ L_1 | submit_j < S_max}
25:     L_1 ← L_1 \ {J_j ∈ L_1 | submit_j < S_max}
26:     for all J_i ∈ L_tmp ∪ L_1 do
27:         Cancel current allocation of J_i
28:     end for
29:     for all J_tmp ∈ L_tmp do
30:         Get_Allocation(J_tmp)
31:     end for
32:     for all J_j ∈ L_1 do
33:         Get_Allocation(J_j)
34:     end for
35: end if
36: for all J_i ∈ L_tmp do
37:     if start_i = current_time then
38:         Start execution of J_i
39:     else
40:         L_0 ← L_0 ∪ J_i
41:     end if
42:     L_tmp ← L_tmp \ J_i
43: end for
44: for all J_i ∈ L_1 do
45:     if start_i = current_time then
46:         Start execution of J_i
47:     end if
48: end for
```

applicability of the resulting algorithm in large-scale production systems. Allocation decisions are taken either when some jobs complete or some new jobs enter the system. These two kinds of events trigger a new scheduling round. The completion of a job, especially if it happens before the expiration of its walltime, makes nodes available that might be used by waiting jobs. New coming jobs, be they regular or not, may also impact the currently planned schedule for different reasons, e.g., candidate for backfilling, priority, tight deadline, ...

From its submission to the beginning of its execution, a job is in a *waiting* state. Our algorithm proposes to store the waiting jobs in two lists. The former, L_0, contains all the jobs whose allocations are definitively determined. It comprises regular jobs but also deadline-driven jobs that either come close to their deadline or improve the backfilling. The latter, L_1, contains only *deadline-driven jobs*, whose allocations can be modified in another scheduling round.

When a *deadline-driven job* is submitted, we determine its allocation according to the CBF algorithm. This allocation takes all the allocations, be they tentative or definitive, of the other waiting jobs into account. If the deadline associated to the job is large enough to prevent its violation from submission, the job is inserted into L_1. On the contrary, the job is considered as regular and inserted into L_0 to be scheduled as early as possible.

When a *regular job* J_r enters the system, we apply Algorithm 1 not only to determine its definitive allocation, but also to reconsider the allocations of waiting deadline-driven jobs. First, if such jobs exist in L_1, we cancel their current allocations (lines 1–3). Second, we build a temporary list L_{tmp} into which J_r is inserted (line 4), and get an allocation for this job. Then, we fill this list with jobs from L_1 whose deadline would be violated because of the allocation of the new regular job J_r. The algorithm proceeds as follows. A new allocation which takes the current allocation of J_r into account is determined for all the jobs in L_1 (lines 6–8). Then, while there is a job J_i in L_1 that does not respect its deadline, we move it from L_1 to L_{tmp} (lines 10–11) and recompute the allocations of both L_{tmp} (lines 15–17) and L_1 (lines 18–20). Note that the allocations for the jobs in L_{tmp} are determined by considering the jobs in an increasing order of submission time. This approach allows us to ensure that if a job can respect of the deadline when it is submitted, none of the modifications of its tentative allocation made by Algorithm 1 would lead to a deadline violation.

At the end of this step, all the deadline-driven jobs are allocated, some of them having been moved forward to avoid deadline violations. However, some jobs in L_{tmp} may still not be able to respect their deadlines. This may come from a different resource fragmentation that appears as we skip some deadline-driven jobs while building L_{tmp}. We thus add an extra step (lines 22–35), in which we move from L_1 to L_{tmp} all the deadline-driven jobs submitted before the last job in L_{tmp} unable to respect its deadline, before recomputing all the allocations.

The next step consists in determining which jobs in L_{tmp} can start their execution in this scheduling round (line 38). Those which cannot are now considered as regular jobs and moved to L_0 (line 40). Finally, our algorithm also starts the execution of some deadline-driven jobs from L_1 (lines 44–48).

5 On the Determination of Deadlines

The main concept underlying the proposed approach is that of *deadline*. This concept raises two important questions: *"Which jobs are considered deadline-driven?"* and *"What are the deadlines associated to these deadline-driven jobs?"*.

In this section, we propose to consider a broad and generic scenario in which deadline-driven jobs can be submitted at any time of the day, for instance by adding an extra submission flag to indicate when a job has to be completed at last. This scenario allows us to answer another question: *"what would users in a hurry gain if other users allowed X% of the jobs to be delayed?"*. Estimating the gain for different values of X will guide the experimental evaluation of our approach given in Sect. 6. For the jobs randomly selected to become deadline-driven, we define the associate deadline as a date that is a maximum between 24 h and 10 times the expressed walltime of the job after the job submission.

The rationale for a delay of at least 24 h comes from an analysis of the daily (and weekly) job arrival pattern in number of jobs submitted every hour, for the four studied workloads. Figure 1 shows a similar, and expected, job arrival pattern for all workloads, with a period (gray area) during which the arrival rate is greater than the daily average arrival rate (horizontal line).

This peak period roughly corresponds to business hours from 9AM to 6PM for all workloads. We note that for SDSC-BLUE and SDSC-DS, this peak period is slightly shifted and starts earlier. This might be explained by the location of the corresponding supercomputers on the U.S. West Coast and submissions

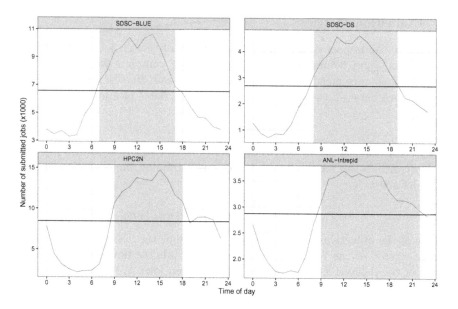

Fig. 1. Daily job arrival for four supercomputers. Gray area depicts a peak period when the arrival rate is greater than the daily average (horizontal line).

from users on the East Coast. Such a usage spanning over several time zones may also explain why the peak period ends later on the ANL-Intrepid machine. The sharp decrease in the arrival rate after business hours is likely to correspond to a lower competition for resources as less jobs are submitted. Weekly arrival shows a similar pattern with a sharp decrease of the number of job submission over the weekend. Then, with a deadline of at least twenty four hours after the submission, we ensure that every deadline-driven job can benefit of a period of lower load to be scheduled earlier than its deadline.

We also propose to set the deadline to be proportional to the expressed wall-time as a way to favor the shortest jobs. Not only they will be less delayed than jobs with a larger walltime but they are also better candidates for backfilling. The chosen factor of 10 comes from the observed average stretch, i.e., how much a job is impacted by its waiting time, in the different workloads.

To favor the adoption of the proposed approach, incentives for users to submit deadline-driven jobs have to be provided. On most platforms managed by a RJMS, the submissions of a given user are often limited by different quotas (e.g., per user, group, resource type) and influenced by earlier submission pattern. A simple incentive would be to loosen these limitations, hence giving a better admission rate, for users accepting to see their jobs delayed by the scheduler. On platform where users have to pay to access resources, we can easily imagine a discount offered to users who set a deadline as part as their SLA.

6   Experimental Evaluation

6.1   Evaluation Metrics

To evaluate the impact of allowing the execution of certain jobs to be delayed provided they end before a given deadline on the complete workload, we use several performance metrics. First we consider the *wait time* of a job, defined as the difference between the starting and submission dates of a job:

$$wait_i = start_i - submit_i. \tag{1}$$

A second classical metric is to compute the *stretch* experienced by a job. This metric quantifies the relative impact of the wait time on the execution of a job and is defined as:

$$stretch_i = (wait_i + walltime_i)/walltime_i. \tag{2}$$

One of the objectives of our proposal is to reduce the *average wait time* and *average stretch* of the regular jobs. This would indicate how much these jobs benefit of the delayed executions of deadline-driven jobs. We also analyze these two metrics over the whole workload to quantify the potential gain offered by deadline-based scheduling.

We also consider performance metrics related to the deadline-driven jobs. First we measure the number of jobs for which the proposed algorithm is not able to respect the deadline. Second we estimate how the deadline has effectively been used by our algorithm. To this end we define a notion of *deadline usage* as:

$$usage_i = (completion_i - submit_i)/(deadline_i - submit_i). \qquad (3)$$

Analyzing the average usage over the entire set of deadline-driven jobs will provide insight about our approach. High values will indicate that regular jobs were scheduled uninterruptedly in the interval left by delaying deadline-driven jobs. Conversely, smaller values will mean that deadline-driven jobs were able to exploit period of lower load before the expiration of their deadlines.

6.2   Simulation Environment

We resort to simulation for our experimental evaluation. Instead of developing an *ad-hoc* simulator, we opted for using an existing simulation framework. Several such tools have been used in the literature to simulate the replay of workloads from the Parallel Workloads Archive. The Alea[1] job scheduling simulator [13] is based on the GridSim toolkit and allows to compare queue-based scheduling algorithms. Alea separates the implementation of the algorithms, defined as independent Java classes, from that of the discrete event simulation itself. However, new algorithms have to be coded in this specific language and embedded into the code base of the tool. Alea also offers an interesting dynamic scheduling feature allowing jobs to be submitted during the simulation and support the management of priority queues [11]. In the early stage of this work, we used the SimBatch tool [14] for our evaluations. This framework, whose maintenance and evolution are no longer supported, was based on the SimGrid toolkit [15]. As for Alea, new algorithms had to be included to the code base, in C, of the tool.

In this work we decided to rely on another recent and promising SimGrid-based tool. Batsim[2] [16] is developed by the team that develops and maintains the OAR RJMS [1]. It decouples the simulation of the resources and the execution of a schedule from the decisions that led to this schedule. Then Batsim can leverage the different network and computing models of SimGrid to adapt the level of realism of the simulation to the needs of the users. In our experiments, we simulate jobs as simple delays defined as the minimum between the execution time as logged in the workload and the expressed walltime. Batsim exposes a simple message interface between the simulation engine and scheduling algorithms written as plugins in various programming languages.

For our experiments we use the latest version of Batsim shipped in a container as recommended by the development team. This container relies on the latest stable version of SimGrid (3.14.159) at the time of writing. We coded the proposed DBF algorithm as a scheduler plugin of Batsim in Python. We also implemented two state-of-the-art algorithms, CBF and EASY, that are used as references to evaluate the performance of our algorithm. To ensure the reproduction and further investigation of the presented results, and thus

---

[1] Alea web site: https://github.com/aleasimulator/alea.
[2] Batsim web site: https://github.com/oar-team/batsim.

favor Open Science, these algorithm implementations, the scripts used to prepare and convert the workloads into the Batsim input format and analyze the outcomes of the simulations, as well as the sources of this paper are made available online [17].

6.3   Results

We begin the evaluation of the proposed deadline-based backfilling approach by assessing its impact on regular jobs. For each workload, we randomly select a number of jobs to become deadline-driven and assign deadlines to these jobs as described in Sect. 5. Table 2 summarizes the respective numbers of regular jobs when the percentage of deadline-driven jobs varies from 20% to 80%.

In all the subsequent analyses, we filter out regular jobs whose wait time (resp. stretch) was 0 (resp. 1) simultaneously for all the three algorithms. Such jobs were lucky enough to obtain the requested resources right on submission independently of the scheduling algorithm used. Keeping them would modify the perception of the actual performance of a given algorithm.

First, we study the evolution of the *average wait time* experienced by the regular jobs shown by Fig. 2. A first observation is that this average wait time remains stable for both the CBF and EASY algorithms when we increase the number of deadline-driven jobs. This indicates that the decreasing number of jobs under consideration does not impact this metric. We also note that EASY consistently leads to a smaller average wait time than CBF, which comes from its more aggressive backfilling strategy. The proposed DBF algorithms outperforms its two contenders in all configurations except for the SDSC-BLUE workload with 20% of deadline-driven jobs where EASY is slightly better.

We also observe that our algorithm leads to a linear decrease of the average wait time of regular jobs when we increase the share of deadline-driven jobs. The best improvement is obtained for SDSC-DS where DBF already reduces the average wait time by more than a factor of two when there are only 20% of deadline-driven jobs. However, the results obtained by EASY in this configuration indicate that CBF obtains poor performance for this workload. It may be explained by a higher resource fragmentation for this workload that EASY can better exploit with its more aggressive backfilling strategy. It is also interesting

Table 2. Number of regular jobs impacted by deadline-based backfilling when the number of randomly selected deadline-driven jobs varies from 20% to 80%.

Workload	Total	Percentage of deadline-driven jobs			
		20%	40%	60%	80%
SDSC-BLUE	157,604	126,084	94,564	63,043	31,522
SDSC-DS	64,715	51,772	38,829	25,886	12,943
HPC2N	202,871	162,297	121,723	81,150	40,576
ANL-Intrepid	68,936	55,149	41,363	27,575	13,789

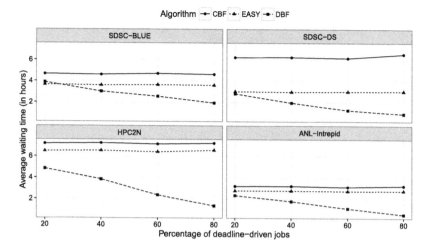

Fig. 2. Evolution of the average wait time experienced by regular jobs with the percentage of deadline-driven jobs.

to note that, even with only 20% of deadline-driven jobs, DBF is at least on par with EASY or reduces the average wait time up to 25% (for the HPC2N workload) but is also able to provide guarantees on job completion times that EASY would not give. Indeed, the scheduling of regular jobs is based on CBF and then the first tentative allocation of regular jobs gives them a completion time than can only be reduced afterwards. Moreover, DBF ensures that a deadline-driven job completes before its deadlines, which is another kind of upper bound.

Figure 3 shows a more detailed view of the wait time experienced by the regular jobs. Each line corresponds to a workload while each column corresponds to a given percentage of deadline-driven jobs. Each panel presents the wait time as an Empirical Cumulative Distributive Function for the three considered algorithms.

These more detailed results globally confirm the trends shown in Fig. 2 but also give us some interesting extra information. For instance, the top-left panel corresponds to the selection of 20% of deadline-driven jobs in the SDSC-BLUE workload. It is the configuration in which EASY leads to a slightly better average wait time than DBF. We observe that this comes from a greater number of jobs (above 25%) that can start immediately with EASY thanks to the aggressive backfilling. However, the first quartile for DBF is only of two and a half minutes. We also note a difference of less than half an hour for the third quartile in favor of EASY, but DBF is able to reduce the maximum wait time of about twelve hours. Again, this is explained by the design of EASY that causes extra wait time for jobs that cannot benefit of backfilling. We observe similar distributions for all the workloads when there are 20% of deadline-driven jobs. When the percentage of deadline-driven jobs increases, DBF competes with EASY with wait times close to zero for at least 25% of the jobs (with 40% of deadline-driven jobs on SDSC-BLUE and SDSC-DS, and 60% for ANL-Intrepid), while the performance

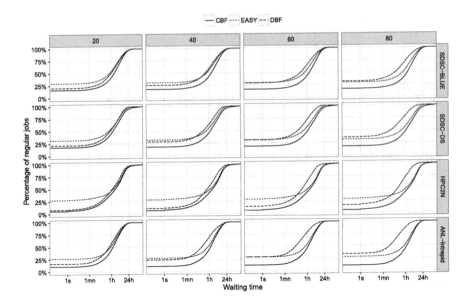

Fig. 3. Wait times experienced by regular jobs.

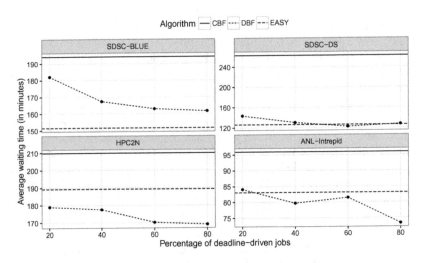

Fig. 4. Evolution of the average wait time experienced by all jobs with the percentage of deadline-driven jobs.

of CBF remains unchanged. A noticeable exception is the HPC2N workload, which is the largest in terms of number of jobs. There we observe a uniform reduction of the wait time when the share of deadline-driven jobs increases.

Figure 4 presents similar results as Fig. 2 but for the entire workload, i.e., regular and deadline-driven jobs combined. Note that this figure also includes the jobs whose wait time is zero with the different algorithms. Moreover and for the sake of clarity, we express the average wait time in minutes.

We can see that, in addition to reducing the average wait time of regular jobs, the proposed DBF algorithm also globally reduces the average wait time of the whole workload with regard to CBF. The improvement over this algorithm, upon which DBF is based, also increases with the proportion of deadline-driven jobs. This means that allowing the scheduler to delay some jobs (as defined in Sect. 5) to favor some others that are more urgent does not come at the price of a global degradation of the schedule quality but actually improves it.

The comparison with EASY does not show a clear winner, even though DBF leads to similar or lower average wait times for most workloads with at least 40% of deadline-driven jobs. We also recall that DBF provides users with an upper bound on job completion time, as CBF does. This valuable information that EASY cannot give may justify a slightly larger average wait time.

We continue our evaluation with the analysis of our second performance metric: the stretch, or slowdown, experienced by jobs when scheduled with the different algorithms. The evolution of the average stretch with the percentage of deadline-driven jobs and the relative performance of the three algorithms are very similar to those in Fig. 2 for the average wait time. This means that, on average, the respective execution time of deadline-driven does not influence this metric which is thus mainly driven by the wait time. Then we also analyze the *maximum stretch* which is a typical indicator of fairness in the literature. Indeed a small maximum stretch, ideally close to the average stretch indicates that the scheduling algorithm does not disfavor some jobs too much in order to reduce the completion time of others. Figure 5 presents the evolution of the maximum stretch for regular jobs with the percentage of deadline-driven jobs.

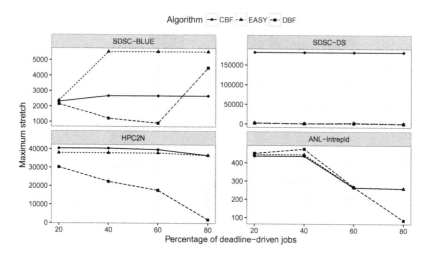

Fig. 5. Evolution of the maximum stretch for regular jobs with the percentage of deadline-driven jobs.

There is a great difference between the maximum and average stretches for all algorithms, which was expected as none of them aims at optimizing fairness among jobs. We also observe important variations of the maximum stretch for all the three algorithms when the percentage of deadline-driven jobs varies. This indicates that this value strongly depends on the subset of jobs that have been selected to become deadline-driven. For instance, the regular job that has the maximum stretch for CBF with 40, 60, and 80% of deadline-driven jobs on the SDSC-BLUE workload belongs to the set of 20% of deadline-driven jobs, hence a smaller maximum stretch. Then we can just comment on the general trends but not on specific values. We can however say that DBF either leads to similar (for SDSC-DS and ANL-Intrepid) or better (for SDSC-BLUE and HPC2N) maximum stretches than those achieved by EASY.

The DBF algorithm has been designed to ensure the respect of the deadlines associated to the jobs. As explained in Sect. 4, deadline violations can only occur when the first tentative allocation determined for a job already fails to respect the deadline, due to heavy load or the occupation of most of the resources by long lasting jobs. Figure 6 shows how many deadlines were not respected for each workload depending on the proportion of deadline-driven jobs. For each configuration, we distinguish short jobs whose deadline was set to 24 h from those whose deadline is proportional to the expressed walltime.

A first comment is that the number of deadline violations is extremely small compared to the number of deadline-driven jobs in the system and, not surprisingly, higher for the two largest workloads. These results show that DBF is able to guarantee the completion of almost all the deadline-driven jobs before

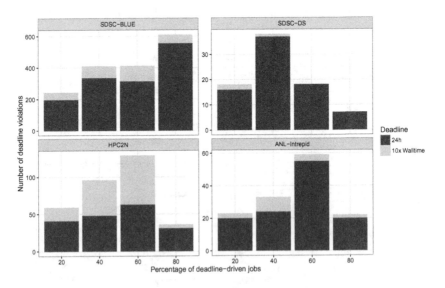

Fig. 6. Evolution of the number of deadline violations for the DBF algorithm with the percentage of deadline-driven jobs.

their deadline. Moreover the evolution with the proportion of deadline-driven jobs does not indicate a direct correlation. For each of the presented experiment, a growing set of jobs to become deadline-driven jobs is randomly selected. However, these sets are not inclusive, e.g., all the jobs in the 20% set are not necessarily in the 80% set. Moreover, a majority of the jobs that cannot respect their deadlines were submitted in heavily loaded period. We also observe that a vast majority of these violations are for jobs with a 24-h deadline, i.e., short jobs with an expressed walltime of less than three hours, which confirms a relation with a heavy load at submission time for these jobs. The HPC2N workload exhibits a different pattern with more violations for longer jobs. A further analysis shows that a few set of jobs experience similar deadline violations which indicates that all these jobs had to wait for the completion of a single job.

When analyzing how the deadlines associated to the jobs were exploited by the DBF algorithm we found that, all simulations combined, almost half of the deadline-driven jobs were executed immediately after their submission. These jobs are uniformly distributed over the workloads and scenarios. Figure 1 showed large periods of lower load every night. As deadline-driven jobs were randomly selected it would not surprising that a large fraction of them were submitted during lower load periods. We decided to removed these jobs from the computation of the average deadline usage shown by Fig. 7.

This graph shows a very similar trend for all the workloads: the more deadline-driven jobs are submitted the less they use their deadlines. Moreover, the percentages of deadline usage are pretty low, with a maximum of 17.3% for SDSC-BLUE with 20% of deadline-driven jobs. This tends to indicate that the chosen deadlines might have been too lazy and could be shortened. Note also that the deadlines were determined from the expressed walltime that are

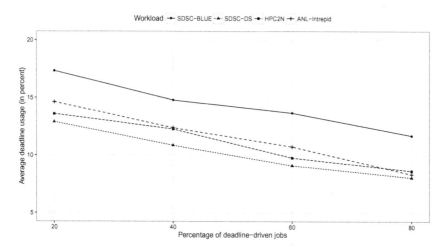

Fig. 7. Evolution of the utilisation of the deadlines of the deadline-driven jobs by the DBF algorithm with the percentage of deadline-driven jobs.

Table 3. Time to simulate the scheduling of four workloads with three algorithms.

	DBF				CBF	EASY
	20%	40%	60%	80%		
SDSC-BLUE	4 min 33 s	4 min 34 s	04 min 38 s	5 min 13 s	3 min 35 s	2 min 18 s
SDSC-DS	2 min	2 min 13 s	2 min 07 s	2 min 02 s	1 min 49 s	58 s
HPC2N	23 min 03 s	29 min 51 s	34 min 26 s	30 min 27 s	7 min 21 s	3 min 03 s
ANL-Intrepid	2 min 20 s	2 min 25 s	2 min 21 s	2 min 04 s	1 min 52 s	1 min 10 s

typically and largely overestimated by users. However, these results also show that associating a (very) large deadline to a job does not necessarily mean that the job will be delayed for a (very) long time. It just gives more freedom to the scheduler which will exploit it only when needed. For instance, less than 1% of the deadline-driven jobs used more than 80% of their deadlines.

We conclude this evaluation by discussing the time needed to simulate the scheduling of the different workloads by the three considered algorithms, as summarized in Table 3. All the simulations were run on a notebook (8-core 2.40 GHz Intel i7-4700MQ CPU) using Batsim in a Docker container hosted by an Ubuntu 16.04 LTS Operating System.

We first observe that varying the percentage of deadline-driven jobs handled by the proposed DBF algorithm does not have any significant impact on the time needed to schedule a full workload. We also note that the time needed to schedule the HPC2N workload is much larger than for the other workloads. It can partially be explained by the greater number of jobs to execute on a relatively small number of processors (202,871 jobs on 240 processors), but also by a large overestimation of walltimes for a fair amount of jobs, i.e., up to 1,000 times greater. This implies a lot of extra rescheduling steps that directly impact the simulation time. However, the average time to schedule a job for this workload remains reasonable in less than 10 ms, and is less than 2 ms for the three other workloads. Compared to CBF, the management of deadline-driven jobs, and the benefits they bring, by DBF induces an affordable overhead of 25%. Finally, EASY that computes less tentative allocations is about twice as fast as DBF but does not provide the same guarantees on job completion times.

7 Related Work

In the scheduling literature, deadlines usually express a Quality of Service requirement. For instance, in (hard) real-time systems the Earliest Deadline First (EDF) policy [18] is a preemptive scheduling algorithm that puts jobs in a priority queue and selects the job with the closest deadline for execution when a scheduling event occurs. Similarly on big data analytics clusters, some jobs require guarantees on their completion time and thus can be seen as deadline-sensitive jobs [19,20]. In these two areas, deadlines act as a constraint the scheduler has to respect, while in our work we primarily see the deadline as an extra degree of freedom for the scheduler. Another main difference is that in both real-time and big data systems, jobs are usually executed on a single compute node and often periodic while in HPC systems jobs are mainly parallel and independent. The associated scheduling challenges and the definition and usage of deadlines are then completely different.

The distinction between urgent (but necessarily important) jobs and less latency-sensitive (but often important) jobs can also be found and characterized in big data workloads and RJMS. For instance the Google's Borg system [5] distinguishes "production" services used for end-user-facing products that show a diurnal usage pattern from "non-production" batch jobs that are less sensitive to short-term performance fluctuations.

In [21], the authors define a concept of flexible backfilling to schedule jobs on heterogeneous HPC resources. They use deadlines to increase the priority of jobs when they are coming close to their deadlines and decrease it when the deadlines expire. In this paper, we use deadlines in a different way, not to increase the priority of a job but on the contrary to further delay its execution.

While the backfilling strategies implemented by CBF and EASY are popular in production systems, they may cause important resource fragmentation. In [22, 23], the authors rely on meta-heuristics, i.e., tabu-search and random selection, to periodically reorganize the schedules. While these modifications improve the average wait time and stretch, they do not preserve one of the most interesting feature of CBF which is to provide an upper bound of job completion time on submission. The proposed Deadline-based backfilling algorithm also builds upon and improves the seminal CBF algorithm, but conserves this feature for both regular and deadline-driven jobs. Finally, in [24] the authors modify the way candidates for backfilling are selected in the list of waiting jobs. As our proposed solution, this approach improves CBF with regard to the performance metrics used in Sect. 6 but differs in the selection criterion. They rely on new priority criteria while we use the deadlines associated to the jobs.

8   Conclusion and Future Work

A common and fundamental principle of Resource and Job Management Systems is to build schedules aiming at making jobs complete as soon as possible, hence minimizing their response time. Backfilling approaches participate to this effort, with a interesting side effect of improving resource usage, by moving jobs ahead in the schedule to fill resources left idle by other jobs.

In this paper, we followed the simple hypothesis that some users may not be willing to get their results as soon as possible to design an original algorithm called *Deadline-based Backfilling* (DBF). If some job is submitted along with a deadline for its execution, this algorithm can delay it up to the expiration of this deadline to leave room to more urgent jobs. We design this algorithm while aiming at keeping its complexity as low as possible to favor its adoption and at preserving the capacity to provide an upper bound on job completion time from the submission. We evaluate the performance of this algorithm in terms of average wait time and average stretch on four workloads extracted from the Parallel Workload Archive. Experimental results shown a clear improvement on both metrics when compared to the classical Conservative Backfilling and EASY scheduling algorithms.

Experiments presented in Sect. 6 study the impact of the proportion of deadline-driven jobs on the quality of the schedule using simple deadline determination rules. Our main future work will be to derive some principles to set the most beneficial deadlines from the characterization of jobs composing the workloads. Patterns in terms of duration, number of processors, periodicity will be investigated. Then we will complete this study by fixing the proportion of deadline-driven jobs and analyzing the impact of the derived deadline on the schedule. Finally we aim at defining policies and incentives to motivate users to be less eager to get their results and give some extra freedom to the scheduler.

References

1. Capit, N., Da Costa, G., Georgiou, Y., Huard, G., Martin, C., Mounié, G., Neyron, P., Richard, O.: A batch scheduler with high level components. In: Proceedings of the 5th International Symposium on Cluster Computing and the Grid (CCGrid), Cardiff, UK, May 2005, pp. 776–783 (2005)
2. Yoo, A.B., Jette, M.A., Grondona, M.: SLURM: simple Linux utility for resource management. In: Feitelson, D., Rudolph, L., Schwiegelshohn, U. (eds.) JSSPP 2003. LNCS, vol. 2862, pp. 44–60. Springer, Heidelberg (2003). https://doi.org/10.1007/10968987_3
3. Staples, G.: TORQUE - TORQUE resource manager. In: Proceedings of the ACM/IEEE SC2006 Conference on High Performance Networking and Computing, Tampa, FL, p. 8, November 2006
4. Boutin, E., Ekanayake, J., Lin, W., Shi, B., Zhou, J., Qian, Z., Wu, M., Zhou, L.: Apollo: scalable and coordinated scheduling for cloud-scale computing. In: Proceedings of the 11th USENIX Symposium on Operating Systems Design and Implementation, (OSDI), Broomfield, CO, pp. 285–300, October 2014
5. Verma, A., Pedrosa, L., Korupolu, M., Oppenheimer, D., Tune, E., Wilkes, J.: Large-scale cluster management at Google with Borg. In: Proceedings of the 10th European Conference on Computer Systems (EuroSys), Bordeaux, France, April 2015
6. Hindman, B., Konwinski, A., Zaharia, M., Ghodsi, A., Joseph, A.D., Katz, R.H., Shenker, S., Stoica, I.: Mesos: a platform for fine-grained resource sharing in the data center. In: Proceedings of the 8th USENIX Symposium on Networked Systems Design and Implementation (NSDI), Boston, MA (2011)
7. Schwiegelshohn, U., Yahyapour, R.: Analysis of first-come-first-serve parallel job scheduling. In: Proceedings of the 9th Annual ACM-SIAM Symposium on Discrete Algorithms, San Francisco, CA, 629–638, January 1998
8. Feitelson, D., Tsafrir, D., Krakov, D.: Experience with using the parallel workloads archive. J. Parallel Distrib. Comput. 74(10), 2967–2982 (2014)
9. Feitelson, D.G., Weil, A.M.: Utilization and predictability in scheduling the IBM SP2 with backfilling. In: Proceedings of the 12th International Parallel Processing Symposium (IPPS), pp. 542–546 (1998)

10. Mu'alem, A.W., Feitelson, D.G.: Utilization, predictability, workloads, and user runtime estimates in scheduling the IBM SP2 with backfilling. IEEE Trans. Parallel Distrib. Syst. **12**(6), 529–543 (2001)

11. Klusáček, D., Tóth, Š.: On interactions among scheduling policies: finding efficient queue setup using high-resolution simulations. In: Silva, F., Dutra, I., Santos Costa, V. (eds.) Euro-Par 2014. LNCS, vol. 8632, pp. 138–149. Springer, Cham (2014). https://doi.org/10.1007/978-3-319-09873-9_12

12. Lifka, D.A.: The ANL/IBM SP scheduling system. In: Feitelson, D.G., Rudolph, L. (eds.) JSSPP 1995. LNCS, vol. 949, pp. 295–303. Springer, Heidelberg (1995). https://doi.org/10.1007/3-540-60153-8_35

13. Klusáček, D., Rudová, H.: Alea 2 - job scheduling simulator. In: Proceedings of the 3rd International ICST Conference on Simulation Tools and Techniques (SIMU-Tools 2010), Malaga, Spain (2010)

14. Caniou, Y., Gay, J.-S.: Simbatch: an API for simulating and predicting the performance of parallel resources managed by batch systems. In: César, E., Alexander, M., Streit, A., Träff, J.L., Cérin, C., Knüpfer, A., Kranzlmüller, D., Jha, S. (eds.) Euro-Par 2008. LNCS, vol. 5415, pp. 223–234. Springer, Heidelberg (2009). https://doi.org/10.1007/978-3-642-00955-6_27

15. Casanova, H., Giersch, A., Legrand, A., Quinson, M., Suter, F.: Versatile, scalable, and accurate simulation of distributed applications and platforms. J. Parallel Distrib. Comput. **74**(10), 2899–2917 (2014)

16. Dutot, P.-F., Mercier, M., Poquet, M., Richard, O.: Batsim: a realistic language-independent resources and jobs management systems simulator. In: Desai, N., Cirne, W. (eds.) JSSPP 2015-2016. LNCS, vol. 10353, pp. 178–197. Springer, Cham (2017). https://doi.org/10.1007/978-3-319-61756-5_10

17. N'takpé, T., Suter, F.: Companion of the don't hurry be happy: a deadline-based backfilling approach article (2017). https://doi.org/10.6084/m9.figshare.4644466

18. Liu, C.L., Layland, J.: Scheduling algorithms for multiprogramming in a hard-real-time environment. J. ACM **20**(1), 46–61 (1973)

19. Jyothi, S.A., Curino, C., Menache, I., Narayanamurthy, S.M., Tumanov, A., Yaniv, J., Mavlyutov, R., Goiri, I., Krishnan, S., Kulkarni, J., Rao, S.: Morpheus: towards automated SLOs for enterprise clusters. In: Proceedings of the 12th USENIX Symposium on Operating Systems Design and Implementation (OSDI), Savannah, GA, pp. 117–134, November 2016

20. Lucier, B., Menache, I., Naor, J., Yaniv, J.: Efficient online scheduling for deadline-sensitive jobs. In: Proceedings of the 25th ACM Symposium on Parallelism in Algorithms and Architectures (SPAA), Montreal, Canada, pp. 305–314, July 2013

21. Baraglia, R., Capannini, G., Pasquali, M., Puppin, D., Ricci, L., Techiouba, A.: Backfilling strategies for scheduling streams of jobs on computational farms. In: Danelutto, M., Fragopoulou, P., Getov, V. (eds.) Making Grids Work, pp. 103–115. Springer, Boston (2008). https://doi.org/10.1007/978-0-387-78448-9_8

22. Klusáček, D., Rudová, H.: Performance and fairness for users in parallel job scheduling. In: Cirne, W., Desai, N., Frachtenberg, E., Schwiegelshohn, U. (eds.) JSSPP 2012. LNCS, vol. 7698, pp. 235–252. Springer, Heidelberg (2013). https://doi.org/10.1007/978-3-642-35867-8_13

23. Klusàček, D., Chlumský, V.: Planning and metaheuristic optimization in production job scheduler. In: Proceedings of the 20th Workshop on Job Scheduling Strategies for Parallel Processing, Chicago, IL, May 2016. https://doi.org/10.1007/978-3-319-61756-5_11
24. Lindsay, A., Galloway-Carson, M., Johnson, C., Bunde, D., Leung, V.: Backfilling with guarantees made as jobs arrive. Concurr. Computat. Pract. Exp. 25(4), 513–523 (2013)

Supporting Real-Time Jobs on the IBM Blue Gene/Q: Simulation-Based Study

Daihou Wang[1], Eun-Sung Jung[2](✉) [ID], Rajkumar Kettimuthu[3], Ian Foster[3,4], David J. Foran[5], and Manish Parashar[1]

[1] Rutgers Discovery Informatics Institute, Rutgers University, Piscataway, NJ, USA
[2] Hongik University, Seoul, South Korea
ejung@hongik.ac.kr
[3] MCS Division, Argonne National Laboratory, Lemont, IL, USA
[4] Department of Computer Science, University of Chicago, Chicago, IL, USA
[5] Rutgers Cancer Institute of New Jersey, New Brunswick, NJ, USA

Abstract. As the volume and velocity of data generated by scientific experiments increase, the analysis of those data inevitably requires HPC resources. Successful research in a growing number of scientific fields depends on the ability to analyze data rapidly. In many situations, scientists and engineers want quasi-instant feedback, so that results from one experiment can guide selection of the next or even improve the course of a single experiment. Such real-time requirements are hard to meet on current HPC systems, which are typically batch-scheduled under policies in which an arriving job is run immediately only if enough resources are available and is otherwise queued. Real-time jobs, in order to meet their requirements, should sometimes have higher priority than batch jobs that were submitted earlier. But, accommodating more real-time jobs will negatively impact the performance of batch jobs, which may have to be preempted. The overhead involved in preempting and restarting batch jobs will, in turn, negatively impact system utilization. Here we evaluate various scheduling schemes to support real-time jobs along with the traditional batch jobs. We perform simulation studies using trace logs of Mira, the IBM BG/Q system at Argonne National Laboratory, to quantify the impact of real-time jobs on batch job performance for various percentages of real-time jobs in the workload. We present new insights gained from grouping the jobs into different categories and studying the performance of each category. Our results show that real-time jobs in all categories can achieve an average slowdown less than 1.5 and that most categories achieve an average slowdown close to 1 with at most 20% increase in average slowdown for some categories of batch jobs with 20% or fewer real-time jobs.

Keywords: Real-time job scheduling · Preemptive scheduling
Scheduler simulation · Supercomputing

© Springer International Publishing AG, part of Springer Nature 2018
D. Klusáček et al. (Eds.): JSSPP 2017, LNCS 10773, pp. 83–102, 2018.
https://doi.org/10.1007/978-3-319-77398-8_5

1 Introduction

Scientific instruments such as accelerators, telescopes, light sources, and colliders generate large amounts of data. Because of advances in technology, the rate and size of these data are rapidly increasing. Advanced instruments such as state-of-the-art detectors at light source facilities generate tens of terabytes of data per day, and future camera-storage bus technologies are expected to increase data rates by an order of magnitude or more. The ability to quickly perform computations on these data sets will improve the quality of science. A central theme in experimental and observational science workflow research is the need for quasi-instant feedback, so that the result of one experiment can guide selection of the next. Online analysis so far has typically been done by dedicated compute resources available locally at the experimental facilities. With the massive increase in data volumes, however, the computational power required to do the fast analysis of these complex data sets often exceeds the resources available locally. Hence, many instruments are operated in a blind fashion without quick analysis of the data to give insight into how the experiment is progressing.

Large-scale high-performance computing (HPC) platforms and supercomputing are required in order to do on-demand processing of experimental data. Such processing will help detect problems in the experimental setup and operational methods early on and will allow for adjusting experimental parameters on the fly [41]. Even slight improvements can have far-reaching benefits for many experiments. However, building a large HPC system or having a supercomputer dedicated for this purpose is not economical, because the computation in these facilities typically is relatively small compared with the lengthy process of setting up and operating the experiments.

We define real-time computing as the ability to perform on-demand execution. The real-time computation may represent either analysis or simulation. Recently NERSC set up a "real-time" queue on its new Cori supercomputer to address real-time analysis needs. It uses a small number of dedicated compute nodes to serve the jobs in the real-time queue, and it allows jobs in the real-time queue to take priority on other resources. It is also possible to preempt "killable" jobs on these other resources.

NERSC is an exception, however. The operating policy of most supercomputers and scientific HPC systems is not suitable for real-time computations. The systems instead adopt a batch-scheduling model where a job may stay in the queue for an indeterminate period of time. Thus, existing schedulers have to be extended to support real-time jobs in addition to the batch jobs. The main challenge of using supercomputers to do real-time computation is that these systems do not support preemptive scheduling. A better understanding of preemptive scheduling mechanisms is required in order to develop appropriate policies that support real-time jobs while maintaining the efficient use of resources.

In this paper, we present our work on evaluating various scheduling schemes to support mixes of real-time jobs and traditional batch jobs. We perform simulation studies using trace logs of Mira, the IBM BG/Q system at Argonne National Laboratory, to quantify the impact of real-time jobs on batch job performance and system utilization for various percentages of real-time jobs in the workload. Parallel job scheduling has been widely studied [13–15]. It includes strategies such as backfilling [23,25,33,35], preemption [19,26], moldability [9,29,36] malleability [5], techniques to use distributed resources [28,37], mechanisms to handle fairness [30,40], and methods to handle inaccuracies in user runtime estimates [39]. Sophisticated scheduling algorithms have been developed that can optimize resource allocation while also addressing other goals such as minimizing average slowdown [16] and turnaround time. We explore several scheduling strategies to make real-time jobs more likely to be scheduled in due time. Although the techniques that we employ are not new, our context and objective are new. Using Mira trace logs, we quantify the impact of real-time jobs on batch job performance for various percentages of real-time jobs in the workload. We present new insights gained from studying the performance of different categories of jobs grouped based on runtime and the number of nodes used. Our results show that real-time jobs in all categories can achieve an average slowdown less than 1.5 (most categories achieve an average slowdown close to 1) with at most 20% increase in average slowdown for some categories of batch jobs (average slowdown for batch jobs in other categories decreases) with 20% or fewer real-time jobs. With 30% real-time jobs, the slowdown for real-time jobs in one of the categories goes above 2, but the impact on batch jobs is comparable to the case with 20% real-time jobs. With 40% or more real-time jobs, the average slowdown of batch jobs in one of the categories increases by around 90%, and the average slowdown of real-time jobs also goes above 3.

The rest of the paper is organized as follows. Section 2 describes the background on parallel job scheduling, checkpointing, the Mira supercomputer, and the simulator used for our study. In Sect. 3 we discuss related work, and in Sect. 4 we give the problem statement. In Sect. 5 we present the scheduling techniques studied, and in Sect. 6 we describe the extensions we did to enable real-time scheduling in the Qsim simulator. Section 7 presents the experimental setup and the simulation results of various scheduling techniques. Section 8 provides the conclusions.

2   Background

We provide in this section some background on parallel job scheduling, Mira, Qsim, and checkpointing.

2.1   Parallel Job Scheduling

Scheduling of parallel jobs can be viewed in terms of a 2D chart with time along one axis and the number of processors along the other axis. Each job can be thought of as a rectangle whose width is the user-estimated runtime and height is the number of processors requested. The simplest way to schedule jobs is to use the first-come, first-served (FCFS) policy. If the number of free processors available is less than the number of processors requested by the job at the head of the queue, an FCFS scheduler leaves the free processors idle even if waiting queued jobs require fewer than the available free processors. Backfilling addresses this issue. It identifies 'holes' in the 2D schedule and smaller jobs that fit those holes. With backfilling, users are required to provide an estimate of the length of the jobs submitted for execution. A scheduler can use this information to determine whether a job is sufficiently small to run without delaying any previously reserved jobs.

2.2   Mira Supercomputer

Mira is a Blue Gene/Q system operated by the Argonne Leadership Computing Facility (ALCF) at Argonne National Laboratory [3]. It was ranked 9th in the 2016 Top500 list, with peak performance at 10,066 TFlop/s. Mira is a 48-rack system, with 786,432 cores. It has a hierarchical structure connected via a 5D torus network. Nodes are grouped into midplanes, each of which contains 512 nodes; and each rack has two midplanes. Partitions on Mira are composed of such midplanes. Thus, jobs on Mira are scheduled to run on partitions that have integer multiples of 512 nodes. The smallest production job on Mira occupies 512 nodes, and the largest job occupies 49,152 nodes. The Cobalt [1] batch scheduler used on Mira is an open-source, component-based resource management tool developed at Argonne. It has been used as the job scheduler on Intrepid (the supercomputer at ALCF before Mira) and is being used in other Blue Gene systems such as Frost at the National Center for Atmospheric Research [2].

2.3   Qsim Simulator

We used the Qsim discrete event simulator [4] because it was designed for the Cobalt scheduler. Job scheduling behavior is triggered by job-submit(Q)/job-start(S)/job-end(E) events. The latest version of Qsim supports three versions of backfilling-based job scheduling policies: first-fit (FF) backfilling, best-fit (BF) backfilling, and shortest-job-first (SJF) backfilling [25]. By design, Qsim supports the simulation only of batch job scheduling. In this study, we extended the Qsim simulator to support real-time job scheduling using a high-priority queue and preemption.

2.4   Checkpointing Applications

Checkpoint and restart mechanisms were first introduced into modern super-computing systems to provide fault tolerance [12]. Checkpointing is the process of saving a running application's state to nonvolatile storage. The saved state can be used to restart the application from when the last checkpoint was taken. Over the years, these mechanisms have evolved along with the new generations of supercomputing architecture and network developments. Among many varia-tions, major checkpointing approaches can be categorized as either application level or system level [12].

In the application-level approach, checkpointing is done by individual applications (the Cornell Checkpoint(pre) Compiler (C3) [31] is an example of this approach, and such works are surveyed in [43]). It requires changes to the application code, but it can significantly reduce the amount of data that need to be saved for restarting.

In the system-level approach, checkpointing is done outside of applications. Checkpointing can be implemented either in the operating systems (MOSIX [7] and BLCR [11] are examples of this approach) or in the runtime library or system. In this approach, checkpointing is done by copying the application's memory into persistent storage without specific knowledge of the application. It does not require any changes to the application.

3 Related Work

Parallel job scheduling has been widely studied [6,17,23,25,38], and a number of surveys [13–15] and evaluations [8,18,20,22] have been published. However, not been much work has been done in the context of supporting on-demand jobs on supercomputers that operate in batch-processing mode.

Although preemptive scheduling is universally used at the operating-system level to multiplex processes on single-processor systems and shared-memory multiprocessors, it is rarely used in parallel job scheduling. Studies of preemptive scheduling schemes have focused on their overheads and their effectiveness in reducing average job turnaround time [8,10,19,21,24,34].

Others have studied preemptive scheduling for *malleable parallel jobs* [10,27, 32,44], in which the number of processors used to execute a job is permitted to vary dynamically over time. In practice, parallel jobs submitted to supercomputer centers are generally rigid; that is, the number of processors used to execute a job is fixed. The work most similar to ours is SPRUCE (Special Priority and Urgent Computing Environment) [42], which investigated mechanisms for supporting *urgent* jobs such as hurricane analysis on HPC resources. The authors define urgent computing jobs as having time-critical needs, such that late results are useless. SPRUCE considered only a basic preemptive scheduling scheme with no checkpointing and assumed that urgent jobs are infrequent. Our work differs in terms of both its job model and the scheduling schemes considered. Our job model assumes that jobs with real-time constraints arrive more frequently and that jobs are not total failure even if the job timing requirements are missed. We evaluate more sophisticated preemptive scheduling schemes.

4 Problem Statement

Our goal is to study the impact of accommodating real-time jobs in (batch) supercomputer systems. We consider two kinds of jobs: *batch jobs* and *real-time jobs*. Real-time jobs expect to execute immediately, whereas batch jobs expect best-effort service. We assume that all jobs are rigid: jobs are submitted to run on a specified fixed number of processors. We assume that a certain percentage

($R\%$) of the system workload will be real-time jobs and that the rest are batch jobs. We study different values of R. We evaluate different scheduling schemes that prioritize real-time jobs over batch jobs in order to meet the expectations of real-time jobs to the extent possible. In addition to performance, we study the impact of various scheduling schemes on system utilization.

5   Scheduling Techniques

We evaluate five scheduling schemes that accommodate real-time jobs in addition to the traditional batch jobs. Detailed description of the schemes is given below.

5.1   High-Priority Queue-Based Scheduling

Real-time jobs are enqueued in a *high-priority queue* (hpQ), whereas batch jobs are enqueued in a *normal queue*. The scheduler gives priority to the jobs in the high-priority queue and blocks all the jobs in the normal queue until all the jobs in the high-priority queue are scheduled.

5.2   Preemptive Real-Time Scheduling

In the preemptive scheduling schemes, if not enough resources are available to schedule a real-time job, the scheduler selects a partition for the real-time job that maximizes system utilization, preempts any batch job running on this partition or its child partitions, and schedules the real-time job. It then resubmits those batch jobs to the normal queue for later restart/resume. The overhead introduced by preemption impacts the jobs that are preempted as well as the system utilization. Checkpointing can help reduce the overhead of preemption, but checkpointing does not come for free. Checkpointing's impact on job run-time and system utilization needs to be accounted for as well. For the preemptive scheduling schemes, $t_{ckpt}^{j}, t_{pre}^{j}, ch_{ckpt}^{j}, ch_{ckpt}^{sys}$, and ch_{pre}^{sys} capture these overheads. Here t_{ckpt}^{j} and t_{pre}^{j} are the additional time incurred for *job j* due to checkpointing overhead and preemption overhead, respectively; ch_{ckpt}^{sys} and ch_{pre}^{sys} are the core-hours lost by the system due to checkpointing overhead and preemption overhead, respectively; and ch_{ckpt}^{j} is core-hours lost by *job j* due to checkpointing overhead.

PRE-REST: PRE-REST corresponds to preemption and restart of batch jobs. No system- or application-level checkpointing occurs. Thus, the preempted jobs have to be restarted from the beginning. Equations 1 to 5 describe the overhead associated with this scheme.

$$t^j_{ckpt} = 0 \tag{1}$$

$$t^j_{pre} = \sum_{i=1}^{\#preemptions_j} t^j_{used_i} \tag{2}$$

$$ch^{sys}_{ckpt} = 0 \tag{3}$$

$$ch^{sys}_{pre} = \sum_{k \ in \ batch \ jobs} t^k_{pre} * nodes_k \tag{4}$$

$$ch^j_{ckpt} = 0 \tag{5}$$

Here, $\#preemptions_j$ is the number of times $job\ j$ is preempted, $t^j_{used_i}$ is the time $job\ j$ (preempted job) has run in its ith execution, and $nodes_j$ is the number of nodes used by $job\ j$.

PRE-CKPT-SYS: This scheme corresponds to the system-level checkpoint support. All batch jobs are checkpointed *periodically* by the system (without any application assistance), and the checkpoint data (the process memory including the job context) are written to a parallel file system (PFS) for job restart. Batch jobs running on partitions chosen for real-time jobs are killed immediately, and they are resubmitted to the normal queue. When the preempted batch job gets to run again, the system resumes it from the latest checkpoint. The system checkpoint interval ($ckpIntv_{sys}$) is universal for all running batch jobs. Equations 6 to 10 describe the overhead incurred by the preempted jobs (in terms of time) and the system (in terms of core-hours).

$$t^j_{ckpt} = \sum_{i=1}^{\lfloor \frac{t^j_{runtime}}{ckpIntv_{sys}} \rfloor} \frac{ckpData^j_i}{bandwidth^{write}_{PFS}} \tag{6}$$

$$t^j_{pre} = \sum_{i=1}^{\#preemptions_j} \frac{ckpData^j_{latest}}{bandwidth^{read}_{PFS}} + ckpTgap^j_i \tag{7}$$

$$ch^{sys}_{ckpt} = \sum_{k \ in \ batch \ jobs} t^k_{ckpt} * nodes_k \tag{8}$$

$$ch^{sys}_{pre} = \sum_{k \ in \ batch \ jobs} t^k_{pre} * nodes_k \tag{9}$$

$$ch^j_{ckpt} = 0 \tag{10}$$

Here $ckpData^j_i$ is the amount of data to be checkpointed for job j for i_{th} checkpoint; $ckpData^j_{latest}$ is the amount of data checkpointed in the most recent checkpoint for $job\ j$; $bandwidth^{write}_{PFS}$ and $bandwidth^{read}_{PFS}$ represent the write and read bandwidth of the PFS, respectively; and $ckpTgap^j_i$ is the time elapsed between the time $job\ j$ was checkpointed last and the time $job\ j$ gets preempted for ith preemption.

PRE-CKPT-APP: This scheme corresponds to the application-level checkpointing. Applications checkpoint themselves by storing their execution contexts and recover by using that data when restarted without explicit assistance from the system. The checkpoint interval ($ckpIntv_{app}^j$) and the amount of data checkpointed ($ckpData^j$) change based on the application. Equations 11 to 15 describe the overhead incurred by the preempted jobs (in terms of time and core-hours) and the system (in terms of core-hours).

$$t_{ckpt}^j = \sum_{i=1}^{\lfloor \frac{t_{runtime}^j}{ckpIntv_{app}^j} \rfloor} \frac{ckpData_i^j}{bandwidth_{PFS}^{write}} \tag{11}$$

$$t_{pre}^j = \sum_{i=1}^{\#preemptions_j} \frac{ckpData_{latest}^j}{bandwidth_{PFS}^{read}} + ckpTgap_i^j \tag{12}$$

$$ch_{ckpt}^{sys} = 0 \tag{13}$$

$$ch_{pre}^{sys} = \sum_{k\ in\ batch\ jobs} t_{pre}^k * nodes_k \tag{14}$$

$$ch_{ckpt}^j = t_{ckpt}^j * nodes_j \tag{15}$$

PRE-CKPT: In this scheme, jobs are checkpointed right before they get preempted. The premise here is that there is interaction between the scheduler and the checkpointing module. When the scheduler is about to preempt a job, it informs the appropriate checkpointing module and waits for a checkpoint completion notification before it actually preempts the job. The checkpoint and preemption overhead in this scheme is minimal since there is no need to checkpoint at periodic intervals and there will not be any redundant computation (since checkpoint and preemption happen in tandem). Equations 16 to 20 describe the overhead incurred by the preempted jobs (in terms of time) and the system (in terms of core-hours).

$$t_{ckpt}^j = \sum_{i=1}^{\#preemptions_j} \frac{ckpData_i^j}{bandwidth_{PFS}^{write}} \tag{16}$$

$$t_{pre}^j = \sum_{i=1}^{\#preemptions_j} \frac{ckpData_i^j}{bandwidth_{PFS}^{read}} \tag{17}$$

$$ch_{ckpt}^{sys} = \sum_{k\ in\ batch\ jobs} t_{ckpt}^k * nodes_k \tag{18}$$

$$ch_{pre}^{sys} = \sum_{k\ in\ batch\ jobs} t_{pre}^k * nodes_k \tag{19}$$

$$ch_{ckpt}^j = 0 \tag{20}$$

6   Qsim Extensions

We used Qsim [4], an event-driven parallel job scheduling simulator, for our study. We extended QSim to support preemption and accommodate real-time

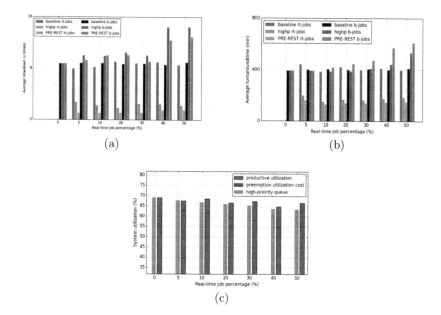

Fig. 1. Performance comparison under different real-time job (RTJ) percentages: (a) *job slowdown* of **PRE-REST**, **hpQ**, and **baseline**; (b) *job turnaround time* of **PRE-REST**, **hpQ**, and **baseline**; (c) *system utilization* of **PRE-REST** and **hpQ** under different RTJ percentages.

jobs. We implemented in Qsim all five scheduling schemes described in the preceding section. Our extensions provide two ways to mark certain jobs in the job log as real-time jobs: *user-specified* and *random*. In the user-specified approach, users can provide an index list, and the jobs with the index provided in the list are picked as real-time jobs. In the *random* approach, $R\%$ of the jobs are picked randomly as real-time jobs. Our extensions also allow the users to provide inputs as the following:

- $ckpData$ - amount of data to be checkpointed
- $bandwidth_{PFS}^{write}$ - write bandwidth of parallel file system
- $bandwidth_{PFS}^{read}$ - read bandwidth of parallel file system
- $ckpIntv_{sys}$ - checkpoint interval for system-level checkpointing
- $ckpIntv_{app}$ - checkpoint interval for application-level checkpointing (percentage of job wall time).

7   Experimental Evaluation

In this section we present details of the experimental setup and the workload traces used for our experiments. We then present the simulation results.

7.1   Workload Trace

For this study, we used four week-long trace logs collected from the Mira super-computer at Argonne. The statistics of the logs are summarized in Table 1. The logs are denoted by Wk-a, Wk-b, Wk-c, and Wk-d to anonymize the specific week; *#Job* represents the number of completed jobs in the trace log; *AvgNum-Core* represents the average number of cores required by completed jobs in the trace log; *AvgWallTime* represents the average wall time (in minutes) required by completed jobs in the trace log; *AvgRsc* represents the average amount of resources (in core-hours) required by completed jobs in the trace log; and *Avg-WallTimeAccu* represents the accuracy of average wall time (in percentage) relative to the average runtime of completed jobs.

Table 1. Statistics of Mira trace logs.

Log	#Job	AvgNumCore (cores)	AvgWallTime (min)	AvgRsc (core hours)	AvgWallTimeAccu (%)
Wk-a	403	2650.9	206.90	7931.1	86.7
Wk-b	1217	2659.8	132.83	5043.5	85.6
Wk-c	852	2437.4	165.39	6206.2	92.3
Wk-d	943	2195.3	235.68	7021.5	81.4

7.2   Experimental Setup

To fully evaluate the performance of all the scheduling schemes under different amounts of real-time jobs, we randomly chose $R\%$ (real-time job percentage) of jobs in the experimental trace log and set them as real-time jobs (RTJ), with the rest $(100 - R)\%$ as batch jobs (BJ). In our experiments we used $R \in \{5, 10, 20, 30, 40, 50\}$. Experimental results were averaged over 20 random sample groups for each R value.

We analyzed the performance of the scheduling schemes in terms of the following performance metrics.

- *Job turnaround time*: time difference between job completion time and job submission time
- *Bounded job slowdown (slowdown)*:

$$Bounded\ slowdown = (Wait\ time + Max(Run\ time, 10))/ \\ Max(Run\ time, 10) \tag{21}$$

The threshold of 10 min was used to limit the influence of very short jobs on the metric.

- *System utilization*: proportion of the total available processor cycles that are used.

$$System\ utilization = \frac{(\sum_j runtime_j \cdot nodes_j + ch_{ckpt}^j) + ch_{pre}^{sys} + ch_{ckpt}^{sys}}{Makespan \cdot nodes_{total}} \tag{22}$$

– *Productive utilization (productive_util)*: proportion of the total available processor cycles that are used for actual job execution, which excludes checkpoint and preemption overhead.

$$Productive\ utilization = \frac{\sum_j runtime_j \cdot nodes_j}{Makespan \cdot nodes_{total}} \tag{23}$$

We compare performance of scheduling schemes described in Sect. 5 with the baseline performance. Baseline performance is obtained by running both *RTJ* and *BJ* as batch jobs on Qsim with the default scheduling algorithm, which is FCFS with first-fit backfilling. Although we gathered experimental results for four week-long traces (Wk-a, Wk-b, Wk-c, Wk-d described in Table 1), we present the results for only Wk-a because of space constraints. We note that the trends for other three logs are similar to that for the log presented here.

7.3   High-Priority Queue and Preemption Without Checkpointing

We first evaluated the performance of the high-priority queue and preemption with no checkpointing (PRE-REST) schemes. Figure 1 shows the average slowdown and average turnaround time of jobs and system utilization for different RTJ percentages. From Figs. 1(a) and (b), we can observe that both the high-priority queue and PRE-REST schemes improve the performance of RTJ significantly without a huge impact on the batch jobs when %RTJ ≤ 30.

With the high-priority queue, RTJ achieve much lower job slowdown and job turnaround time compared with their baseline metrics. But the absolute values are still much higher than the desired values. For example, job slowdown ranges from 1.72 to 3.0, significantly higher than the desired slowdown of 1. Even though RTJ have higher priority than BJ have, they must wait for the running batch jobs to finish if not enough free nodes are available for RTJ to start immediately.

From Fig. 1(a), we see that preemptive scheduling can achieve a slowdown close to 1 for RTJ for workloads with up to 30% RTJ. For workloads with a higher percentage of real-time jobs (40% and 50%), however, as more system resources are occupied by RTJ, some RTJ have to wait for the required resources, resulting in a higher average slowdown (~1.5) for RTJ.

Comparing hpQ with PRE-REST, we see that PRE-REST is consistently better than hpQ for RTJ in terms of both slowdown and turnaround time. This result is expected because RTJ can preempt the running BJ in PRE-REST while they cannot do that in hpQ. Regarding BJ, we note that PRE-REST is almost always better than hpQ in terms of average slowdown, whereas hpQ is almost always better than PRE-REST in terms of average turnaround time. We conjecture that preemption of batch jobs to schedule RTJ in PRE-REST benefits the shorter BJ indirectly. In other words, preemption creates opportunities for shorter BJ to backfill. Of the batch jobs that are preempted, longer jobs will likely have a hard time backfilling and thus will suffer the most in PRE-REST. Since hpQ does not allow any batch job to be scheduled if an RTJ is waiting, the shorter jobs will not be able to backfill even if they could. The average job slowdown is influenced significantly by the short jobs. In contrast, the average job turnaround time tends to be influenced much more by the long jobs. Since PRE-REST causes relatively more negative impact on longer BJ and indirectly benefits shorter BJ, and since high-priority queue causes more negative impact on shorter BJ by denying the backfill opportunities that they would have otherwise had, PRE-REST is better in terms of average slowdown, and high-priority queue is better in terms of average turnaround time for BJ. The PRE-REST scheme having a lower productive utilization than hpQ has (see Fig. 1(c) and the text below) also supports our theory.

Figure 1(c) shows overall utilization and productive utilization of PRE-REST and high-priority queue. We note that overall utilization includes all the usage of the system, including the redundant cycles used by the preempted jobs (if any) and the cycles spent on checkpointing and preemption (if applicable). In contrast, productive utilization includes only the cycles used for the productive execution of the jobs. For high-priority queue, the overall utilization is the same as that of productive utilization since it does not have any redundant computations or any other additional overhead. In PRE-REST, portions of preempted jobs get executed more than once since they have to start from the beginning after each preemption. In Fig. 1(c), the bars on the leftmost end (0% RTJ) correspond to the baseline utilization. We can see that the overall (productive) utilization for high-priority queue decreases with the increasing percentage of RTJ. We also see that High-priority queue blocks the batch jobs and prevents them from backfilling whenever one or more real-time jobs are waiting. Thus, batch jobs suffer more with increasing numbers of real-time jobs. Although the overall utilization of PRE-REST is higher than that of high-priority queue, its productive utilization is lower because of the cycles wasted by the restart of preempted jobs from scratch. Productive utilization for high-priority queue reduces by 5% (compared with the baseline) when there are 20% real-time jobs and by 10% when there are 50% real-time jobs. In contrast, for PRE-REST, productive utilization reduces by 15% when there are 20% real-time jobs and by 20% when there are 50% real-time jobs.

7.4 Performance of Checkpoint-Based Preemptive Scheduling

We compare the performance of preemptive scheduling schemes with the baseline and hpQ schemes in Fig. 2. From Fig. 2a, we can see that for RTJ, all preemptive scheduling schemes can maintain an average slowdown in the range of [1.0, 1.4], as opposed to slowdowns around 2.0 or above with hpQ and around 8.0 or above with the baseline. Even for BJ, preemptive scheduling schemes with checkpointing (PRE-CKPT, PRE-CKPT-SYS, and PRE-CKPT-APP) perform significantly better than hpQ and the baseline when the %RTJ ≤ 30 (see Fig. 2b). We note that the average turnaround time results have similar trends as the average slowdown, and we expect that the improvement for batch jobs for 30% RTJ is modest. Based on these results, there is no reason not to support up to 30% RTJ in the workloads. The performance of RTJ is as expected, but the performance improvement for batch jobs when %RTJ ≤ 30 is both surprising

and counterintuitive. We suspect that certain categories of BJ are benefiting at
the expense of certain other categories of BJ. Also, not all RTJ are getting the
same amount of benefit. To understand these results better, we divided the jobs
into four categories: two partitions for the number of nodes used (narrow and
wide) and two partitions for the runtime (short and long). The criteria used for
classification is as follows:

- Narrow: number of nodes used is in the range [512, 4096] inclusive (note that
  the number of nodes allocated on Mira is a multiple of 512).
- Wide: number of nodes used is in the range [4608, 49152] inclusive.
- Short: jobs with runtime ≤ 120 min.
- Long: jobs with runtime > 120 min.

The performance of the baseline, hpQ, and preemptive scheduling schemes
for narrow-short, narrow-long, wide-short, and wide-long categories of RTJ and
BJ is shown in Figs. 3, 4, 5, and 6, respectively. We can see from Figs. 3b and
d that narrow-short batch jobs slowdown and that turnaround times with the
preemption schemes are significantly better than the baseline and hpQ for cases
where the %RTJ ≤ 30. For the same cases, however, the performance of the
preemption schemes for narrow-long BJ is comparable to that of the baseline
and hpQ, and for wide-short and wide-long BJ is (significantly) worse than
baseline and hpQ. Since 63% of the total jobs (57% of RTJ and 64% of BJ) are
narrow-short, the overall performance of all jobs shown in Fig. 2 is influenced by
the performance of narrow-short jobs much more than the performance of jobs
in other categories.

7.5   Impact of Checkpointing Implementations

In this section, we further evaluate the performance of preemptive scheduling in
terms of checkpoint data size and checkpoint interval.

First, to evaluate the performance impact of checkpoint data size, we conducted experiments with different checkpoint data file size for PRE-CKPT. We
define checkpoint data file size per node as $dsize$, with $dsize \in \{1$ GB, 4 GB, 16
GB$\}$, which represent checkpoint data with a compress rate of $\{92.75\%, 75\%,
0\%\}$ when the system memory size is assumed to be 16 GB. Based on the I/O
performance benchmarks for Mira, we set the I/O bandwidth per node to 2
GB/s while we set the parallel file system bandwidth cap for checkpoint/restart
data write/read to 90% of the PFS bandwidth (240 GB/s). The results of the
BJ slowdown are illustrated in Fig. 7(b). From the results, we can see the general trend: the average slowdown for BJ increases as the checkpoint data size
increases. For example, the average slowdown for BJ increases from 6.2 to 7.8
when the checkpoint data size varies from 1 GB to 16 GB for the workload with
10% RTJ. The results of the RTJ slowdown are illustrated in Fig. 7(a). No clear
trend is evident, which is expected since the checkpoint data size should not
affect RTJ.

Next, we study the impact of different checkpoint intervals for PRE-CKPT-
SYS and PRE-CKP-APP. We study the performance of PRE-CKP-SYS for

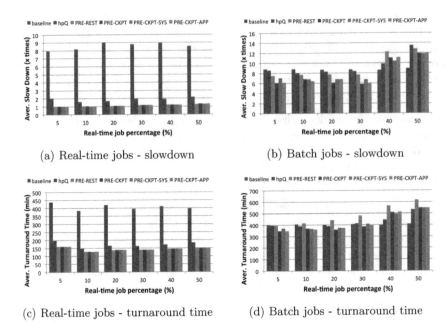

(a) Real-time jobs - slowdown

(b) Batch jobs - slowdown

(c) Real-time jobs - turnaround time

(d) Batch jobs - turnaround time

Fig. 2. Performance comparison of baseline, hpQ, PRE-REST, PRE-CKPT, PRE-CKPT-SYS, and PRE-CKPT-APP schemes.

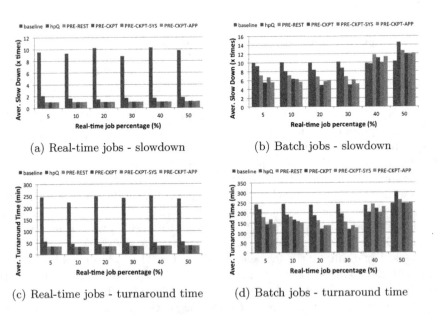

(a) Real-time jobs - slowdown

(b) Batch jobs - slowdown

(c) Real-time jobs - turnaround time

(d) Batch jobs - turnaround time

Fig. 3. Performance comparison of baseline, hpQ, PRE-REST, PRE-CKPT, PRE-CKPT-SYS, and PRE-CKPT-APP schemes for narrow-short jobs.

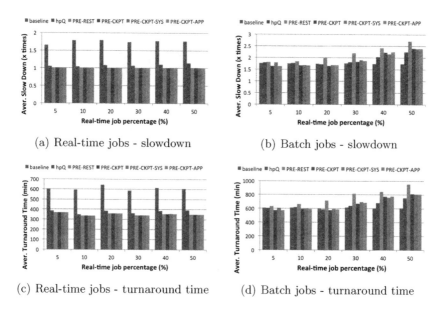

(a) Real-time jobs - slowdown   (b) Batch jobs - slowdown

(c) Real-time jobs - turnaround time   (d) Batch jobs - turnaround time

Fig. 4. Performance comparison of baseline, hpQ, PRE-REST, PRE-CKPT, PRE-CKPT-SYS, and PRE-CKPT-APP schemes for narrow-long jobs.

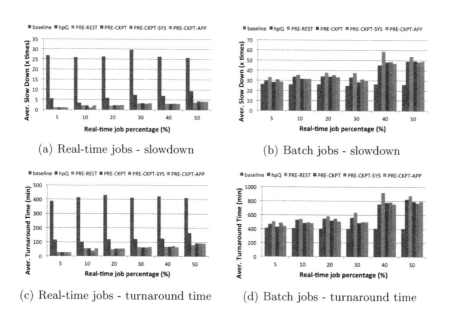

(a) Real-time jobs - slowdown   (b) Batch jobs - slowdown

(c) Real-time jobs - turnaround time   (d) Batch jobs - turnaround time

Fig. 5. Performance comparison of baseline, hpQ, PRE-REST, PRE-CKPT, PRE-CKPT-SYS and PRE-CKPT-APP schemes for wide-short jobs.

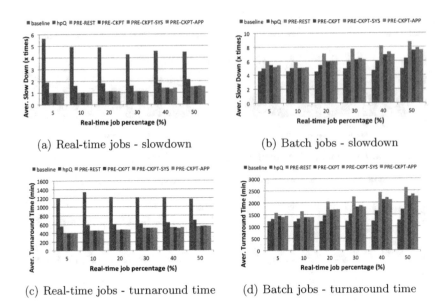

Fig. 6. Performance comparison of baseline, hpQ, PRE-REST, PRE-CKPT, PRE-CKPT-SYS, and PRE-CKPT-APP schemes for wide-long jobs.

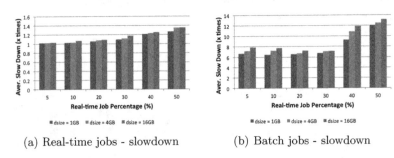

Fig. 7. Performance of PRE-CKPT-SYS for different checkpoint data sizes.

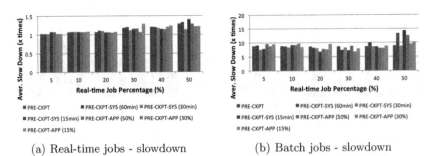

Fig. 8. Performance comparison of PRE-CKPT, PRE-CKPT-SYS, and PRE-CKPT-APP for different checkpoint intervals.

checkpoint intervals $int \in \{15\,\text{min}, 30\,\text{min}, 60\,\text{min}\}$. These interval values are selected based on the average wall time of 207 min. We study the performance of PRE-CKP-APP by setting checkpoint intervals to different percentages of wall time ($pcent$). We use $pcent \in \{15\%, 30\%, 50\%\}$. Figure 8 shows RTJ and BJ slowdowns for PRE-CKPT and for different checkpoint intervals for PRE-CKP-SYS and PRE-CKP-APP. These results are for checkpoint data file size per node $dsize = 4$ GB (I/O bandwidth per node and the PFS bandwidth cap are set to the same values mentioned before). No clear trend is seen from these results. The checkpoint interval should not affect the RTJ performance since only BJ are checkpointed. A longer checkpoint interval will result in a lower checkpoint overhead for BJ but a potentially higher restart overhead for preempted BJ. The amount of restart overhead is highly dependent on the schedule. From the results in Fig. 8(b), a checkpoint interval of 30 min for PRE-CKP-SYS and 30% wall time for PRE-CKP-APP perform better for most cases.

7.6   Summary of the Results

Even though the non-preemptive hpQ scheme can dramatically reduce the slowdown of RTJ (4× or more) compared with the baseline scheme that treats all jobs equally, the absolute values of average slowdown of RTJ is still around 2, which may not be acceptable for RTJ. Preemption is required to bring the average slowdown of RTJ close to 1. Surprisingly, both non-preemptive and preemptive schemes that favor RTJ benefit BJ also when %RTJ ≤ 30. Further analyses reveal that in addition to RTJ, narrow-short BJ also benefit significantly from the schemes that favor RTJ. With preemptive schemes, preemption of wide and long BJ can help narrow-short BJ (in addition to RTJ) through new backfilling opportunities. With hpQ, prioritizing RTJ over BJ (and making wide BJ wait) possibly creates additional backfilling opportunities for narrow-short BJ. When %RTJ ≤ 20, average slowdowns for narrow-short, narrow-long, and wide-long RTJ remain very close to 1 for all preemptive schemes; and the average slowdown for wide-short RTJ is ≤ 1.5 at least for some of the preemptive schemes. Checkpointing definitely helps reduce the negative impact on BJ. The BJ slowdown increases with increasing checkpoint data size, but no clear trend is seen with respect to the checkpoint interval (a checkpoint interval of 30 min or, when the interval is a percentage of wall time, 30% works best).

8   Conclusions

We have presented a simulation-based study of trade-offs that arise when supporting real-time jobs on a batch supercomputer. We studied both preemptive and non-preemptive scheduling schemes to support real-time jobs using production job logs by varying the percentage of real-time jobs in the workload. We compared both slowdown and turnaround time of real-time and batch jobs observed with these schemes against the ones observed with a baseline, which is the scheduling policy used in production for the system we studied. We also analyzed the performance of different categories of jobs and provided detailed insights. We showed that preemptive scheduling schemes can help real-time jobs in all categories achieve an average slowdown less than 1.5 with at most a 20% increase in average slowdown for some categories of batch jobs when the workload has 20% or fewer real-time jobs.

Acknowledgments. This material is based upon work supported by the U.S. Department of Energy, Office of Science, Advanced Scientific Computing Research, under Contract DE-AC02-06CH11357. We thank the Argonne Leadership Computing Facility at Argonne National Laboratory for providing the Mira trace log used in this study.

References

1. Cobalt project. http://trac.mcs.anl.gov/projects/cobalt
2. Frost, NCAR/CU BG/L System. https://wiki.ucar.edu/display/BlueGene/Frost
3. Mira. https://www.alcf.anl.gov/mira
4. Qsim. http://trac.mcs.anl.gov/projects/cobalt
5. Allen, G., Angulo, D., Foster, I., Lanfermann, G., Liu, C., Radke, T., Seidel, E., Shalf, J.: The cactus worm: experiments with dynamic resource selection and allocation in a grid environment. IJHPCA **15**(4), 345–358 (2001)
6. Anastasiadis, S., Sevcik, K.: Parallel application scheduling on networks of workstations. J. Parallel Distrib. Comput. **43**(2), 109–124 (1997)
7. Barak, A., Guday, S., Wheeler, R.G. (eds.): The MOSIX Distributed Operating System: Load Balancing for UNIX. LNCS, vol. 672. Springer, Heidelberg (1993). https://doi.org/10.1007/3-540-56663-5
8. Chiang, S.-H., Vernon, M.K.: Production job scheduling for parallel shared memory systems. In: Proceedings of the 15th International Parallel & Distributed Processing Symposium, Washington, DC, USA, p. 47 (2001)
9. Cirne, W., Berman, F.: Adaptive selection of partition size for supercomputer requests. In: Feitelson, D.G., Rudolph, L. (eds.) JSSPP 2000. LNCS, vol. 1911, pp. 187–207. Springer, Heidelberg (2000). https://doi.org/10.1007/3-540-39997-6_12
10. Deng, X., Gu, N., Brecht, T., Lu, K.: Preemptive scheduling of parallel jobs on multiprocessors. In: Proceedings of the Seventh Annual ACM-SIAM Symposium on Discrete Algorithms, SODA 1996, Philadelphia, PA, USA, pp. 159–167 (1996)
11. Duell, J.: The design and implementation of Berkeley Labs Linux checkpoint/restart. Technical report (2003). http://www.nersc.gov/research/FTG/checkpoint/reports.html
12. Egwutuoha, I.P., Levy, D., Selic, B., Chen, S.: A survey of fault tolerance mechanisms and checkpoint/restart implementations for high performance computing systems. J. Supercomput. **65**(8), 885–900 (2005)
13. Feitelson, D.G.: Job scheduling in multiprogrammed parallel systems. Research Report RC 19790 (87657), IBM T. J. Watson Research Center, October 1994
14. Feitelson, D.G., Rudolph, L.: Parallel job scheduling: issues and approaches. In: Feitelson, D.G., Rudolph, L. (eds.) JSSPP 1995. LNCS, vol. 949, pp. 1–18. Springer, Heidelberg (1995). https://doi.org/10.1007/3-540-60153-8_20
15. Feitelson, D.G., Rudolph, L., Schwiegelshohn, U.: Parallel job scheduling — a status report. In: Feitelson, D.G., Rudolph, L., Schwiegelshohn, U. (eds.) JSSPP 2004. LNCS, vol. 3277, pp. 1–16. Springer, Heidelberg (2005). https://doi.org/10.1007/11407522_1

16. Feitelson, D.G., Rudolph, L., Schwiegelshohn, U., Sevcik, K.C., Wong, P.: Theory and practice in parallel job scheduling. In: Feitelson, D.G., Rudolph, L. (eds.) JSSPP 1997. LNCS, vol. 1291, pp. 1–34. Springer, Heidelberg (1997). https://doi.org/10.1007/3-540-63574-2_14

17. Jones, J.P., Nitzberg, B.: Scheduling for parallel supercomputing: a historical perspective of achievable utilization. In: Feitelson, D.G., Rudolph, L. (eds.) JSSPP 1999. LNCS, vol. 1659, pp. 1–16. Springer, Heidelberg (1999). https://doi.org/10.1007/3-540-47954-6_1

18. Ward Jr., W.A., Mahood, C.L., West, J.E.: Scheduling jobs on parallel systems using a relaxed backfill strategy. In: Feitelson, D.G., Rudolph, L., Schwiegelshohn, U. (eds.) JSSPP 2002. LNCS, vol. 2537, pp. 88–102. Springer, Heidelberg (2002). https://doi.org/10.1007/3-540-36180-4_6

19. Kettimuthu, R., Subramani, V., Srinivasan, S., Gopalsamy, T., Panda, D.K., Sadayappan, P.: Selective preemption strategies for parallel job scheduling. IJHPCN **3**(2/3), 122–152 (2005)

20. Lawson, B.G., Smirni, E.: Multiple-queue backfilling scheduling with priorities and reservations for parallel systems. In: Feitelson, D.G., Rudolph, L., Schwiegelshohn, U. (eds.) JSSPP 2002. LNCS, vol. 2537, pp. 72–87. Springer, Heidelberg (2002). https://doi.org/10.1007/3-540-36180-4_5

21. Leung, V.J., Sabin, G., Sadayappan, P.: Parallel job scheduling policies to improve fairness: a case study. In: Lee, W.-C., Yuan, X. (eds.) ICPP Workshops, pp. 346–353. IEEE Computer Society (2010)

22. Leutenneger, L.T., Vernon, M.K.: The performance of multiprogrammed multiprocessor scheduling policies. In: ACM SIGMETRICS Conference on Measurement and Modelling of Computer Systems, pp. 226–236, May 1990

23. Lifka, D.A.: The ANL/IBM SP scheduling system. In: Feitelson, D.G., Rudolph, L. (eds.) JSSPP 1995. LNCS, vol. 949, pp. 295–303. Springer, Heidelberg (1995). https://doi.org/10.1007/3-540-60153-8_35

24. Motwani, R., Phillips, S., Torng, E.: Non-clairvoyant scheduling. In: Proceedings of the Fourth Annual ACM-SIAM Symposium on Discrete Algorithms, SODA 1993, Philadelphia, PA, USA, pp. 422–431 (1993)

25. Mu'alem, A.W., Feitelson, D.G.: Utilization, predictability, workloads, and user runtime estimates in scheduling the IBM SP2 with backfilling. IEEE Trans. Parallel Distrib. Syst. **12**(6), 529–543 (2001)

26. Niu, S., Zhai, J., Ma, X., Liu, M., Zhai, Y., Chen, W., Zheng, W.: Employing checkpoint to improve job scheduling in large-scale systems. In: Cirne, W., Desai, N., Frachtenberg, E., Schwiegelshohn, U. (eds.) JSSPP 2012. LNCS, vol. 7698, pp. 36–55. Springer, Heidelberg (2013). https://doi.org/10.1007/978-3-642-35867-8_3

27. Parsons, E.W., Sevcik, K.C.: Implementing multiprocessor scheduling disciplines. In: Feitelson, D.G., Rudolph, L. (eds.) JSSPP 1997. LNCS, vol. 1291, pp. 166–192. Springer, Heidelberg (1997). https://doi.org/10.1007/3-540-63574-2_21

28. Ranganathan, K., Foster, I.: Decoupling computation and data scheduling in distributed data-intensive applications. In: Proceedings of the 11th IEEE International Symposium on High Performance Distributed Computing, HPDC 2002, p. 352. IEEE Computer Society, Washington, DC (2002)

29. Sabin, G., Lang, M., Sadayappan, P.: Moldable parallel job scheduling using job efficiency: an iterative approach. In: Frachtenberg, E., Schwiegelshohn, U. (eds.) JSSPP 2006. LNCS, vol. 4376, pp. 94–114. Springer, Heidelberg (2007). https://doi.org/10.1007/978-3-540-71035-6_5

30. Sabin, G., Sadayappan, P.: Unfairness metrics for space-sharing parallel job schedulers. In: Feitelson, D., Frachtenberg, E., Rudolph, L., Schwiegelshohn, U. (eds.) JSSPP 2005. LNCS, vol. 3834, pp. 238–256. Springer, Heidelberg (2005). https://doi.org/10.1007/11605300_12

31. Schulz, M., Bronevetsky, G., Fernandes, R., Marques, D., Pingali, K., Stodghill, P.: Implementation and evaluation of a scalable application-level checkpoint-recovery scheme for MPI programs. In: Proceedings of the ACM/IEEE SC 2004 Conference Supercomputing, pp. 38–38, November 2004

32. Sevcik, K.C.: Application scheduling and processor allocation in multiprogrammed parallel processing systems. Perform. Eval. **19**(2–3), 107–140 (1994)

33. Shmueli, E., Feitelson, D.G.: Backfilling with lookahead to optimize the packing of parallel jobs. J. Parallel Distrib. Comput. **65**(9), 1090–1107 (2005)

34. Snell, Q.O., Clement, M.J., Jackson, D.B.: Preemption based backfill. In: Feitelson, D.G., Rudolph, L., Schwiegelshohn, U. (eds.) JSSPP 2002. LNCS, vol. 2537, pp. 24–37. Springer, Heidelberg (2002). https://doi.org/10.1007/3-540-36180-4_2

35. Srinivasan, S., Kettimuthu, R., Subramani, V., Sadayappan, P.: Selective reservation strategies for backfill job scheduling. In: Feitelson, D.G., Rudolph, L., Schwiegelshohn, U. (eds.) JSSPP 2002. LNCS, vol. 2537, pp. 55–71. Springer, Heidelberg (2002). https://doi.org/10.1007/3-540-36180-4_4

36. Srinivasan, S., Subramani, V., Kettimuthu, R., Holenarsipur, P., Sadayappan, P.: Effective selection of partition sizes for moldable scheduling of parallel jobs. In: Sahni, S., Prasanna, V.K., Shukla, U. (eds.) HiPC 2002. LNCS, vol. 2552, pp. 174–183. Springer, Heidelberg (2002). https://doi.org/10.1007/3-540-36265-7_17

37. Subramani, V., Kettimuthu, R., Srinivasan, S., Sadayappan, P.: Distributed job scheduling on computational grids using multiple simultaneous requests. In: Proceedings of the 11th International Symposium on High Performance Distributed Computing, p. 359. IEEE Computer Society, Washington, DC (2002)

38. Talby, D., Feitelson, D.G.: Supporting priorities and improving utilization of the IBM SP scheduler using slack-based backfilling. In: Proceedings of the 13th International Parallel Processing Symposium, pp. 513–517 (1999)

39. Tang, W., Desai, N., Buettner, D., Lan, Z.: Job scheduling with adjusted runtime estimates on production supercomputers. J. Parallel Distrib. Comput. **73**(7), 926–938 (2013)

40. Tang, W., Ren, D., Lan, Z., Desai, N.: Toward balanced and sustainable job scheduling for production supercomputers. Parallel Comput. **39**(12), 753–768 (2013)

41. Thomas, M., Dam, K., Marshall, M., Kuprat, A., Carson, J., Lansing, C., Guillen, Z., Miller, E., Lanekoff, I., Laskin, J.: Towards adaptive, streaming analysis of X-ray tomography data. Synchrotron Radiat. News **28**(2), 10–14 (2015)

42. Trebon, N.: Enabling urgent computing within the existing distributed computing infrastructure, Ph.D. thesis. University of Chicago (2011). AAI3472964

43. Walters, J.P., Chaudhary, V.: Application-level checkpointing techniques for parallel programs. In: Madria, S.K., Claypool, K.T., Kannan, R., Uppuluri, P., Gore, M.M. (eds.) ICDCIT 2006. LNCS, vol. 4317, pp. 221–234. Springer, Heidelberg (2006). https://doi.org/10.1007/11951957_21

44. Zahorjan, J., McCann, C.: Processor scheduling in shared memory multiprocessors. In: ACM SIGMETRICS Conference on Measurement and Modelling of Computer Systems, pp. 214–225, May 1990

Towards Efficient Resource Allocation for Distributed Workflows Under Demand Uncertainties

Ryan D. Friese[1(✉)], Mahantesh Halappanavar[1], Arun V. Sathanur[1], Malachi Schram[1], Darren J. Kerbyson[1], and Luis de la Torre[2]

[1] Pacific Northwest National Laboratory, Richland, WA, USA
{ryan.friese,mahantesh.halappanavar,arun.sathanur,
malachi.schram,darren.kerbyson}@pnnl.gov
[2] Universidad Metropolitana, San Juan, PR, USA
delatorre11@suagm.edu

Abstract. Scheduling of complex scientific workflows on geographically distributed resources is a challenging problem. Selection and scheduling of a subset of available resources to meet a given demand in a cost efficient manner is the first step of this complex process. In this paper, we develop a method to compute cost-efficient selection and scheduling of resources under demand uncertainties. Building on the techniques of Sample Average Approximation and Genetic Algorithms, we demonstrate that our method can lead up to 24% improvement in costs when demand uncertainties are explicitly considered. We present the results from our preliminary work in the context of a high energy physics application, the Belle II experiments, and believe that the work will equally benefit other scientific workflows executed on distributed resources with demand uncertainties. The proposed method can also be extended to include uncertainties related to resource availability and network performance.

Keywords: Cost-efficient scheduling · Uncertainty quantification
Large scale workflows · Sample average approximation

1 Introduction

Efficient utilization of computing resources is an important goal for the design and execution of complex scientific workflows. However, scheduling of these workflows on distributed computing resources is fraught with several uncertainties that lead to poor utilization of resources. In this work, we introduce the notion of uncertainties in forecasted demand and develop strategies for cost-efficient utilization of distributed resources. The three main components of our work are: (*i*) a prototypical scientific workflow from the Belle II experiments containing aspects of data generation through experiments and simulations, and analysis of this data; (*ii*) a methodology based on Sampled Average Approximation (SAA) to generate scenarios and select efficient strategies; and (*iii*) a Genetic Algorithm

© Springer International Publishing AG, part of Springer Nature 2018
D. Klusáček et al. (Eds.): JSSPP 2017, LNCS 10773, pp. 103–121, 2018.
https://doi.org/10.1007/978-3-319-77398-8_6

(GA) based method to compute efficient strategies to meet forecasted demand given a set of resources and their usage costs.

The Belle II experiments probe the interactions of fundamental constituents of our universe. The experiments will generate about 25 peta bytes (a peta byte is 10^{15} bytes) of raw data per year with an anticipated stored data of over 350 peta bytes at the end of the experiment (2022) [1,10]. Data is generated not only from the physical experiments conducted through the Belle II detector, but also from Monte Carlo simulations and user analysis. Similar to many large-scale experiments, the users, data, storage and computational resources related to the experiment are geographically distributed across the globe. Therefore the Belle II experiment is an ideal case study for our work.

Intuitively, the Sample Average Approximation (SAA) provides a mechanism to optimize functions with variables that are subject to uncertainties. Two key ideas in SAA are the use of sampling and optimization under certainty [15]. Given a particular demand, in terms of the number of compute units, a cost-efficient mix of resources can be chosen to meet this demand, where the cost of using each type of resource is different. We provide a rigorous formulation of this optimization problem in Sect. 2. However, this deterministic optimization problem becomes hard when the demand is subject to uncertainties. Note that

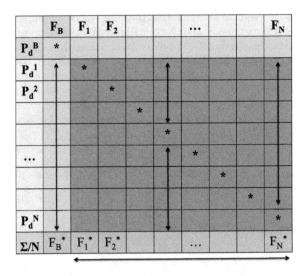

Fig. 1. An illustration of our approach using the Sample Average Approximation method. Different scenarios (represented along the rows: $P_d^1 - P_d^N$) are created by drawing random samples from the distribution of a given base demand (P_d^B). Solutions (represented along the columns: $F_B, F_1 - F_N$) are generated using a Genetic Algorithm based optimizer for each scenario. The asterisks on the diagonal correspond to the scenario used to create a solution. Each solution is used to solve every other scenario (non-diagonal entries). The bottom row represents the mean value for each solution over every scenario. The minimum mean value provides an optimal solution.

the supply (availability of resources) is also subject to uncertainties that we will ignore in this work and note that our work can be extended to include such uncertainties. Assuming the probability distribution functions for demands are known apriori from the application domain, we first generate several scenarios by drawing random samples from these distributions. We then solve each scenario as a deterministic case using a Genetic Algorithm (GA) based approach. We implement a modified version of the popular Nondominated Sorted Genetic Algorithm II (NSGAII) [3]. We detail this method in Sect. 3.

The optimal strategy (the mix of resources to meet the demand) for a given scenario is used to compute the cost of meeting the demand from all the other scenarios. A mean cost for each strategy is computed, and the minimum of these means is chosen as the optimal strategy that is robust to different scenarios. A base case is also computed and compared against the optimal solution (in terms of solving different scenarios). The proposed SAA based method is illustrated in Fig. 1. We discuss the experimental setup and results in Sects. 4 and 5, respectively.

Contributions

We make the following contributions in this preliminary work paper:

- Present a scheduling framework for Belle II workflows under demand uncertainties.
- Present a novel Genetic Algorithm based approach for computing cost-efficient selection of resources based on the analogy of unit commitment problem in electric power grids.
- Present a Sample Average Approximation based method to develop scenarios and compute solutions that are optimal across different scenarios. We demonstrate the effectiveness of this approach using a prototypical workflow from high energy physics application.
- We demonstrate a cost benefit of up to 24% relative to the optimal base case, and thus, make a case for the utility of considering demand uncertainties in scheduling of complex scientific workflows executed on distributed resources.

The paper is organized as follows. We provide a rigorous formulation of the cost-efficient selection of resources to meet a given demand in Sect. 2. We present the proposed methodology in Sect. 3 and explain the details of Sample Average Approximation and Genetic Algorithm based methods. We provide our experimental setup in Sect. 4 and experimental results in Sect. 5. We present related work in Sect. 6, and our conclusions in Sect. 7.

2   Problem Formulation

Given that a variety of distributed resources are available to meet a certain demand, the question we address is: *What is the most cost-effective allocation of resources to meet the given demand?* We address this question using the analogy of Unit Commitment problem in the context of electric power grids [22]. We first introduced this idea in our previous work [9] using linear programming approaches to develop solutions. In this paper, we develop a genetic algorithm based approach and introduce the notion of *uncertain demand*. An important assumption we make is that only a subset of available resources is sufficient to meet the demand for a given time period. We note that this is a fair assumption when cloud computing resources are being utilized and when multiple dedicated resources are used to support several scientific applications.

For Belle II experiments, several types of distributed resources including dedicated and opportunistic on-demand resources are available. The cost structures (both fixed (start up) and operating) vary significantly for different kinds of resources. As an example, while dedicated resources have a fixed operating cost, cloud computing resources such as Amazon EC2 have a variety of resources with different fixed and usage based costs [23]. A similar problem of resource utilization also arises in the context of electric power grids that is popularly known as the Unit Commitment problem. Consider a power grid operator with access to several power generators with different start-up and operating costs, and demand (load) that varies significantly over a period of time including seasonal fluctuations. For a given period of time, generally from several hours to a few days, the objective of unit commitment is to determine a subset of power generators that will used and the amount of power they will generate to meet the demand at a *minimum cost*. Using the notation introduced by Wright [30], we can formally express the objective function as:

$$\min F = \sum_{t=1}^{T} \sum_{j=1}^{N} C_j(P_j(t)) + S_j(x_j(t), u_j(t)), \tag{1}$$

subject to constraints:

$$\sum_{j=1}^{N} P_j(t) = P_d(t) \tag{2}$$

$$\sum_{j=1}^{N} r_j(x_j(t), P_j(t)) \geq P_r(t), \tag{3}$$

where F is the total system cost for N power generators with operating (fuel) cost C_j and start-up cost S_j to generate P_j units of power. The variable x_j represents the number of time units (for example, hours) that a given generator is on (positive) or off (negative). Similarly, the variable u_j represents the state of a generator at a given time unit $t + 1$. It is positive (+1) if the state is up and negative (−1) if the state is down. The constraints enforce that the demand, $P_d(t)$ at time t, is satisfied. Further, the system is also required to meet a certain additional (reserve) unanticipated demand P_r, and r_j is the reserve available from generator j for time period t. The total time period under consideration is T.

For the purposes of this paper, we define $P_j(t)$ as the computing power of a resource v_j for time unit t. A metric for expressing power in the context of Belle II is HEP SPEC – a metric derived from SPEC CPU 2006 standard[1]. Different costs for resources available for Belle II experiments can be potentially modeled using machine specifications (energy and power consumption) and operation policies, in a method described in Singer *et al.* [23]. Demand for computing resources arise from several tasks including Monte Carlo simulation campaigns with given number of events (P_d) that are simulated over a given period of time. The user analysis jobs are generally chaotic and lead to uncertainties in demand that need additional resources to satisfy. This situation is equivalent to the spinning reserve (P_r) in a power grid. A key problem addressed in this paper is that we consider demand uncertainties explicitly and solve the optimization problem. We will discuss our proposed methodology to solve the unit commitment based formulation using genetic algorithm in Sect. 3. An advantage of using the analogy of unit commitment is that a large body of work is available to solve the problem efficiently. We discussed a linear programming based approach in [9], and note that several other approaches are available in literature [22].

3   Proposed Methodology

We formulated the cost-efficient resource selection problem using the analogy of unit commitment problem in Sect. 2. In this section, we develop a method to handle demand uncertainties in this formulation using Sample Average Approximation (SAA), and then develop a genetic algorithm based method to compute efficient solutions for the optimization problem.

3.1   Sample Average Approximation (SAA)

The optimization problem described in Eq. 1 cannot be computed exactly when demand is uncertain. Therefore, we employ the SAA technique, which is based on the ideas of sampling and deterministic optimization, to solve this problem. Formally, the problem can be expressed as:

$$\min f(x) = f(x, \xi), \tag{4}$$

where x represents the scheduling strategy for resources (which resources to commit and at what level to run) and ξ represents demand that is random and independent of x. $f(x, \xi)$ is therefore the total cost. Given a probability distribution function for demand, we randomly sample different values for demand $\xi_1, \xi_2, \ldots, \xi_n$, and set

$$\min f_n(x) = \frac{1}{n} \sum_{i=1}^{n} f(x, \xi_i). \tag{5}$$

---

[1] HEP SPEC is based on SPEC CPU 2006. Further information is available from http://w3.hepix.org/benchmarks/doku.php/.

For a given value of demand, the optimization problem becomes deterministic, which we solve using a genetic algorithm based approach (described next). We then pick the minimum value from Eq. 4 ($\min f(x) = \min f_n(x)$), as illustrated in Fig. 1. The SAA method converges to an optimal solution as the number of samples n increases [15]. We conduct our experiments with 5000 samples that we detail in Sect. 4. We note that in this particular formulation of the problem, our solution space is limited to the $(n+1)$ solutions corresponding to the n scenarios and the base case. The eventual solution (commitment strategy) is chosen to be the minimum mean solution among $(n+1)$ solutions. We plan to modify our current method to account for the objective function at each step as the expectation over $(n+1)$ scenarios to develop a globally optimal solution in our future work. We also plan to explore mathematical programming based methods to compute optimal solutions.

3.2   Genetic Algorithm

Genetic algorithms (GAs) are common evolutionary optimization techniques useful in solving problems that contain large and complex search spaces (e.g., [11,18,24,27,29]). GAs try to emulate the process of natural selection; i.e., producing better (fitter) solutions as time progresses. Typical GAs maintain a population of individuals called chromosomes. Each chromosome is a solution to the problem being solved. Chromosomes are compared with one another by evaluating their fitness. Fitness functions are often, but not always, the objective function to optimized (this paper presents two fitness functions, one is the direct objective (i.e. Eq. 1), while the other is a relaxed version). Chromosomes are further composed of genes, the base component of a solution, their representation is highly dependent on the problem being solved. Our paper implements a popular multi-objective GA, the NSGAII [3].

Better solutions in a GA are produced as the population evolves through time. Evolution occurs due to three genetic-operators: selection, crossover, and mutation. During selection, chromosomes are chosen as parents to "mate" and produce offspring chromosomes. Typically, selection operators are biased towards selecting more fit chromosomes. The crossover operation takes the chromosomes chosen during selections and swaps a portion of the genes of each parent into one another, resulting in offspring chromosomes that contain genetic information from both parents. Finally, mutation operates on chromosomes individually, with individual genes in a chromosome being randomly mutated to introduce new genetic information. Selection, crossover, and mutation are applied to the population until some stopping criteria is met, e.g., the population converges, or a given number of iterations have been performed.

Numerous techniques can be used to speed up the process of finding fit chromosomes by taking advantage of parallel systems. One approach is an island model, which has numerous populations evolving simultaneously with occasional migration of chromosomes from population to population [8,26]. Our GA implements a variation of the island model.

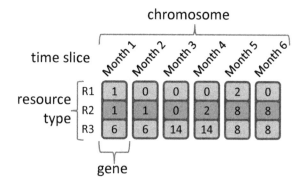

Fig. 2. Unit Commitment chromosome structure. Each gene represents the number of resources of each type used in a given month.

Chromosome Structure for Unit Commitment: As stated previously in Sect. 2, our goal is to select a combination of machines that meet a given demand and minimize cost over an N-month time period. Every month has an associated demand that must be met.

Due to the month-by-month decomposition of the problem, we can easily construct chromosomes where each gene will represent a specific month within the time period. Furthermore, for each month we indicate the number of resources of each type to be used. As a result, each chromosome can be represented as a $M \times R$ matrix, where M is the number of months, and R is the number of resource types available. For this paper, we assume machines can only be used in integer quantities, but accounting for "partial" machines is a trivial change. Figure 2 presents the chromosome and gene structure used in our GA. In this example we are purchasing resources for a 6 month period, and have 3 resource types to choose from.

In the case where the computing resources specified by a given chromosome do not meet the required demand (Eq. 2), additional on-demand resources are "purchased" to make up the difference and produce a valid solution. Typically on-demand resources are more expensive per unit of compute performance, thus it is desirable to not have to purchase additional resources.

Genetic Operators: The selection operator used in our GA is a binary tournament selection [19] with replacement. Two randomly selected chromosomes are compared against one another and the fitter chromosome is selected as a parent for crossover.

Crossover is performed using a two-point crossover scheme [11]. In this scheme, the indices of two genes are randomly selected, and the genes between these two points are swapped between parent chromosomes to produce two new offspring chromosomes.

Finally, the mutation operator we implemented operates on individual genes. During this operation, each gene within a chromosome may mutate with a given probability. When a gene is selected for mutation, each resource type has a $\frac{1}{\text{\# Resource Types}}$ probability of having the number of allocated resources changed. When a resource type mutates, a normal distribution with the mean equal to the current number of resources and a standard deviation of .5 is used to create a new value for the allocated resources of that type. We set negative allocations to zero.

Island Model Implementation: In island model GAs there exist P multiple populations that evolve concurrently. After a given number of iterations, the populations will migrate chromosomes from one population to another, introducing new genetic material into each population. The idea is that the individual populations will explore and optimize different areas of the search space. During migration events, new genetic material is introduced that has been optimized for a different sub-spaces. By combining optimized genetic material for two different sub-spaces, the hope is that new solutions will be created that span the sub-spaces and result in solutions that are more fit overall.

The rate of migration can significantly impact the performance of the GA. When a migration event occurs after every iteration, the individual populations essentially form a single larger population. This is because the constant exchange of genetic material from neighboring populations prevents diversity and exploration within the individual populations. When migration events never occur, no genetic material is exchanged between the populations, and the result is the same as if P regular populations were executed and the best solution was chosen from among them. Selecting an appropriate migration rate is generally related to the convergence rates of the individual populations, and is thus highly dependent on the problem being solved. We used an empirically determined static migration rate.

We implement a modified island model GA, where we have a central population, and several satellite populations. The satellite populations migrate chromosomes with one another using a ring pattern and also perform an one-way many-to-one communication with the central population (Fig. 3). The satellite (blue) populations both send and receive chromosomes (blue arrows) while the central (orange) population only receives chromosomes (orange arrows). During a migration event, each population (excluding the central population) will send copies of its *most fit* chromosome. When a new chromosome is received by a population, it will replace its *least fit* chromosome with the new one.

The number of chromosomes are the same for every population and should be at least equal to the number of populations themselves (this guarantees the central population has enough space to hold a chromosome from every satellite population). By using same sized populations, the execution time to perform n iterations between migration events will be very similar for each population. Thus, we have implemented the communication between populations using synchronized MPI send/recvs. For our problem, idle time due to load unbalance (from some populations finishing before others) and communication overhead is negligible compared to the compute cost between migration events.

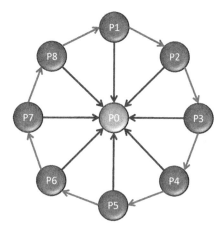

Fig. 3. Illustration of GA Island Model. The ring communication pattern is represented as the blue arrows connecting the satellite populations. The many-to-one communication between the central population and satellite populations is represented as the orange arrows. (Color figure online)

Objective Functions (Minimize Total and Base Cost): We optimized for two objectives simultaneously. The first objective is the total cost to purchase the machines required to meet a given demand, while the second cost is what we call the "base" cost. The <u>total</u> cost includes both the cost due to purchasing the machines specified by a chromosome, and any cost incurred when extra on-demand machines are required to be purchased. The <u>base</u> cost does not include the cost for additional machines. Recall, chromosomes may potentially create solutions that do not meet the required demand, thus extra machines need to be purchased to make these chromosomes valid solutions. Minimizing total cost is the exact objective we are trying to minimize (Eqs. 1 and 2), while minimizing base cost is a relaxation.

We use the base cost as the second objective instead of only optimizing for total cost for multiple reasons. First, minimizing the base cost (in addition to total cost) allows the GA to more directly explore areas of the search space that contain (potentially high performing) invalid solutions (i.e. compute resources that do not meet required demand). Typically, the base cost should have a higher contribution towards the total cost (for good solutions), by explicitly optimizing the base cost we more directly optimize the total cost as well. Finally, any solution that requires extra resources to be purchased can actually be represented by a number of valid solutions, thus minimizing the base cost covers larger areas of the search space than minimizing the total cost alone.

Algorithm 1 shows the method for calculating the costs (base and extra) of a given chromosome, To calculate the base cost of a chromosome we iterate over each month, summing the on-demand cost of any used resource (applies to on-demand and hybrid cost resources) as well as the start-up cost for any newly purchased subscription based resources. To accurately account for hybrid

Algorithm 1. Calculating the costs (base and extra) of a chromosome

---

Input: machinesToPurchase[months][numResourceTypes],   demand[months],
extraResource
Output: cost,extraCost
1: $baseCost = 0$
2: $extraCost = 0$
3: $purchased[months][numResourceTypes]$
4: **for** m in $months$ **do**
5:     $availCompute = 0$
6:     **for** r in $resourceTypes$ **do**
7:         **for** $t \leftarrow m..(m + r.contractLength - 1)$ **do**
8:             $purchased[t][r.type]+ = machinesToPurchase[m][r.type]$
9:             $baseCost+ = purchased[m][r.type] * r.onDemandCost$ ▷ 0 for up-front resources
10:            $baseCost+ = machinesToPurchase[m][r.type] * r.upFrontCost$ ▷ 0 for on-demand resources
11:        $availCompute+ = purchased[m][r.type] * r.compute$
12:        $neededCompute = demand[m] - availCompute$
13:        **if** $neededCompute > 0$ **then**
14:            $extraCost+ = ceil(neededCompute/extraResource.compute) * extraResource.onDemandCost$
15: **return** $baseCost, extraCost$

---

resources that incur an on-demand cost when used, we keep track of previously purchased resources for the length of their contract (line 8). Note, for purely on-demand machines, their contract length is one month.

Calculating extra cost also iterates over each month, but the sum of compute power supplied by each purchased resource is compared to the demand required for that month. If the supplied compute power is greater than or equal to the demand, no additional resources are purchased. Otherwise the supplied compute power does not meet the required demand, and additional extra (on-demand) resources must be purchased. Typically, this extra resource has a higher cost than other resources. The total cost of a chromosome would simply be the sum of the base and extra costs.

4   Experimental Setup

Computation in Belle II experiments arise from three kinds of activities: (*i*) processing of raw data from the Belle II detector, (*ii*) Monte Carlo simulations of physical phenomena, and (*iii*) physics analysis of experimental and simulation data. Both data storage and computation span a geographically distributed set of resources covering several continents. While the computational demand for Monte Carlo campaigns is fairly stable, the demand for user analysis tends to be chaotic leading to uncertainties in demand. Inspired from this setting, we use a representative setup for demand and supply in our experiments that are detailed in this section.

Table 1. Representative subscription costs for Amazon EC2 resources. The third column EC2 Compute Unit (ECU) provides the relative measure of the processing power of an Amazon EC2 machine instance. The fourth column represents the subscription time for a specific machine subscription plan. The fifth column S_j represents the fixed (set up) cost (in dollars) for the period specified in the fourth column. The sixth column represents the monthly usage cost C_j (in dollars per month).

Machine	Cost type	ECU	Time (month)	S_j (\$)	C_j (\$/month)
1	On-demand	0.2	1	0	13.14
2	Hybrid	0.2	12	102	4.38
3	Subscription	0.2	12	151	0
4	Hybrid	0.2	36	218	2.92
5	Subscription	0.2	36	303	0
6	On-demand	0.8	1	0	26.28
7	Hybrid	0.8	12	204	8.76
8	Subscription	0.8	12	302	0
9	Hybrid	0.8	36	436	5.84
10	Subscription	0.8	36	607	0
11	On-demand	6.5	1	0	63.51
12	Hybrid	6.5	12	324	27.01
13	Subscription	6.5	12	635	0
14	Hybrid	6.5	36	657	18.25
15	Subscription	6.5	36	1235	0
16	On-demand	13	1	0	126.29
17	Hybrid	13	12	648	54.02
18	Subscription	13	12	1271	0
19	Hybrid	13	36	1314	36.5
20	Subscription	13	36	2470	0
21	On-demand	26	1	0	252.58
22	Hybrid	26	12	1296	108.04
23	Subscription	26	12	2541	0
24	Hybrid	26	36	2628	73
25	Subscription	26	36	4941	0
26	On-demand	53.5	1	0	505.89
27	Hybrid	53.5	12	2593	216.08
28	Subscription	53.5	12	5082	0
29	Hybrid	53.5	36	5256	146
30	Subscription	53.5	36	9881	0
31	On-demand	124.5	1	0	1264.36
32	Hybrid	124.5	12	6482	540.2
33	Subscription	124.5	12	12706	0
34	Hybrid	124.5	36	13150	365
35	Subscription	124.5	36	24703	0

We present two sets of simulations, the first is a small illustrative example while the second is a larger simulation inspired from the Belle II experiment. For the large simulations, we use models of cloud computing resources based

Table 2. Resource costs for illustrative example.

Machine	Cost typ	ECU	Time (month)	S_j (\$)	C_j (\$/month)
1	On-demand	1.3	1	0	10.0
2	Hybrid	1.3	4	11.5	2.9
3	Subscription	1.3	4	22.8	0

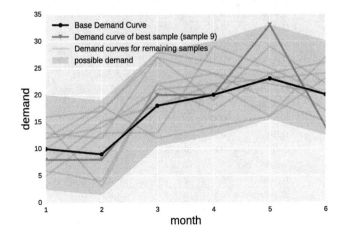

Fig. 4. Demand curves for the illustrative example. The base demand curve is shown as the black line. The demand curve for best sample is the dark blue line, while the light blue lines show the demand curves for all other samples. The shaded area represents the possible demand values $(d_m - 7.5, d_m + 10)$. (Color figure online)

on Amazon EC2, as shown in Table 1 (note that the prices in the table may not reflect current Amazon EC2 prices). The resource costs for the illustrative example are presented in Table 2. Each compute resource has an associated ECU (compute power), contract length, and up-front (S_j) and on-demand costs (C_j).

Multiple demand curves are constructed as follows. For our illustrative example, we simulate a 6-month workflow using 10 sampled scenarios. The base demand curve for this example is the black line in Fig. 4. To create a new scenario, for each month, we used the demand d_m from the base curve as the seed value and sample a new value from a uniform distribution $U(d_m - 7.5, d_m + 10)$. In Fig. 4, the sampled demand curves are the blue lines while the area of possible demands is shown as the shaded area. For the larger experiments, we simulated a 24-month workflow and executed two 5000-scenario campaigns. The base demand curve, upon which all the other scenarios drew their demand curves from, is presented as the solid line in Fig. 7. For the first campaign, the range for the uniform distribution is $a = d_m - 15, b = dm + 20$. The range for the second campaign is half that of the first, i.e., $a = d_m - 7.5, b = d_m + 10$. Sample demand curves and possible demand values for the higher (blue line and shaded area) and lower variation (green line and shaded area) campaigns are presented in Fig. 7. In future work, we plan to examine base curves for additional workflows, and different sampling distributions.

All simulations were run on a 20-node cluster with an InfiniBand interconnect. Each node is equipped with dual 10-core Intel IvyBridge CPUs (Intel E5-2680 v2, 2.8 GHz) and 128 GB RAM (DDR3-1866). Each scenario fully occupied one node (one population per core), and multiple scenarios were executed across the cluster concurrently.

The following parameters were used in the genetic algorithm to produce solutions for each scenario. The number of populations in the island model was set to 20 (19 satellite populations and a single central population). Each population contained 25 chromosomes. Each chromosome starts with a random initial state. Migration events were performed every 200 generations. The probability that an individual gene would be selected for mutation was set to 1%. If two chromosomes were selected for crossover, they would always mate and produce two offspring. Finally, we terminated the algorithm and took the best solution found after 60 s. Given these parameters and our cluster configuration, each population performed roughly 30,000 iterations, resulting in 300 migration events. The compute-to-communication ratio is between 10–12.

5 Experimental Results and Discussion

We now present the experimental results for the two simulations, a smaller illustrative example and larger simulations, as detailed in Sect. 4. We will start with a detailed presentation of the illustrative example and then present the key details of the larger simulations. Our goal in this section is to highlight the substantial gains that can be obtained by carefully considering demand uncertainties relative to a solution obtained without uncertainties (base case).

As an illustration, we present the cost of computing all the scenarios (represented as rows) with the most optimal strategy (represented as columns) for a given scenario (diagonal entries) in Fig. 5 for the small illustrative example. Note that the diagonal entry will be the best solution for a given scenario (P_d^i) among solutions computed by different strategies (F_i). The final strategy is selected by picking a strategy that provides the minimum mean value across different scenarios, represented in the bottom-most row of the matrix. Further details of the optimal strategy (F_9) are provided in Fig. 6. We show the difference between the mean values of base case (F_B) and the optimal strategy as the expected benefit of the proposed method.

We consider two variants of the larger simulation by varying the probability distribution functions for demand relative to the base case. While one variation is small, the other is relatively large. We capture the key results in Fig. 7. First, we show the base demand curve (black line) and the regions of possible demand for the high (blue shaded area) and low (green shaded area) variations. The demand curves for the best performing solutions for the high (blue line) and low (green line) variants show that both solutions tend to have higher demands (per month) than the base curve. In general, the monthly demand is met by

	F_B	F_1	F_2	F_3	F_4	F_5	F_6	F_7	F_8	F_9	F_{10}
P_d^B	510.7	572.1	588.5	618.4	620.1	558.9	535.7	574.3	550.2	529.4	538.7
P_d^1	640.7	597.9	661.7	705.8	653.3	674.7	644.4	614.3	651.8	639.4	647.4
P_d^2	707.8	697.9	636.5	780.0	689.1	734.7	718.6	680.1	726.0	709.4	707.4
P_d^3	616.2	633.4	644.3	575.8	679.1	622.8	605.7	642.7	642.8	646.5	631.3
P_d^4	800.7	767.9	764.9	865.8	689.4	806.3	814.4	730.1	797.6	799.4	807.4
P_d^5	617.8	652.1	661.4	668.4	663.0	527.9	618.6	634.3	606.0	609.4	615.8
P_d^6	549.1	583.4	605.6	614.2	631.7	590.2	524.4	592.7	567.3	566.5	577.1
P_d^7	650.7	629.2	664.6	722.9	637.5	677.6	654.4	570.1	647.6	649.4	657.4
P_d^8	573.3	606.0	638.2	622.6	620.1	611.5	558.6	559.8	497.6	543.6	542.9
P_d^9	586.2	651.8	627.2	672.6	690.1	620.2	575.7	639.8	586.0	549.4	585.8
P_d^{10}	523.3	576.3	564.0	601.0	605.6	544.4	527.0	578.5	483.1	496.4	457.4
$\Sigma/10$	614.0	633.5	641.5	677.1	652.6	633.6	616.1	619.7	614.2	(612.6)	615.3

Fig. 5. Complete set of results for the illustrative example. Different scenarios are represented as rows, the diagonal entries represent the best strategy (solution) for the corresponding scenario. A column indicates the cost for each scenario for a given strategy. The bottom-most row represents the mean cost for a given strategy. The final strategy picked is the one that is minimum (F_9) in this row.

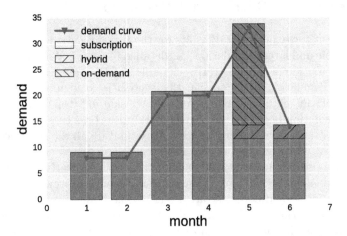

Fig. 6. Resource allocation (and demand curve) of best solution for illustrative example. The different hatches within a bar represent the amount of each resource cost type (subscription, hybrid, on-demand) used.

a higher contribution of subscription and hybrid machines, using few (costly) on-demand machines. It is cheaper to buy a subscription or hybrid resource and let it sit idle for a couple of months, than to replace that resource with an equivalent on-demand resource. Thus, the best performing solutions are those that are over-provisioned when applied to other demand scenarios.

In order to highlight the main benefits of incorporating uncertainties, we capture the benefit (difference between the mean costs of base and optimal

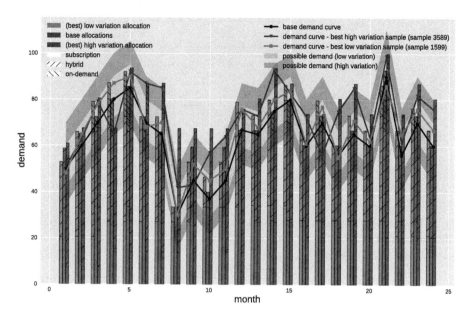

Fig. 7. Demand curves and allocations for Belle II based simulation. The base demand curve is shown as the black line. The demand curve for high variation best sample is the blue line, while the green line shows the demand curve for low variation best sample. The blue shaded area represents the possible demand values for the high variation experiment $(d_m - 15, d_m + 20)$. The green shaded area represents the possible demand values for the low variation experiment $(d_m - 7.5, d_m + 10)$. The vertical bars show resource allocations for the base (black), the best high variation (blue) and best low variation (green). The different hatches within a bar represent the amount of each resource cost type (subscription, hybrid, on-demand) used. (Color figure online)

strategies) in Figs. 8 and 9. We present the difference as a percentage relative to the base case in Fig. 8. The difference is presented as a function of the number of samples and variation in demand. We present the benefits as absolute numbers (along Y-axis) in Fig. 9 and provide the identity of the optimal strategy for a given number of samples plotted along X-axis.

We observe that the accuracy of the proposed method increases as the number of samples increase (plotted along X-axis), and the strategies change providing different (nonlinear) amounts of benefit relative to the base case. Further, we note that for the small variation simulation, the optimal strategy remains constant (Strategy 1599) after a certain number of samples (about 1700). The difference between the base case and the optimal strategy also increases when the amount of variation increases. We note that we are able to clearly demonstrate the benefits of incorporating demand uncertainties by using a rather simplistic setting with uniform distributions. Since real-world scenarios vary significantly and have different kinds of probability distributions, we anticipate that the proposed method will result in significant cost benefits for such situations.

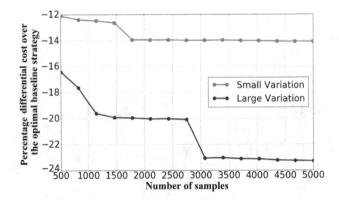

Fig. 8. Percentage differential costs between optimal base case and optimal strategy. Different number of samples are used along X-axis for two different scenarios – small variation and large variation.

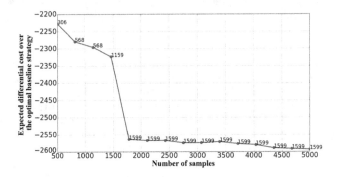

Fig. 9. Expected differential costs between optimal base case and optimal strategy for the small variation scenario with different number of samples. The numbers indicate the identity of the strategy that was chosen as an optimal strategy.

6   Related Work

Our work is inspired from the unit commitment problem in power grids in developing a strategy for cost-efficient resource allocation for complex scientific workflows on distributed computing resources [9]. In this work, we introduced the notion of demand uncertainties that arise due to several different reasons including uncertainties in estimations and chaotic use of resources. Given the roots of our work in unit commitment problem, a natural area of related work lies in a large body of work on modeling and quantification of uncertainties for the unit commitment problem [7,21,28]. We note that the underlying physics of a power grid makes modeling uncertainties in that area a relatively challenging problem. However, we can derive from the existing work to model uncertainties in scheduling and resource allocation. Furthermore, the use of genetic algorithms to solve the unit commitment problem has been presented in [14,25].

The notion of demand uncertainty has also been explored in the area of grid computing by Batista *et al.* [2], and in resource allocation by Johansson and Sternad [13]. Unlike the previous work, we develop cost-efficient strategies for resource selection for distributed workflows that have access to a large set of resources with diverse cost structures for usage. Our work becomes especially relevant in the context of cloud computing. The notion of uncertain demand has also been explored for cloud based resources. Johannes *et al.* explored the use of fuzzy optimization for resource allocation with uncertain demand [12]. Related work on cloud resource allocation work has been explored in [16, 17, 31]. Genetic algorithms have been used extensively for resource allocation [4–6, 20].

To the best of our knowledge, we believe this work is the first in exploring cost-efficient resource allocation as the first step in an integrated approach to schedule and manage HEP workflows, such as Belle II, under demand uncertainties.

7   Conclusions

We presented our preliminary work on incorporating demand uncertainties in computing cost-efficient resource selection as the first step of an integrated approach for efficient scheduling of complex workflows on distributed computing platforms. Using the technique of Sample Average Approximation, we demonstrate upto 24% improvement in costs relative to an optimal base case without uncertainties. We also presented a Genetic Algorithm based technique to compute efficient solutions for optimization problems when demands are certain. We developed our experiments within the context of a high energy physics workflow, the Belle II experiments, that execute on geographically distributed resources.

In our future work, we plan to extend our work through rigorous modeling of uncertainties and develop computationally efficient techniques based on stochastic programming. We believe that the benefits of our work will not only prepare us for the forthcoming Belle II experiments but also lead to significant reduction in costs in the utilization of available resources with varying cost structures. We also believe that our work will benefit a large number of complex workflows that utilize distributed computing resources in general and cloud computing resources in particular.

Acknowledgment. This work was supported by the Integrated End-to-end Performance Prediction and Diagnosis for Extreme Scientific Workflows (IPPD) Project. IPPD is funded by the U. S. Department of Energy Awards FWP-66406 and DE-SC0012630 at the Pacific Northwest National Laboratory. Pacific Northwest National Laboratory is operated by Battelle for the DOE under Contract DE-AC05-76RL01830. The work of Luis de la Torre was supported in part by the U.S. Department of Energy, Office of Science, Office of Workforce Development for Teachers and Scientists (WDTS) under the Visiting Faculty Program (VFP).

References

1. Asner, D.M., Dart, E., Hara, T.: Belle II experiment network and computing. arXiv preprint arXiv:1308.0672 (2013)
2. Batista, D.M., Drummond, A.C., da Fonseca, N.L.S.: Scheduling grid tasks under uncertain demands. In: Proceedings of the 2008 ACM Symposium on Applied Computing, SAC 2008, pp. 2041–2045. ACM, New York (2008)
3. Deb, K., Pratap, A., Agarwal, S., Meyarivan, T.: A fast and elitist multiobjective genetic algorithm: NSGA-II. IEEE Trans. Evol. Comput. **6**(2), 182–197 (2002)
4. Dogan, A., Ozguner, F.: Genetic algorithm based scheduling of meta-tasks with stochastic execution times in heterogeneous computing systems. Cluster Comput. **7**(2), 177–190 (2004)
5. Friese, R.D.: Efficient genetic algorithm encoding for large-scale multi-objective resource allocation. In: 9th Workshop on Large-Scale Parallel Processing (LSPP 2016), in the Proceedings of the IPDPS 2016 Workshops and PhD Forum (IPDPSW), May 2016
6. Garshasbi, M.S., Effatparvar, M.: High performance scheduling in parallel heterogeneous multiprocessor systems using evolutionary algorithms. Int. J. Intell. Syst. Appl. **11**, 89–95 (2013)
7. Gholami, A., Shekari, T., Aminifar, F., Shahidehpour, M.: Microgrid scheduling with uncertainty: the quest for resilience. IEEE Trans. Smart Grid **7**(6), 2849–2858 (2016)
8. Gorges-Schleuter, M.: Explicit parallelism of genetic algorithms through population structures. In: 1st Workshop on Parallel Problem Solving from Nature (PPSN), pp. 150–159 (1990)
9. Halappanavar, M., Schram, M., de la Torre, L., Barker, K., Tallent, N.R., Kerbyson, D.J.: Towards efficient scheduling of data intensive high energy physics workflows. In: Proceedings of the 10th Workshop on Workflows in Support of Large-Scale Science, WORKS 2015, pp. 3:1–3:9. ACM, New York (2015)
10. Hara, T.: Belle II: computing and network requirements. In: Proceedings of the Asia-Pacific Advanced Network, pp. 115–122 (2014)
11. Holland, J.: Adaptation in Natural and Artificial Systems: An Introductory Analysis with Applications to Biology, Control, and Artificial Intelligence, 1st edn. The University of Michigan, Ann Arbor (1975)
12. Johannes, A., Borhan, N., Liu, C., Ranjan, R., Chen, J.: A user demand uncertainty based approach for cloud resource management. In: 2013 IEEE 16th International Conference on Computational Science and Engineering, pp. 566–571, December 2013
13. Johansson, M., Sternad, M.: Resource allocation under uncertainty using the maximum entropy principle. IEEE Trans. Inf. Theor. **51**(12), 4103–4117 (2005)
14. Kazarlis, S.A., Bakirtzis, A., Petridis, V.: A genetic algorithm solution to the unit commitment problem. IEEE Trans. Power Syst. **11**(1), 42–51 (1996)
15. Kim, S., Pasupathy, R., Henderson, S.G.: A guide to sample average approximation. In: Fu, M. (ed.) Handbook of Simulation Optimization, pp. 207–243. Springer, New York (2015)
16. Li, Z., Ierapetritou, M.: Process scheduling under uncertainty: review and challenges. Comput. Chem. Eng. **32**(4–5), 715–727 (2008)
17. Medernach, E., Sanlaville, E.: Fair resource allocation for different scenarios of demands. Eur. J. Oper. Res. **218**(2), 339–350 (2012)

18. Michalewicz, Z., Fogel, D.B.: How to Solve It: Modern Heuristics, 2nd edn. Springer, Heidelberg (2004). https://doi.org/10.1007/978-3-662-07807-5
19. Miller, B., Goldberg, D.: Genetic algorithms, tournament selection, and the effects of noise. Complex Syst. **9**, 193–212 (1995)
20. Oxley, M., Pasricha, S., Siegel, H.J., Maciejewski, A.A., Apodaca, J., Young, D., Briceno, L., Smite, J., Bahirat, S., Khemka, B., Ramirez, A., Zou, Y.: Makespan and energy robust stochastic static resource allocation of a bag-of-tasks to a heterogeneous computing system. IEEE Trans. Parallel Distrib. Syst. **26**(10), 2791–2805 (2015)
21. Ruiz, P.A., Philbrick, C.R., Zak, E., Cheung, K.W., Sauer, P.W.: Uncertainty management in the unit commitment problem. IEEE Trans. Power Syst. **24**(2), 642–651 (2009)
22. Saravanan, B., Das, S., Sikri, S., Kothari, D.: A solution to the unit commitment problem - a review. Front. Energy **7**(2), 223–236 (2013)
23. Singer, G., Livenson, I., Dumas, M., Srirama, S.N., Norbisrath, U.: Towards a model for cloud computing cost estimation with reserved instances. In: Proceedings of the 2nd International ICST Conference on Cloud Computing, CloudComp 2010 (2010)
24. Singh, H., Youssef, A.: Mapping and scheduling heterogeneous task graphs using genetic algorithms. In: 5th Heterogeneous Computing Workshop (HCW 1996), pp. 86–97, April 1996
25. Swarup, K.S., Yamashiro, S.: Unit commitment solution methodology using genetic algorithm. IEEE Trans. Power Syst. **17**(1), 87–91 (2002)
26. Tanese, R.: Distributed genetic algorithms. In: 3rd International Conference on Genetic Algorithms, pp. 434–439 (1989)
27. Wang, L., Siegel, H.J., Roychowdhury, V.P., Maciejewski, A.A.: Task matching and scheduling in heterogeneous computing environments using a genetic-algorithm-based approach. J. Parallel Distrib. Comput. **47**(1), 8–22 (1997). Special Issue on Parallel Evolutionary Computing
28. Wang, Q., Wang, J., Guan, Y.: Stochastic unit commitment with uncertain demand response. IEEE Trans. Power Syst. **28**(1), 562–563 (2013)
29. Whitley, D.: The genitor algorithm and selective pressure: why rank based allocation of reproductive trials is best. In: 3rd International Conference on Genetic Algorithms, pp. 116–121, June 1989
30. Wright, B.: A review of unit commitment (2013)
31. Zhang, Q., Gürses, E., Boutaba, R., Xiao, J.: Dynamic resource allocation for spot markets in clouds. In: Proceedings of the 11th USENIX Conference on Hot Topics in Management of Internet, Cloud, and Enterprise Networks and Services, Hot-ICE 2011, p. 1. USENIX Association, Berkeley (2011)

Programmable In Situ System for Iterative Workflows

Erich Lohrmann[1], Zarija Lukić[2], Dmitriy Morozov[2(✉)], and Juliane Müller[2]

[1] Georgia Institute of Technology, Atlanta, GA, USA
elohrmann3@gatech.edu
[2] Lawrence Berkeley National Laboratory, Berkeley, CA, USA
{zarija,dmorozov,JulianeMueller}@lbl.gov

Abstract. We describe an in situ system for solving iterative problems. We specifically target inverse problems, where expensive simulations are approximated using a surrogate model. The model explores the parameter space of the simulation through iterative trials, each of which becomes a job managed by a parallel scheduler. Our work extends Henson [1], a cooperative multi-tasking system for in situ execution of loosely coupled codes.

1 Introduction

The growing gap between the speed of I/O and computation is widely recognized in the HPC community. Already on today's architectures the slow I/O is responsible for major bottlenecks; the problem will only get worse as we move to exascale, where data movement will dominate all design decisions.

The response to this problem is also well-known by now: in situ and in transit processing. If two codes (e.g., simulation and analysis) need to exchange data, they should do so directly, without going through disk. When running on the same nodes, they should share memory and access one another's data directly. When the rates of processing differ, it's logical to run different codes on different nodes, but they should send data directly to each other, without saving it to disk.

A number of in situ frameworks have been designed to address the I/O problem following this principle: ADIOS [2], DataSpaces [3], GLEAN [4], Damaris/Viz [5], ParaView's Catalyst [6], VisIt's libsim [7], Decaf [8], Henson [1], to name a few — we refer the reader to a community effort comparing four of these frameworks [9]. In all cases, the general pattern of the execution is the same: a simulation produces data and passes it to a chain of analysis codes that transform it, identify its salient features, visualize them, or save them to disk in significantly reduced, scientifically meaningful summaries.

Such chained pipelines support *direct simulations*, which have been invaluable tools in computational science: given a complete description of a physical system, they let a user predict an outcome of a measurement. The aim of our paper is to bring a different execution regime to the attention of the community and

© Springer International Publishing AG, part of Springer Nature 2018
D. Klusáček et al. (Eds.): JSSPP 2017, LNCS 10773, pp. 122–131, 2018.
https://doi.org/10.1007/978-3-319-77398-8_7

to describe our (partial) solution to the problems that it presents. We focus on the class of *inverse problems*, where the measurement result is known, and one tries to infer the values of parameters which characterize the underlying physical system. For example, in experiments we present in this paper, we try to reconstruct thermal parameters of the intergalactic gas in the universe using Lyman α power spectrum measurement [10].

As each simulation can be expensive, it is beneficial to explore parameter spaces by constructing surrogate models, i.e., computationally cheap approximations of the simulated phenomena. These models help identify those parameters that are likely to produce the most scientific insight. Crucially, these models facilitate automatic *iterative* parameter sweeps: the decisions about the input parameters to the simulations can be made automatically based on the results of the previous runs. Furthermore, the input data (either observational or finer simulation output) is usually shared between different parameters. Together, these features offer an opportunity for in situ automation, which we explore in this paper.

Related work. Besides the aforementioned in situ frameworks, we briefly note Swift/T [11], a system that allows the user to script complex workflows. It is much more advanced than our work, and we believe can be used to implement the kind of iterative execution described in this paper. We do emphasize one significant difference. To include user code, implemented in C or C++, into Swift/T, the code has to be organized and compiled into Swift modules (via SWIG wrappers). Because we rely on Henson [1], described in the next section, we are able to work with the separate executable directly.

2   Background

Henson. Our solution extends Henson [1], a cooperative multi-tasking system that lets multiple distinct executables run on the same node and share memory, without any changes to their memory management facilities.

Henson is built on two main ingredients: position-independent executables and coroutines. Individual codes are compiled as position-independent executables, making them simultaneously stand-alone executables and dynamic libraries. Henson loads multiple such codes as dynamic libraries, using `libdl` facilities. This puts them in the *same address space*, letting them access each other's memory directly.

The individual codes, referred by Henson as puppets, are treated as coroutines: each one gets its own stack. To coordinate execution, the codes call `henson_yield` function, which returns control to Henson (e.g., after every time step of a simulation). Crucially, when the control returns back to the puppet, its execution resumes exactly where it left off — all state is preserved. This way Henson provides low-overhead context switching and lets the user coordinate execution of multiple codes from an external script.

Henson includes facilities to help puppets exchange data. It provides a shared map of symbolic names to memory addresses to make it easy for puppets to identify important memory segments. For example, if simulation saves an address of an array by calling `henson_save_array("particles",  &particles, ...)`, an analysis code can later access this array directly by calling `henson_load_array("particles", ...)` — the memory is shared, so only addresses are exchanged.

Henson also provides auxiliary facilities to help users work with MPI. Different codes can be organized into *execution groups*, which are given symbolic names (e.g., "producer" and "consumer") and are assigned to run on different processes. To exchange data between the two groups (e.g., to support in transit analysis), Henson provides `henson_get_intercomm` function that returns an MPI inter-communicator connecting the two groups.

Henson's major limitation is the domain-specific language used to express its scripts. It supports only while-loops and if-statements: both help express the order in which execution should alternate between the puppets, but are too limited in general. To support more complicated workflows, we have extended Henson to use ChaiScript[1], a general purpose scripting language, implemented as a C++ header-only library. The interpreter, including its standard library, is compiled directly into Henson. This offers a major benefit over Python (another natural choice): the interpreter does not search for modules on the filesystem; this automatically obviates a major difficulty with using Python in an HPC environment.

Finally, the most significant addition to Henson, made as part of this work, is the addition of a scheduler that lets the user iteratively launch multiple jobs (that themselves can use in situ and in transit processing), depending on the decisions made by one of the puppets, in our case a surrogate model. We describe the scheduler in detail in the next section.

Surrogate models. Surrogate models are computationally cheap approximations of expensive simulations models [12]. They are widely used in derivative-free optimization, when objective function values are computed based on the output of computationally expensive black-box simulation models, and thus no analytic description of the objective function and its derivatives are available. In general, we use the representation $f(x) = s(x) + e(x)$, where $f(x)$ is the expensive objective function, $s(x)$ is the surrogate model, and $e(x)$ is the difference between the two. Surrogate model optimization algorithms start by generating an initial experimental design of size n_0, for example, using Latin hypercube sampling. The expensive function $f(x)$ is evaluated at the points in the initial design, and we fit the surrogate model $s(x)$ to the data pairs $\{(x_i, f(x_i))\}_{i=1}^{n_0}$. Then, in each iteration of the algorithm, we use the surrogate model $s(x)$ to select one or multiple new points x_*, at which we will do the next expensive evaluations. We update the surrogate model with the new data $(x_*, f(x_*))$ and iterate until the stopping criterion has been met. Typically used stopping criteria are a maximum CPU time or a maximum number of allowed expensive function evaluations.

---

[1] http://chaiscript.com/.

Theorem 3. *In the generic case, a system of m quadratic polynomials in n variables over $\mathbb{F}_q$ is o-reconcilable when $m(o+1)/2 \leq n$.*

Proof. The number of coefficients of S^{-1} that are involved in the $mo(o+1)/2$ equations that set the oil-times-oil coefficients to zero is no, corresponding the rightmost $n \times o$ block of S^{-1}. The other elements of S^{-1} do not affect these coefficients. This leads to a system of $mo(o+1)/2$ quadratic equations in no variables which generically has solutions when $mo(o+1)/2 \leq no$, or equivalently when $m(o+1)/2 \leq n$. $\square$

4.3   Generating Small Solutions

After obtaining an o-reconciliation $(\mathcal{F}, S)$, the task is to obtain a solution $\mathbf{x}$ such that $\mathcal{F}(\mathbf{x}) = \mathbf{0}$ and such that $S^{-1}\mathbf{x}$ is small. The partitioning of $\mathbf{x}$ into the vinegar variables $x_0, \ldots, x_{v-1}$ and the oil variables $x_v, \ldots, x_{n-1}$ separates the shortness objective into two parts. On the one hand, the *vinegar contribution*

$$\left(S^{-1}\right)_{[:,0:(v-1)]} \mathbf{x}_{[0:(v-1)]} \tag{9}$$

must be small; on the other hand, the *oil contribution*

$$\left(S^{-1}\right)_{[:,v:(n-1)]} \mathbf{x}_{[v:(n-1)]} \tag{10}$$

must be small as well. The reason for this separation is not just that the vinegar variables and oil variables are determined in separate steps; in fact, determining vinegar variables that lead to a small vinegar contribution is easy. The form of Eq. 8 guarantees that small vinegar variables will map onto a small vinegar contribution. Therefore, the only requirement for selecting vinegar variables is that they be small enough, say roughly $q^{1/2}$. By contrast, the process of finding suitable oil variables is far more involved.

A quadratic map where $o > m$ can be thought of as a UOV$^-$ map, *i.e.*, a UOV map with $o - m$ dropped components. This gives the signer, or an attacker who possesses the reconciliation, $o - m$ degrees of freedom for selecting the oil variables. Coupled with the freedom afforded by the choice of vinegar variables, the signer or attacker can generate a vector $\mathbf{x}$ such that $S^{-1}\mathbf{x}$ is short.

The task is thus to find an assignment to the oil variables such that (a) $\mathcal{F}(\mathbf{x}) = \mathbf{0}$ is satisfied; and (b) $\left(S^{-1}\right)_{[:,v:(n-1)]} \mathbf{x}_{v:(n-1)}$ is small as well. Constraint (a) is satisfiable whenever $m \leq o$ (in the generic case, *i.e.*, assuming certain square matrices over $\mathbb{F}_q$ are invertible). Constraint (b) requires $o > m$ and the resulting vector can be made shorter with growing $o - m$.

The matrix representation of a quadratic form is equivalent under addition of skew-symmetric matrices, which in particular means that it is always possible to choose an upper-triangular representation even of UOV maps such as Eq. 6. The ith equation of $\mathcal{F}(\mathbf{x}) = \mathbf{0}$ can therefore be described as

$$f_i(\mathbf{x}) = \mathbf{x}^\mathsf{T} \left(\begin{array}{|c|c|} \hline Q_i & L_i \\ \hline & \\ \hline \end{array} \right) \mathbf{x} + \ell^{(i)\mathsf{T}}\mathbf{x} + c_i = 0 \tag{11}$$

$$\left(\mathbf{x}^\mathsf{T}_{[0:(v-1)]} L_i + \ell^{(i)\mathsf{T}}_{[v:(n-1)]} \right) \mathbf{x}_{[v:(n-1)]} = -\mathbf{x}^\mathsf{T}_{[0:(v-1)]} Q_i \mathbf{x}_{[0:(v-1)]} - \ell^{(i)\mathsf{T}}_{[0:(v-1)]}\mathbf{x}_{[0:(v-1)]} - c_i. \tag{12}$$

All m equations can jointly be described as $A\mathbf{x}_{[v:(n-1)]} = \mathbf{b}$ for some matrix $A \in \mathbb{F}_q^{m \times o}$ and vector $\mathbf{b} \in \mathbb{F}_q^m$, because the vinegar variables $\mathbf{x}_{[0:(v-1)]}$ assume constant values. Let $\mathbf{x}^{(p)}$ be any particular solution to this linear system, and let $\mathbf{x}_0^{(k)}, \ldots, \mathbf{x}_{o-m-1}^{(k)}$ be a basis for the right kernel of A. Any weighted combination of the kernel vectors plus the particular solution, is still a solution to the linear system:

$$\forall (w_0, \ldots, w_{o-m-1}) \in \mathbb{F}_q^{o-m} . \ A \left(\mathbf{x}^{(p)} + \sum_{i=0}^{o-m-1} w_i \mathbf{x}_i^{(k)} \right) = \mathbf{b}. \tag{13}$$

This means we have $o-m$ degrees of freedom with which to satisfy constraint (b).

In fact, we can use LLL for this purpose in a manner similar to the clever selection of the vinegar variables. The only difference is that the weight associated with the vector $\mathbf{x}^{(p)}$ must remain 1 because otherwise constraint (a) is not satisfied. This leads to the following application of the embedding method.

Identify $\mathbf{x}^{(p)}$ and all $\mathbf{x}_i^{(k)}$ by their image after multiplication by $(S^{-1})_{[:,v:(n-1)]}$, thus obtaining $\mathbf{z}^{(p)} = (S^{-1})_{[:,v:(n-1)]} \mathbf{x}^{(p)}$ and $\mathbf{z}_i^{(k)} = (S^{-1})_{[:,v:(n-1)]} \mathbf{x}_i^{(k)}$. Then append q^2 to $\mathbf{z}^{(p)}$ and 0 to all $\mathbf{z}_i^{(k)}$, and stack all these vectors in column form over a diagonal of q's to obtain the matrix C:

$$C = \left(\begin{array}{cccc|ccc} - & \mathbf{z}^{(p)\mathsf{T}} & - & & q^2 & & \\ - & \mathbf{z}_0^{(k)\mathsf{T}} & - & & 0 & & \\ & \vdots & & & \vdots & & \\ - & \mathbf{z}_{o-m-1}^{(k)\mathsf{T}} & - & & 0 & & \\ \hline q & & & & & & \\ & & \ddots & & & & \\ & & & q & & & \end{array} \right). \tag{14}$$

Run LLL on this matrix to obtain a reduced basis matrix $B \in \mathbb{Z}^{(o-m+1+n)\times(n+1)}$ of which the first n rows are zero, and a unimodular matrix U satisfying $B = UC$. The appended q^2 element guarantees that the row associated with the particular solution will never be added to another row because that would increase the size of the basis vectors. As a result, there will be one row in the matrix B that ends in q^2. Moreover, this row will be short because it was reduced by all other rows. We now proceed to derive an upper bound for the size of this vector considering only the first n elements, *i.e.*, without the q^2. Unfortunately, the best upper bound

Different surrogate model types have been developed in the literature. We focus here on radial basis function (RBF) models although other models may work in our context. An RBF interpolant is defined as follows:

$$s(x) = \sum_{i=1}^{n} \lambda_i \phi(\|x - x_i\|_2) + p(x), \tag{1}$$

where n denotes the number of points for which we have already evaluated the objective function, $\phi(\cdot)$ is a radial basis function (we use the cubic, $\phi(r) = r^3$), and $p(\cdot)$ denotes the polynomial tail (here, $p(x) = a + b^T x, a \in \mathbb{R}, b \in \mathbb{R}^d$, d is the number of dimensions). The model parameters are determined by solving a linear system of equations.

Different strategies have been developed to iteratively select one or more new sample points. For example, Gutmann [13] uses a target value for the surrogate model and defines a merit function which he (cheaply) optimizes in order to determine the next sample point. Regis and Shoemaker [14] use a stochastic approach in which they create candidate points by perturbing the best point found so far and based on scoring criteria, the best candidate is selected for evaluation. Müller and Shoemaker [15] use a similar approach and in addition to candidates created by perturbation, they also create candidates by uniformly sampling points from the whole variable domain. More examples of surrogate model algorithms and their application to engineering design problems can be found in the literature [16].

3 Scheduler

To support iterative workflows, we have added a `Scheduler` class to Henson. Scheduler takes over a given execution group (a set of MPI ranks). It dedicates one process as a controller and the rest as workers. The controller loads a puppet in charge of the overall execution logic (the surrogate model in our case). That puppet generates a set of trials and, over time, receives results of expensive evaluations, updates the model, and generates new trials. Given the trial points from a surrogate model, a user can `schedule` a new job by specifying an arbitrary ChaiScript function to call, together with its arguments, how many processes it needs to execute, and how those processes should be partitioned into execution groups. The job is placed in the queue on the controller process.

The controller maintains the state of worker processes (whether they have a job assigned to them or whether they are available). If there are jobs in the queue and enough available workers to execute them, it sends out the job (the previously queued function) to the workers. When the workers are done with the job, one of them (e.g., the root) returns a value, which is sent back to the controller. The result of the execution (in our case, expensive evaluation $f(x_*)$) is placed in a results queue to be retrieved and processed by the surrogate model. Listing 1.1 illustrates a sample ChaiScript using the scheduler. Figure 1 illustrates a possible break down of processes between execution groups within and outside the scheduler.

```chaiscript
var pm = ProcMap()
var nm = NameMap()

def world(args)
{
    var sim = load("./simulation ...", pm)
    var ana = load("./analysis    ...", pm)

    sim.proceed()
    while (sim.running())
    {
        ana.proceed()
        sim.proceed()
    }

    if (pm.local_rank() == 0)
    {
        var result = nm.get("result")
        return result
    }
}

var sched = Scheduler()
if (sched.is_controller())
{
    var surrogate = load("./surrogate-model ...", pm)
    surogate.proceed()

    // schedule jobs
    for (/* initial trials */)
    { sched.schedule("job-${i}", "world", args,
                        ["all" : 0], sched.workers()/2) }

    while (sched.control())
    {
        if (!sched.results_empty())
        {
            var x = sched.pop()
            // pass x back to the surrogate
            surrogate.proceed()
            // get new trials and schedule new jobs
        }
    }
    sched.finish()  // signal to workers
} else { scheduler.listen() }
```

Listing 1.1. A sample scheduler ChaiScript.

We highlight some technical ingredients that are crucial for this system to operate properly. When a set of processes is selected to execute a job, we need to construct an MPI communicator on those processes — this communicator acts as the job's MPI_COMM_WORLD. Unfortunately, all (intra-)communicator creation functions provided by MPI are collective, meaning that all the workers, even those that are not assigned to the given job, have to execute them. In our case, this would mean synchronizing all the workers to create a communicator for a new job — clearly undesirable behavior.

To work around this problem, we use the algorithm of Dinan et al. [17] that allows for non-collective communicator creation — or, more accurately, it's collective only on the processes that participate in the newly created communicator. Unlike MPI_Comm_split that constructs a communicator by splitting a larger communicator, the non-collective algorithm builds a communicator from the bottom up. Starting from MPI_COMM_SELF, it alternates between intra- and inter-communicators, using MPI_Intercomm_create and MPI_Intercomm_merge functions, and merges the local communicators from the participating ranks

MPI_COMM_WORLD

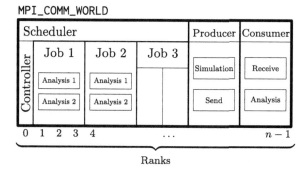

Fig. 1. Schematic partition of the processes with the scheduler.

into the desired communicator. We refer the reader to the original paper [17] for details.

Once the processes construct the communicator, they split it into sub-communicators corresponding to the execution groups specified by the user. Within the job, the user can access the inter-communicators between the groups by calling henson_get_intercomm, mentioned in the previous section. The advantage of this design is that the puppets become oblivious to whether they are running in a job inside the scheduler or over all the ranks. As a result, the user can take advantage of in transit analysis *inside a job*, where separate execution groups are responsible for data generation and analysis. As the earlier work on Henson [1] illustrates, such an execution regime can be beneficial when analysis is computationally expensive: the overhead of data movement pales in comparison to the gains of better strong scaling.

4   Surrogate Model Experiment

In cosmology, spatial correlations of the Lyman α flux offer a promising route to measuring the cosmological and thermal parameters at high redshifts and small scales [18]. The measure we use is the Fourier-space analog of the two-point correlation function — the power spectrum. Given a cosmological model and a model for the ultraviolet background emission from galaxies, we can predict the resulting flux power spectrum, using the Nyx code [19]. The full parameter space of interest consist of 5 cosmological and 4 thermal parameters; to test our computational workflow system, we work with only 3 thermal parameters, thus significantly reducing the dimensionality of the problem. In addition, instead of running full Nyx simulation for every function evaluation (approximately 100,000 CPU hours), we use outputs of a single run and rescale 3 thermal parameters before calculating the power spectrum (approximately 100 CPU hours). This rescaling is an approximation of what a full Nyx run would yield, and is ∼10% accurate (Lukić et al. in prep.), which suffices for the purpose of this work.

We ran our experiments on NERSC's Edison, a Cray XC30 supercomputer with 5,576 nodes with 24 cores each. Each run requested wall clock time of thirty minutes and 3585 processors (150 nodes). This allocation is just enough to run seven simultaneous jobs of 512 processes each, with an extra process reserved for the controller. The input data, a snapshot of a cosmological simulation, is a 193 GB HDF5 file. The individual jobs consist of two separate executables: the power spectrum calculation for the given input parameters and comparison of the resulting spectrum to the given target in L^2-norm. The latter value is returned to the scheduler, which passes it to the surrogate model on the controller process to update its internal state and generate new trials.

Explicit caching. To avoid re-reading the input file, we implemented a stand-alone puppet that reads the data and stores it in memory. It's executed on all the worker processes before they come under the control of the scheduler. Because every job uses 512 processes, each process requires the same data for every job, and we can pre-load the data, save it in memory, and let individual jobs access it directly without re-loading it from disk. In two separate experiments, the average I/O time was 113.47 and 116.98 s. The subsequent calculation of the power spectrum took 322.39 and 423.16 s on average, respectively.

Implicit caching. Re-running the job without explicit caching, where each job re-loads the data directly from disk, we identified an implicit caching mechanism: Linux kernel's page cache. The average I/O time for the first seven jobs was 114.70 and 105.25 s, across two experiments. However, in the subsequent batch of jobs, executing on the same processes, the I/O time went down to 1.57 and 0.75 s. Forcing the kernel to drop its caches by allocating a sufficiently large array brought the average I/O time up to roughly 20 s, presumably the rest of the difference (115 vs 20 s) is due to other caching within the I/O subsystem.

Although in this case explicit caching offers virtually no benefit, it still has advantages. First, it gives the user explicit control over which data is stored between job invocations — the kernel is far less predictable. Second, it allows the user to cache data coming not only from disk, but from any other source — in the full simulation pipeline (that we ultimately aim to implement), the data would come directly from the simulation, without being saved to disk first.

Alternatives. One could implement iterative job execution using the supercomputer's workload manager directly (SLURM in case of Edison). Submitting jobs into the queue, waiting for their execution and results, updating the surrogate model, and iterating would incur the extra overhead of queue wait times (and, of course, the extra I/O overhead). To get a fair comparison we consider the difference in queue wait times, when requesting the same number of nodes for a different amount of time.

Figure 2 shows the average and maximum queue wait times, in non-debug queues of Edison, as a function of requested wall clock, for 100 to 200 nodes, over the six months from February through July 2016. The salient point is that the average time grows sub-linearly. For example, requesting the nodes for 60 min gave an average queue wait time of 14 h, while requesting the nodes for 600 min resulted in average wait time of 63 h. In other words, it's advantageous to request more time and manage the jobs within the allocation.

Edison Queue Wait Times

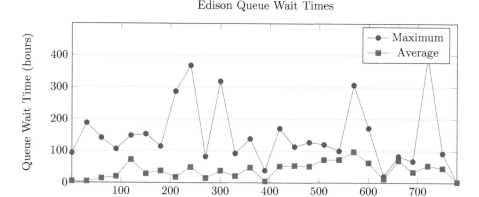

Fig. 2. A graph of queue wait times as a function of requested wall clock. The times tally all requests for 100 to 200 nodes, over six months (February through July 2016).

It is possible to run multiple simultaneous jobs within the allocation directly, using MPI's MPMD mode. Besides again incurring I/O overheads, doing so would synchronize the jobs running simultaneously and would force all of them to take as much time as the slowest job. In our case, although the average calculation time was around 415 s, the fastest calculation finished in roughly 250 s, making the synchronization overhead unreasonable.

5   Conclusion

Iterative workflows — for example, for parameter search in inverse problems — are important in computational science, and we urge the community to not neglect them. The system presented in this paper takes the first step towards their support. In situ processing confers multiple advantages in this context. Besides the illustrated savings in I/O time, Henson lets us monitor the execution of the analysis codes by directly accessing their memory and thus avoiding unnecessary overheads. Such capability can be useful for terminating the code early. For example, if we are interested in an L^∞-norm of a time-varying measurement, we can stop computation once the maximum difference exceeds the current best guess.

Our system also supports more complicated experiments than presented in the previous section. For example, the full analysis we would like to run involves taking snapshots of a live Nyx simulation and fitting parameters to them. To do so, it's essential for the jobs managed by the scheduler to interact with execution groups outside of it. The necessary ingredients are already built into the system (`henson_get_intercomm` can access inter-communicators across execution group levels), and we plan to experiment with such more complicated execution regimes in the near future.

Acknowledgements. We are grateful to Jack Deslippe for providing us the raw data on Edison queue times. This work was supported by Advanced Scientific Computing Research, Office of Science, U.S. Department of Energy, under Contract DE-AC02-05CH11231, and by the use of resources of the National Energy Research Scientific Computing Center (NERSC).

References

1. Morozov, D., Lukić, Z.: Master of puppets: cooperative multitasking for in situ processing. In: Proceedings of High-Performance Parallel and Distributed Computing, pp. 285–288 (2016)
2. Liu, Q., Logan, J., Tian, Y., Abbasi, H., Podhorszki, N., Choi, J.Y., Klasky, S., Tchoua, R., Lofstead, J., Oldfield, R., Parashar, M., Samatova, N., Schwan, K., Shoshani, A., Wolf, M., Wu, K., Yu, W.: Hello ADIOS: the challenges and lessons of developing leadership class I/O frameworks. Concurr. Comput. Pract. Exp. **26**(7), 1453–1473 (2014)
3. Sun, Q., Jin, T., Romanus, M., Bui, H., Zhang, F., Yu, H., Kolla, H., Klasky, S., Chen, J., Parashar, M.: Adaptive data placement for staging-based coupled scientific workflows. In: Proceedings of the International Conference for High Performance Computing, Networking, Storage and Analysis, SC 2015, pp. 65:1–65:12. ACM, New York (2015)
4. Vishwanath, V., Hereld, M., Morozov, V., Papka, M.E.: Topology-aware data movement and staging for I/O acceleration on Blue Gene/P supercomputing systems. In: Proceedings of 2011 International Conference for High Performance Computing, Networking, Storage and Analysis, SC 2011, pp. 19:1–19:11. ACM, New York (2011)
5. Dorier, M., Sisneros, R., Peterka, T., Antoniu, G., Semeraro, D.: Damaris/Viz: a nonintrusive, adaptable and user-friendly in situ visualization framework. In: 2013 IEEE Symposium on Large-Scale Data Analysis and Visualization (LDAV), pp. 67–75, October 2013
6. Bauer, A.C., Geveci, B., Schroeder, W.: The ParaView Catalyst User's Guide v2.0. Kitware Inc., New York (2015)
7. Whitlock, B., Favre, J.M., Meredith, J.S.: Parallel in situ coupling of simulation with a fully featured visualization system. In: Proceedings of the 11th Eurographics Conference on Parallel Graphics and Visualization, pp. 101–109 (2011)
8. Dorier, M., Dreher, M., Peterka, T., Antoniu, G., Raffin, B., Wozniak, J.M.: Lessons learned from building in situ coupling frameworks. In: First Workshop on In Situ Infrastructures for Enabling Extreme-Scale Analysis and Visualization, Austin, United States, November 2015
9. Ayachit, U., et al.: Performance analysis, design considerations, and applications of extreme-scale in situ infrastructures. In: Proceedings of the International Conference on High Performance Computing, Networking, Storage and Analysis (SC) (2016)
10. Viel, M., Becker, G.D., Bolton, J.S., Haehnelt, M.G.: Warm dark matter as a solution to the small scale crisis: new constraints from high redshift Lyman-α forest data. Phys. Rev. D **88**(4), 043502 (2013)
11. Wozniak, J.M., Armstrong, T.G., Wilde, M., Katz, D.S., Lusk, E., Foster, I.T.: Swift/T: large-scale application composition via distributed-memory dataflow processing. In: IEEE/ACM International Symposium on Cluster, Cloud and Grid Computing (CCGrid), pp. 95–102 (2013)

12. Booker, A.J., Dennis Jr., J.E., Frank, P.D., Serafini, D.B., Torczon, V., Trosset, M.W.: A rigorous framework for optimization of expensive functions by surrogates. Struct. Multi. Optim. **17**, 1–13 (1999)
13. Gutmann, H.-M.: A radial basis function method for global optimization. J. Global Optim. **19**, 201–227 (2001)
14. Regis, R.G., Shoemaker, C.A.: A stochastic radial basis function method for the global optimization of expensive functions. INFORMS J. Comput. **19**, 497–509 (2007)
15. Müller, J., Shoemaker, C.A.: Influence of ensemble surrogate models and sampling strategy on the solution quality of algorithms for computationally expensive black-box global optimization problems. J. Global Optim. **60**, 123–144 (2014)
16. Wang, G.G., Shan, S.: Review of metamodeling techniques in support of engineering design optimization. J. Mech. Des. **129**, 370–380 (2007)
17. Dinan, J., Krishnamoorthy, S., Balaji, P., Hammond, J.R., Krishnan, M., Tipparaju, V., Vishnu, A.: Noncollective communicator creation in MPI. In: Cotronis, Y., Danalis, A., Nikolopoulos, D.S., Dongarra, J. (eds.) EuroMPI 2011. LNCS, vol. 6960, pp. 282–291. Springer, Heidelberg (2011). https://doi.org/10.1007/978-3-642-24449-0_32
18. Lukić, Z., Stark, C.W., Nugent, P., White, M., Meiksin, A.A., Almgren, A.: The Lyman α forest in optically thin hydrodynamical simulations. Mon. Not. R. Astron. Soc. **446**, 3697–3724 (2015)
19. Almgren, A.S., Bell, J.B., Lijewski, M.J., Lukić, Z., Van Andel, E.: Nyx: a massively parallel AMR code for computational cosmology. Astrophys. J. **765**, 39 (2013)

A Data Structure for Planning Based Workload Management of Heterogeneous HPC Systems

Axel Keller[(✉)]

Paderborn Center for Parallel Computing,
Paderborn University, 33098 Paderborn, Germany
axel.keller@uni-paderborn.de

Abstract. This paper describes a data structure and a heuristic to plan and map arbitrary resources in complex combinations while applying time dependent constraints. The approach is used in the planning based workload manager OpenCCS at the Paderborn Center for Parallel Computing (PC^2) to operate heterogeneous clusters with up to 10000 cores. We also show performance results derived from four years of operation.

Keywords: Scheduling · Planning · Mapping · Workload management

1 Introduction

Today's HPC systems are heterogeneous, they consist of different node types and accelerators (e.g., GPUs or FPGAs) are used to increase the application performance. Disk storage, software licenses, virtual machines, or software containers are additional resources to be scheduled by a workload management system (WLM). In the past Grid and Cloud computing brought challenges in form of inter system applications, running on more than one system at the same time or consecutively steered by a workflow-manager. The merge of HPC and Big-Data already started and more complex workflows will arise and enhance the complexity of scheduling. Keywords are for example: data aware scheduling, co-allocations, provisional reservations, or SLAs.

Planning based WLMs are well prepared for such environments. In 2003, we published a paper [6] which compared queueing and planning based WLMs on a high level and introduced OpenCCS as a completely planning based WLM. Since then, OpenCCS implemented some features mentioned in [6], like for example, job-migration using Globus, or SLA negotiation and compliance. This work was primarily done in the EU funded projects HPC4U [1] and AssessGrid [1].

However, all work done there was based on scheduling only entire nodes, all of the same type. At that time, we used a generic scheduler and a system-specific mapping instance which verified the schedule. We learned, that planning and mapping has to be done in the scheduler because the mapper had no info about

© Springer International Publishing AG, part of Springer Nature 2018
D. Klusáček et al. (Eds.): JSSPP 2017, LNCS 10773, pp. 132–151, 2018.
https://doi.org/10.1007/978-3-319-77398-8_8

limits or fairness and the scheduler did not consider the requested topology in a satisfying manner (e.g., a 2×4 grid on a system with a 2D-torus topology). Additionally, the scheduler performance collapsed if managing several hundreds of nodes and thousands of jobs.

In 2009, we redesigned OpenCCS. We aimed on supporting time shared operation (i.e., more than one job on a node) on large heterogeneous clusters with thousands of jobs, that is fast online planning of an arbitrary number of resources. It should be easy to integrate commercial applications. Users should be able to reserve resources, submit jobs with a deadline, and steer the mapping. Users and groups should be automatically (un)locked by the system. This paper reports the results of this redesign. Its central contribution is the basic data structure and the planning and mapping heuristic based on this.

We start with a brief comparison of the queueing and planning approach and name challenges of planning based WLMs. In Sect. 3 we introduce OpenCCS focusing on terms which are related to the scope of this paper. Section 4 explains the central data structure used in the OpenCCS scheduler and its basic operations. Based on this, Sect. 5 focuses on the principle process of planning and mapping and describes some resulting aspects in more detail. Section 6 is devoted to performance results derived from real operation over four years. In Sect. 7 we compare the introduced method with other approaches and Sect. 8 summarizes the paper.

2   Queueing vs. Planning

The major criterion for the differentiation of WLMs is the planned time frame. *Queueing systems* try to utilize currently free resources with waiting resource requests and future resource planning for all waiting requests is not done. Hence, waiting resource requests have no assigned start time. *Planning systems* in contrast plan for the present and future. Start times are assigned to all requests and a complete schedule about the future resource usage is computed and made available to the users.

Queueing. In principle there are several queues with different limits on the number of requested resources and the duration (e.g., min, max, defaults, etc.). Jobs within a queue are ordered according to a scheduling policy (e.g., FCFS (first come, first serve)) and users may also order their jobs. Queues might be activated only for specific times (e.g., prime time or weekend).

The task of a queueing system is to assign free resources to waiting requests. The job with the highest priority is always the queue head. If it is possible to start more than one queue head, further criteria, like queue priority, are used to choose a request. If not enough resources are available to start any of the queue heads, the system waits until enough resources become available.

These idle resources may be utilized with less prioritized requests by backfilling mechanisms. Two backfilling variants are commonly used: (1) Conservative backfilling [11]: Requests are chosen so that no other waiting request (including the queue head) is further delayed. (2) EASY backfilling [10]: This variant is more aggressive than conservative backfilling since only the waiting queue head must not be delayed.

Although, it is not mandatory for queueing systems to know the maximum duration of requests, it is often required by the administration, to decrease job waiting times. The "cost of scheduling" is low and choosing the next request to start is fast.

Planning. Planning systems assign start times to all requests. Obviously, duration estimates are mandatory for planning. With this knowledge reservations are easily possible and planning systems are well suited to participate in multi-site application runs.

Fair share [8,9] is often used in queueing systems for prioritizing jobs on the basis of a share of the machine and past and current usage. In planning systems, controlling the usage of the machine is often done differently. One way is to use time dependent constraints for the planning process. For example, during prime time 25% of the system is kept free for "small" jobs. Also project or user specific limits are possible, so that the system is virtually partitioned. Job priorities and even more job dependencies (e.g., job B may start only after job A has terminated with an error) have a stronger impact on the complexity of the planning process than in queueing systems.

Planning based WLMs are real time systems. Assume two successive requests (A and B) using the same nodes and B has been planned one-second after A. Then, A has to be released in at most one-second. Otherwise B will be started while A is still occupying the nodes. This delay would also affect all subsequent requests, since their planned allocation times depend on the release times of their predecessors. Hence, timeouts are necessary for such operations and the WLM has to concern them while planning and adhere to the planned slots while executing jobs.

Planning often implies mapping, because although the number of requested resources (e.g., cores) may be free in the requested time interval, we cannot be sure that always the same resources are free. Additionally, if planning complex resource sets, comprising several resource types, we have to ensure that the whole set can be mapped to a host and of course using placing directives directly enforces mapping. Mapping is not mandatory while planning a start time, if the requested resource set is provided by all hosts of the system and can be mapped to a single host (e.g., requesting one core).

Changes in the resource configuration implies replanning all affected jobs. Possible reasons are: a node fails or is set offline, or the amount of available nodes resources changes (e.g., a memory DIMM or a network card fails).

The "cost of scheduling" is higher than in queueing systems. And as users can view the current schedule and know when their requests are planned, questions like "Why is my request not planned earlier? Look, it would fit in here." are likely to occur. In the next section we briefly describe OpenCCS focusing on the terms, which are necessary to understand the following sections. A more detailed description can be found in the OpenCCS manual [3].

3   The Computing Center Software

OpenCCS has a long history starting in the 1990s at the Paderborn Center for Parallel Computing (PC^2) [13]. Today, OpenCCS consists of several modules, which may run on multiple hosts to improve the response time. OpenCCS is based on events (e.g., timers, messages, signals), and the communication is state-less and asynchronous. The modules are multi-threaded but single-tasked. The submission syntax is strongly PBSPro [12] compatible to ease the integration of commercial applications. Figure 1 depicts the OpenCCS modules (described below) and the event handling.

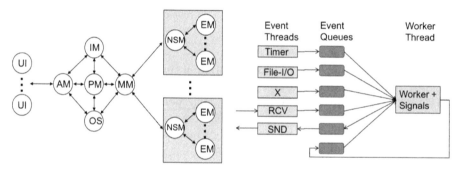

Fig. 1. The OpenCCS modules (left) and event type handling (right)

UI (User Interface): Provides a single access point to one or more systems via command line interfaces.

AM (Access Manager): Manages the user interfaces and is responsible for authentication, authorization, and accounting.

PM (Planning Manager): Schedules and maps the user requests onto the machine.

MM (Machine Manager): Provides machine specific features like node management or job controlling.

IM (Island Manager): Provides OpenCCS internal name services and watchdog facilities to keep OpenCCS in a stable condition.

OS (Operator Shell): The main interface for system administrators to control OpenCCS.

NSM (Node Session Manager): Runs with root privileges on each node managed by OpenCCS. The NSM is responsible for node access and job controlling. At allocation time, the NSM starts an EM for each job.

EM (Execution Manager): Establishes the user environment (UID, shell settings, environment variables, etc.) and starts the application.

OpenCCS uses the Resource and Service Description (RSD) [2] language to specify all system specific hardware and software attributes like node properties, network topology, timeouts, or custom resources.

The planning based approach, implemented in OpenCCS, has some implications. There are no explicit queues in OpenCCS. The "waiting room" is the only equivalent to a queue. A request is moved to this queue if OpenCCS was not able to assign a start time to an already accepted request. Possible reasons are, for example, that resources become unavailable while a request is in state PLANNED or ALLOCATING and there are no comparable resources available. If the resources become available again, OpenCCS automatically tries to replan waiting requests.

Users are supposed to specify the expected runtime of their requests. If no duration is specified, OpenCCS assigns a site specific one.

Privileges, default values, and limitations are attached to groups and users. Entities like user, group, resource, or limit may have a validity period. If the validity is exceeded, the entity is disabled. The rest of the section explains some of this implications in more detail.

Validity. Planning provides an explicit notion of time, and this is also reflected in limits, resource availability, etc. Hence, in OpenCCS entities like resources, users, groups, or limits all may have a validity period. It can be given as an absolute end date, an absolute start and end date, or a cron string, specifying repeated intervals. Validities are mandatory to map time dependent constraints to the data structure described in Sect. 4.

Limit. Limits are assigned to a consumer (i.e., a user or a group) and there may be a different limit for each resource. If a consumer has no limits assigned this means all resources are available forever. A limit consists of the following items:

Validity: The validity period of a limit.
Items: The maximum number of allocatable items.
    Syntax: $< \text{min}[/\text{max}] >$
    min is a integer and max specifies the percent of currently available items. If both given, OpenCCS takes the maximum of min, max. Example: 30/45% denotes a limit 30 items or 45% of the available items.
Duration: The maximum timespan the resource may be used.
Area: The maximum area.
    For example, the area limit 1024h for the resource cores, allows a consumer to request one core for 1024 h, 1024 cores for one hour, or any matching combination in between.

If a time dependent limit is exceeded, the affected request will be scheduled to a later or earlier slot (depending on the request type). In Example 1, the ncpus and tesla limits override the (∗) limit (meaning all resources).

```
Resource     Items       Duration Area  Validity
================================================================
*            unlimited 7d         none  always
ncpus        640         4d3h      none  01.08.17-31.08.17
tesla        unlimited none        500h  always
arrayjobs    1000        none      none  always
jobs         5000        none      none  always
```

Example 1: Some possible limits

FreePool. FreePools are like limits, but describe the conditions for resources to be kept free (i.e., they constrain the access to resources). A FreePool consists of the following items: The validity period, the resource to be kept free, how many of the resource should be kept free, and conditions to get access to the resources. FreePools may be used to:

- Keep free 20% of the available cores but at minimum 10 cores for jobs which request less than four cores for less than one hour.
- Keep all GPUs free for the groups *G1*, *G2* and user *alice*. All others may use the GPUs only for a maximum of two hours.
- Reserve all nodes hosting GPUs for maintenance each two months on Monday from 8am to 6pm.

Requesting Resources. In OpenCCS, users specify the resources needed by a job by using chunks and job-wide resources (e.g., licenses or disk space). A chunk specifies resources that have to be allocated as a unit on a single node. Chunks cannot be split across nodes. Syntax: rset=[N:]chunk[+[N:]chunk...]

A chunk comprises one or more res=value statements separated by a colon. res is one of the OpenCCS built-in resources (e.g., cores, memory, or ompthreads) or one of the customized specified via the RSD language. Chunks may be combined with a placement specification to control how the chunks should be placed on the nodes. Example 2 may illustrate what is possible (Table 1).

Table 1. Possible placement specifications

Modifier	Meaning
Free	No restriction
Pack	All chunks must be placed on one node
Scatter	Only one chunk per node
Exclusive	Only this job may use the node
Shared	This chunk may share the node with other chunks

```
rset=8:ncpus=2:mem=10g:rack=8
rset=ncpus=27:vmem=20g:arch=linux+4:acc=fpga
rset=5:ncpus=16:mem=12g:net=IB+ncpus=1:mem=4g,sw=g03,place=scatter:excl
```

Example 2: Resource requests using chunks

4   The Resource Usage Vector

In Sect. 2, we outlined challenges of a planning based WLM and in Sect. 3 the way OpenCCS is realizing the goals drafted in the introduction. The data structure introduced here, is our central approach to tackle these issues. It is used to represent time dependent limits, FreePools, reservations, and the available resources in the whole managed system and on its nodes.

We store slots of used or free items sorted by time for each used resource. We call this a resource usage vector ($RUSV$).

A *slot* comprises three components. The start time, the stop time, and the number of items, which are used or free within the interval $[start, stop]$. If stop time is 0, this means $[start, \infty[$.

A $RUSV$ additionally has the following components:

maxAvl: the maximum available number of items,
avl: the currently available number of items (i.e., maxAvl - defect),
minDist: the minimal time distance between two slots, normally 1 s.

In the following $R_i[j]$ denotes the $slot_j$ in $RUSV_i$. We do not store slots which are completely "free" (i.e., if storing used items and $slot$.items ≤ 0 or, if storing free items and $slot$.items $\geq RUSV$.avl). Figure 2 depicts a simple example. Please note, that in all intervals, except the specified ones, the number of used items is 0, since this $RUSV$ stores used items.

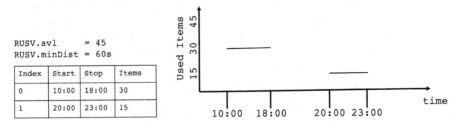

Fig. 2. A simple example of a $RUSV$

4.1   Basic Operations

On $RUSV$s we apply the following basic operations:

Increment ($\oplus$) Adds a slot to a $RUSV$.
Notation: $RUSV \oplus slot$
Increments the number of items of $RUSV$ in the interval $[slot$.start, $slot$.stop$]$ by $slot$.items. Missing slots are added.

Decrement ($\ominus$) Subtracts a slot from a $RUSV$.
Notation: $RUSV \ominus slot$
Decrements the number of items of $RUSV$ in the interval [$slot$.start, $slot$.stop] by $slot$.items. "Free" slots are removed.

Addition (+) Adds two $RUSV$s.
Notation: $R_3 = R_1 + R_2$
This is done by $\forall i \in R_2$: $R_1 \oplus R_2[i]$.

Subtraction ($-$) Subtracts two $RUSV$s.
Notation: $R_3 = R_1 - R_2$
This is done by $\forall i \in R_2$: $R_1 \ominus R_2[i]$.

minFree (mf) Minimum of free slots in R_1 and R_2.
Notation: $R_3 = \mathrm{mf}(R_1, R_2)$
This is done by: $\forall i \in R_2$: $R_3[i] = \max(R_2[i].\text{items}, (R_1.\text{avl} - R_2[i].\text{items}))$.
We do not add new slots, and gaps in R_1 are processed. We use this operation to integrate a resource limit into a $RUSV$. For example, R_1 is the number of available resources in the system and R_2 is the limit for this resource.

Intersection ($\cap$) Intersects R_1 and R_2. R_1 and R_2 store free items.
Notation: $R_3 = R_1 \cap R_2$
This is done by: $\forall i \in R_2$: $R_3[i].\text{items} = min(R_1[i].\text{items}, R_2[i].\text{items})$.
As a result R_3 holds all slots for which at least $R_3[i]$.items are free in R_1 and R_2 at the same time.

getFreeSlots (R_1, F, D, T_1, T_2) Search in R_1 for slots with at least F free items with a duration $\geq$ D in the interval $[T_1, T_2]$.
Notation: $R_2 = \mathrm{getFreeSlots}(R_1, F, D, T_1, T_2)$

For all operations, the following is valid: If the $RUSV$ stores free items, then slots with $slot$.items $\geq RUSV$.avl are removed. If the $RUSV$ stores used items, then slots with $slot$.items ≤ 0 are removed. Consecutive slots are joined if their items are equal and their distance is $\leq$ rus.minDist. Figure 3 depicts the possible overlaps, we have to handle. The actions done are of course specific to the combination of operation and case. For example, assume a $RUSV$ storing used items. Then operation $\ominus$ and case (1) leads to act.items $-=$ new.items and if act.items ≤ 0, slot b will be removed. Operation $\oplus$ and case (1) leads to new slots a and c and b.items $+=$ new.items.

Before we explain the principle planning and mapping process, we introduce the following terms.

sRS (System Resource Set) For each known resource (e.g., cores, memory, GPUs, licenses, etc.), we have one $RUSV$ to reflect the usage of the whole system. The sRS $RUSV$s hold used items.
Notations: sRS_r is the RUSV of resource r and $sRS_r[i]$ is $slot$ i in sRS_r.

nRS (Node Resource Set) For each known resource, a node has one RUSV to reflect its usage. The nRS has the same structure as the sRS. If a resource of the sRS is not available on a node the related $RUSV$ is empty (i.e., nRS_r.avl = 0).

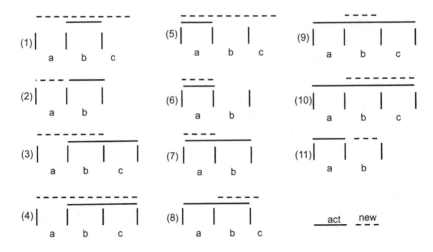

Fig. 3. Possible slot overlap cases

rRS (**Reservation Resource Set**) It is a subset of the *sRS* depending on what resources are reserved. All planning and mapping routines, described in Sect. 5, are the same for normal jobs and for jobs running in a reservation.

reqRS (**Requested Resource Set**) The user requested resources (chunks and job wide) in an internal format. Please note, there are no *RUSV*s in a *reqRS*.

jRS (**Job Resource Set**) For each requested resource of a job, we summarize all requested chunk and job wide resources.
E.g., requesting 8:ncpus=2:mem=10g, results in a *jRS* of ncpus=16:mem=80g.

usdRS (**Used Resource Set**) The resources which are already assigned to a consumer. The *usdRS* has the same structure as the *sRS* and is used while processing consumer specific limits.

uRS (**User Resource Set**) For each requested resource we have a *RUSV* reflecting the users view on the system related to limits, FreePools, and already assigned resources. The *uRS* has the same structure as the *sRS* and is built in the planning process.

5   Planning and Mapping

Here, we describe the principle process of planning and mapping requests using *RUSV*s. At submit time the user specifies the resources which should be used (i.e., chunks and job wide resources) and when and how long the resources will be used (e.g., provisional, best-effort, deadline, fixed start time, slot-aware start time, SLAs, duration, etc.). Additionally, the user may specify how the chunks should be placed (e.g., pack, scatter, free, shared, exclusive) and how the job should be processed (e.g., checkpointing, re-start, etc.). Based on this specifications, the *PM* starts the planning which is divided into three phases.

Phase 1 checks if and when enough resources are free concerning all constraints like limits, FreePools, or already assigned resources.

Phase 2 does the mapping. If the resources can be mapped to all nodes, mapping is postponed to allocation time. Mapping is a separate layer to allow different mapping policies.

Phase 3 updates the $usdRS$, the sRS, and the nRS of all affected nodes. In the following, we describe these steps in more detail.

5.1 Planning

When a new job comes in, we first scan the resource request and build internal data structures. Thereafter, we add missing default and force values (overwriting user given values), and check if all requested resources are known and available (requested $\leq$ maxAvl). Default and force values may be assigned to the system, the group, or the user. As a result, we get the $reqRS$ and the jRS.

We then determine the search interval $[T_1, T_2]$ which depends on the job type (e.g., best effort, reservation, deadline). For example, the search interval of a reservation is of course given by the user, whereas the search interval of a best effort job starts at submit time and ends never. All subsequent operations are working in this search interval.

After determining FreePools and limits matching the resource request and $[T_1, T_2]$, we create the uRS by computing: $\forall r \in jRS$:

$$uRS_r = sRS_r + FreePool_r \text{ and then}$$
$$uRS_r = \mathrm{mf}(uRS_r, limit_r - usdRS_r).$$

Processing a resource set (e.g., the sRS), means that for all resources in question the related $RUSV$ operations, introduced in Sect. 4, are performed.

The uRS reflects now the user's view on the amount of available resources in the search interval. Hence, we are able to search for slots where all requested resources are available at the same time in the requested amount for the requested duration. This is done by computing:

$$\forall r \in jRS : R_{freeSlots} = R_{freeSlots} \cap getFreeSlots_r(uRS_r, F_r, D, T_1, T_2).$$

If $R_{freeSlots}$ is not empty, we try to find a valid mapping.

The complexity of the planning process without mapping is independent of the number of jobs in the system, since we process only $RUSV$s.

5.2 Mapping

The input is the job's duration D, the $reqRS$, the jRS, and $R_{freeSlots}$ as a result of the planning process described in the last section. Mapping is also done in two phases. Phase 1 determines a candidate list comprising nodes on which at least one chunk $\in reqRS$ is unused for the duration D, in the search interval. Phase 2 then uses this list to select nodes according to a policy (e.g., greedy, energy efficiency, etc.). For this purpose, a weight (i.e., a scalar value) is computed for all nodes. The weight is used to rank the nodes from "cheap" to "expensive".

It is computed by: $\forall r \in$ consumable resources provided by the node:

$$W_{node} = max\left(W_{node}, \frac{r}{r_{system}}\right)$$

and then $W_{node} = W_{node} * cores_{system} + prio_{node} * cores_{system}.$
$cores_{system}$ is the number of available cores in the system.
$prio_{node}$ is an integer value and may be specified by the administrator via RSD.
   The basic steps of phase 1 are:

1. Build N_{cand}: A list of all usable nodes providing the required chunks in principle. N_{cand} is then sorted by the node's weight.
2. Build $FCN_{n,c}$: $\forall n \in N_{cand}$ and for each requested chunk c build a $RUSV$ where the chunk is free for at least duration D on the node:

$$\forall r \in chunk_c : FCN_{n,c} \cap getFreeSlots(nRS_r, F_r, D, T_1, T_2).$$

If $FCN_{n,c}$ for a node n is empty, this node is removed from N_{cand}. To get a good node utilization, we first compute a weight for each requested chunk related to a node, similar to the node's weight, and sort the chunks by their weight in descending order. As a result we get X $RUSVs$ per node. X is the number of requested chunks and $FCN_{n,c}[i]$.items holds the number of free chunks.
3. Build FCJ_c: For each requested chunk build a $RUSV$ holding the sum of all related $FCN_{n,c}$ by computing:

$$\forall n \in N_{cand} \text{ and } \forall c \in reqRS : FCJ_c = \sum_{c,n} FCN_{n,c}$$

and removing all intervals with less than the required number of chunks or a duration < D. We then check if enough chunks are available. If not then the job cannot be mapped within the search interval.
4. Build FS: The intersection of all FCJ_c by computing:

$$\forall c \in reqRS : FS \cap FCJ_c.$$

FS then holds all slots with a duration $\geq$ D, where all chunks are available at the same time.

The result of phase 1 is: A $RUSV$ (FS) with available time slots $\geq$ D and a list of nodes (N_{cand}) and for each node $FCN_{n,c}$ (a RUSV for each chunk with free time slots $\geq$ D).

   If FS is not empty, we have found a set of nodes which provide the resources. We then enter phase 2. Until now, we do a greedy mapping. The Greedy mapper tries to map expensive chunks on cheap nodes first. If mapping was not possible for all slots in FS, we try another slot of $R_{freeSlots}$ else, we build the mapping-data $njRS$. For each mapped host, it holds information which resources in what amount the host provides. The $njRS$ can be seen as a node specific jRS.

   The complexity of the mapping process is independent of the number of jobs in the system. It depends on the number of nodes and the job's chunk complexity. For example mapping a chunk requesting one core can be done in more ways than mapping a chunk comprising 32 cores and a GPU.

5.3   Booking

The last step is to commit the planned resources for the planned interval in
$usdRS$, sRS, and nRS by computing:

$$\forall r \in jRS \text{ and } \forall s \in \{\text{sRS}, \text{usdRS}\} : s_r \oplus jRS_r.$$

For nRS, we book on all mapped nodes:

$$\forall r \in \text{ node's } njRS : nRS_r \oplus njRS_r.$$

The inverse operation (i.e., revoke) is done by computing $\ominus$ instead of $\oplus$. Revoke
is used if a job is removed or while scanning for a better plan.

5.4   Notable Aspects

Of course, there are a lot of pitfalls and exceptions to cope with, while applying
the heuristic outlined above. In the following, we describe some aspects.

Backfilling. Backfilling is invoked whenever a job has been removed from the
plan. It affects all jobs with a planned start time after the removed job. To
avoid long answer times (e.g., 100,000 planned jobs), backfilling is done in the
background controlled by a special backfilling thread. The basic two steps are:

1. Sample affected jobs and sort them (by job-priority, submit-time, etc.) A job's
   priority is computed automatically at submit time. Criteria are for example:
   job type, requesting expensive or "special" resources, or node parallelism.
2. For each job try to find a "better" place in the plan. Following a First-Fit
   strategy, we first unbook the job's resources and plan it again. If the planned
   start time is earlier than the previous one, we book the new time interval,
   else the old one. Other strategies are possible but not yet implemented. Jobs
   are started immediately if possible.

Replanning. Replanning is invoked if a job cannot be allocated due to an
allocation error or a timeout. We then displace jobs with a lower priority to
ensure that the job in question can be allocated at the planned start time.
Replanning is also necessary if a user altered the job specification, an already
assigned resource becomes unavailable (e.g., if a node is set offline or a node
monitors a resource change), or a node is available again. In the latter case all
waiting and matching jobs are then replanned.

Estimation of job runtime. Overestimation is handled by backfilling. Under-
estimation results normally in aborting the running job. However, users may
increase the runtime via altering the job. There exists also a limit which we normally set to 10% of the initial runtime. Additionally, users may specify that the
running job is notified by OpenCCS X minutes before the maximum duration
ends. This is done by running a script or sending a signal to the job. The job
then can react.

Reservations. Users may reserve resources in advance and submit then jobs to the reservation. If planning a job for a reservation, we use rRS instead of sRS and the maximum search interval is the duration of the reservation. Hence, for the scheduler, a reservation is an own system.

Exclusive node access. To be able to compute $R_{freeSlots}$ for exclusive node access, we need to know the number of free cores to be searched for. For example, assume a cluster with nodes having 16, 32, and 240 cores and the user requests 10:npcus=12, place=free:excl. How many cores should be free?

Since arrangement is free, we could map more than one chunk on a node with 32 or 240 cores. Here, the planning phase needs mapping data to be accurate which is not possible because we cannot map before planning. To circumvent this, we compute an average number of cores for all nodes.

Timeouts. Since a planning based WLM is a real time system, we have to use timeouts for nearly all operations. For example, the administrator specifies how long allocating or releasing a job may last. If a timeout is exceeded, the node in question is set "down" in the scheduler and all related requests are replanned.

"Expensive" resources. Jobs using a GPU often also need at least one CPU core on the host. To avoid that a job which does not need the GPU blocks all CPU cores on the host, it may be specified in RSD that X cores are kept free for jobs requesting GPUs. Jobs not requesting GPUs, only get $min(availableCores - X, requestedCores)$. While building $FCN_{n,c}$, we also ensure that exclusive node access is not possible for jobs not using a GPU.

To avoid that expensive nodes (e.g., an SMP node with 32 cores and 1 TB RAM) get blocked by long running cheap chunks, but still are usable, the administrator my define node specific limits. For example jobs may only be mapped to an SMP node if they request at least 80 g virtual memory, or 66 g memory, or 17 cores, or their duration is ≤ 12 h. This is applied while building N_{cand}.

Accelerating planning and mapping. If we have FreePools and limits with a cron based validity, we accelerate the planning process, by building a template $RUSV$ for the validity and then transpose it to the respective needed time interval. For this purpose, we use the routine: $R_2 = \texttt{cronToRUSV}(R_1, I, T_1, T_2, P)$. R_1 is the template $RUSV$ starting at 1.1.1970 (i.e., (time_t) 0) and holding one period. P is the cron's period length (hour, day, or week). To get a $RUSV$ with absolute times, we add a time offset (derived by T_1, T_2, and P) to each $R_1[i]$.start and stop and set $R_1[i]$.items to I. We do this in a loop with step size P until $[T_1, T_2]$ is filled. If we assume a validity of "every Monday and Friday from 7am to 11am" and T_1 is 1.1.2018 and T_2 is 31.12.2025. P is then a week.

To accelerate the mapping the N_{cand} list is built only once. It is rebuilt, whenever a node becomes available again. The node specific $FCN_{n,c}$ in the mapping process are built in parallel because they are independent. For this purpose the scheduler module PM uses a dynamic thread pool. The nodes to process are put in a queue and each of the threads takes a node and computes $FCN_{n,c}$ for this node until the queue is empty.

6   Performance Results

All numbers in this section are derived from real operation over four years on our OCuLUS and ARMINIUS clusters [13].

OCuLUS is running Scientific Linux and consists of 616 compute nodes with in total 9.920 CPU cores, 8 Xeon-Phis, and 32 GPUs. The nodes have 64 GB, 256 GB, or 1 TB RAM. All nodes are connected by Infiniband and Ethernet. The Xeon-Phis may be used in offload or native mode. The scheduler module *PM* is running on a host equipped with two Intel Xeon CPUs E5-2670, 2.60 GHz and 64 GB RAM. The *PM* is configured to pin on the cores 8–15, the thread-pool maximum size is 8.

ARMINIUS is running Scientific Linux and consists of 62 compute nodes with in total 660 CPU cores. All nodes are connected by Infiniband and Ethernet. The *PM* is running on a host equipped with two Intel Xeon CPUs X5650, 2.67 GHz and 36 GB RAM. The *PM* is configured to pin on the cores 8–10 (ARMINIUS has only 62 nodes) and the thread-pool size is limited to 8.

OpenCCS on OCuLUS processed about 4.5 million jobs for about 200 different users in about 70 groups. The job sizes ranged from one to 4,096 cores. The runtimes ranged from seconds to 60 days. The initial duration limit for a new project at PC^2 is set to 7 days. The average number of processed jobs per day was 3,082 and the maximum was 196,217. 94% of the submitted jobs completed, 6% were removed by the users before they started. The average runtime was 184 m, the average waiting time 191 m. The average accuracy of the job's duration estimation was 22%. The plan normally comprises a time interval of 8 to 10 weeks and the *sRS* holds about 300 to 400 slots. The bad accuracy is mainly driven by the large number of one core jobs, submitted as job arrays. Example 3 from the OpenCCS reporting tool gives an overview of the job distribution related to requested cores. The data was sampled in 2016.

```
================================================================
      Req.             Avg.    Avg.     Avg.    %Total   Sum
Rank  cores    Jobs  Walltime Accuracy Waiting Occupied  Occ.
================================================================
   1    16   57,516     10h    41.67%      7h   17.75%  17.75%
   2    32    9,701   1d50m    39.68%     20h   14.19%  31.93%
   3 1,024      277     19h    65.30%    8d18h  10.34%  42.27%
   4   768      468     10h    55.91%   12d10h   6.63%  48.90%
   5    64    3,883     13h    46.00%     11h    6.30%  55.20%
   6   128   14,002      1h    26.43%      5h    4.74%  59.94%
   7   256      684     13h    39.30%     14h    4.40%  64.34%
   8 1,536       77     16h    64.01%   22d22h   3.62%  67.96%
   9     1 1,480,565     1h    21.39%      2h    3.55%  71.51%
  10   512      151     16h    62.61%     17h    2.33%  73.83%
```

Example 3: OCuLUS job distribution related to requested cores, ranked by occupied core hours.

```
-----------RUSV INFO -------------------------
Number of RUSV-create calls      : 95,766,132
Number of RUSV-free calls        : 169,898,098
Number of RUSV-slot-new calls    : 250,851,576
Number of RUSV-slot-free calls   : 233,838,317


-----------VECTOR INFO -----------------------
Vectors (used/avail)             : 5,780,091 / 6,291,456
Elements(used/avail/filling)     : 11,014,670/ 61,465,796 / 17.92%
Memory  (sum/payload/overhead)   : 663.87MB / 153.44MB / 510.43MB
Allocs/Reallocs/Frees            : 11,518,320/ 16,711,065 / 0
```

Example 4: Memory consumption of the OCuLUS *PM*

The *PM* on OCuLUS uses about 6 GB RAM if 15 k jobs are in the system. Based on the data structure introduced in Sect. 4, the *PM* uses a large number of *RUSV*s. Example 4 gives an overview of the memory usage logged by the *PM*. There are 10 k jobs in the plan, the first backfill has been processed and *sRS* holds 345 slots.

On OCuLUS, we measured up to about 100 processed job submissions per second by running 30 clients on the two access nodes. Each client submitted best effort jobs in a loop. The jobs requested chunks with two cores and a maximum runtime of 2 m. Since the jobs were also running on the cluster, this is the OpenCCS performance.

The performance of the *PM* itself is higher. As described in Sect. 5.2, the runtime of the mapping process depends on the number of nodes and the complexity of the requested chunks. This is reflected if we look on the number of backfills per second which is continuously measured by the *PM*. On OCuLUS, we see numbers up to 500 and sorting of 60 k jobs by job priority takes about 20 ms. The time to plan a job array with 10 k jobs takes about 30 s. Job array planning is done in chunks of 500 sub-jobs. On ARMINIUS, we see up to 1500 backfills per second.

Core pinning is essential for the performance of the *PM*. The number of backfills per second increases by a factor of about two if pinning is activated. This is related to the large amount of *RUSV* accesses.

OpenCCS modules may be restarted at any time and if an OpenCCS module crashed, it will be automatically restarted by the *IM*. At restart a module reads its status data and synchronizes the job states with its partners. The time the *PM* needs to recover 5000 jobs takes about 20 s.

7   Related Work

There are a lot of papers related to the planning based approach. Since this paper is more a result of practical work, this section does not cover the whole area of planning based scheduling. We only relate to similar work.

Cluster and Grid. In [4], Chlumský et al. propose a similar approach as presented here. They extend the Torque [15] scheduler to allow planning jobs to different clusters. Their approach uses job lists, holding start and completion time and gap lists, representing unused periods of CPU time and the amount of free RAM across nodes within a cluster. Both list types are sorted by time. The gap list may be seen as a kind of *RUSV*. A gap list entry points to the appropriate node, the node's free RAM, and to the nearest following job. Planning an incoming job is done by finding a place in the gap list, backfilling is done by shifting jobs into earlier "slots". The authors use a Tabu Search heuristic to optimize the current schedule. Compared to the work presented here, the approach of [4] is restricted to plan only two resources (cores and memory). Requesting complex resource sets comprising different chunk types or job wide resources is not possible. They also neglect limits, reservations, and placing directives.

In [14], Schneider et al. propose a list based data structure to support advance reservations in Grid environments and local WLMs for HPC systems. Lists hold information about the summed up booked capacity and for each node mapping information. The list entries represent a range of free resources. Such a list may be organized in three ways:

1. As time exclusive list. For each point in time there is only one item, representing the current available capacity. The list is ordered by the start time of the blocks, that is, adjacent blocks follow each other in the free list.
2. As capacity list. Each item spans the whole time span where at least the given capacity is free. During this time span, there may be other sub time spans with more capacity available; these time spans are managed as sub lists of the longer block. Hence, a hierarchical data structure is used.
3. As mixed list. The splitting of the list items does not follow any rule. The items may be ordered by the start time and the available capacity. The list items should have references to all adjacent free blocks.

For their evaluations, the authors simulate a cluster with 128 CPUs and use the time exclusive list type. They compare three ways of organizing the lists: slotted time, list based, and AVL tree.

Schneider et al. use an approach which is very close to the one introduced here. The information about the summed up booked capacity corresponds to our *sRS*, the mapping information to the *nRS*, and the list entries are structured similar to a *slot* in a *RUSV*. The time exclusive list is nearly the same as our resource sets, except that we handle slots of used instead of free resources and do not store slots where all resources are in use.

Schneider et al. support only exclusive booking of nodes, and, just as in [4], complex resource sets comprising different chunk types or job wide resources, limits, and placing directives are not available. Additionally, they do not describe how planning and mapping should work if more than one resource type is requested, like for example ncpus=5:gpus=3.

Both, the authors of [4, 14], compared their approach with other papers and assessed them all weaker, related to their approaches. Hence, and for the lack of space, we do not consider them here.

Big-Data. The following WLM examples are, in principle, all based on the MapReduce model and schedule jobs on a Hadoop platform focusing on the need for locality and elasticity of MapReduce jobs. Such jobs often consist of multiple tasks (e.g., map or reduce) that are run on different cluster nodes, where the unit of per-task resource allocation is a container (i.e., a bundle of resources such as CPU, RAM and disk I/O). An OpenCCS chunk is like a container related to scheduling. Due to the MapReduce model, tasks are often loosely coupled, malleable and may be preempted. MapReduce jobs are mainly characterized by a start time, a deadline, and a collection of stages. Each stage has a total demand of containers and may also have a minimum parallelism constraint (or gang size) of containers. The most important SLO is the job deadline.

YARN [17] schedules jobs on a Hadoop platform and comprises three basic blocks. The Resource Manager (RM), the Application Manager (AM), and, on each node, a Node Manager (NM). The RM is scheduling containers bound to a particular node.

There is on AM for each job. The AM is the head of a job, managing all lifecycle aspects including dynamically increasing and decreasing resource consumption, managing the flow of execution, handling faults and computation skew, and performing other local optimizations. Hence, the AM can be seen as a kind of workflow engine dividing a job into tasks and mapping tasks to containers. An AM is requesting containers from the RM and then starting job-tasks on such containers by using the NMs which are responsible for establishing, observing, and removing containers on a node. A container request to the RM includes: the number of containers, the resources per container, locality preferences, and priority of requests within the application. An AM may request containers to be killed when the corresponding work is not needed any more.

In contrast to OpenCCS, YARN does not plan to the future and it does not know maximum runtimes of a container. To our best knowledge YARN can only handle containers consisting of CPUs and memory and is not able to schedule job-wide resources like licenses. However, YARN supports preemption of containers which is not supported by OpenCCS.

In [16] the authors describe TetriSched, a scheduler integrated in the YARN reservation system. It considers both, job-specific preferences and estimated job runtimes in its allocation of resources. Job-specific preferences are provided by tenants as composable utility functions. They allow TetriSched to understand which resources are preferred, and by how much, over other acceptable options. Estimated job runtimes and constraints on job execution times (e.g., deadlines or reservations) allow TetriSched to plan ahead in deciding whether to wait for a busy preferred resource to become free or to assign a less preferred resource. TetriSched translates the given requirements into a Mixed Integer Linear Problem (MILP) that is solved by an external solver to maximize the overall utility.

The main advantage of TetriSched over OpenCCS is its ability to compute a global schedule by simultaneously considering the placement and temporal preferences of all the jobs in each compute cycle, and to support user given utility functions (e.g., the job needs two time units on GPUs and three on CPUs) which allow a greater scheduling flexibility. OpenCCS does a greedy job-by-job planning. However, it is not quite clear how long it takes to solve a MILP, if there are tens of thousands of jobs in the system. In [5] the authors use heuristics due to the very long runtime of the MILP solver. TetriSched seems to support only space-sharing (i.e., a job is occupying a node exclusively).

Rayon [5] is another extension to YARN. It provides reservation-based scheduling which leverages explicit information about the deadline and time-varying resource needs of a job. Rayon comes with a declarative reservation definition language (RDL), that allows users to express a rich class of constraints, including deadlines, malleable and gang parallelism requirements, and inter-job dependencies.

The scheduler itself comprises a framework for planning SLA jobs by using fast, greedy heuristics, and a component for the dynamically assignment of cluster resources to the planned and best-effort jobs, which also adapts to changing cluster conditions. Rayon makes use of planning in two ways: online, to accept/reject jobs on arrival, and offline, to reorganize sets of accepted jobs.

Rayon immediately plans incoming SLA jobs and assigns a start time. Best effort jobs are filled in the remaining gaps by the adaptive scheduler component. The Rayon RDL is automatically transferred to a MILP formulation like in [16]. However, for the authors solving MILPs is not practical for online scenarios, and cannot scale to large problem sizes (solver runtime ranged from 80 s to 3200 s). Hence, Rayon, just like OpenCCS does, plans one job at a time, and never reconsiders placement decisions for previously jobs. A job is divided in containers with a minimum runtime of X time-units. In case of under-reservation, an SLA job will run with guaranteed resources up to a point, and then continue as a best-effort job until completion.

OpenCCS also supports reservations and deadline scheduling but does not support neither malleable jobs nor preemption. Jobs in the HPC world are still mainly rigid. Best-efforts jobs in OpenCCS are not starving which may happen in Rayon. OpenCCS also allows renegotiation of accepted jobs.

It seems that Rayon, like YARN does, mainly supports CPUs and memory as container parts. Customizable resources are not possible. It is also not clear if Rayon supports time dependent limitations and heterogeneous clusters.

Morpheus [7], which is integrated in YARN, aims on lowering the number of deadline violations while retaining cluster-utilization. It builds on three key ideas: (1) automatically deriving SLOs and job resource models from historical data, (2) relying on recurrent reservations and packing algorithms to enforce SLOs, and (3) dynamic reprovisioning to mitigate inherent execution variance. The job resource model is a time-varying skyline of resource demands. It employs a MILP formulation, that explicitly controls the penalty of over/under provisioning and balances predictability and utilization. As in [5] Morpheus does not use an external MILP solver due to the long runtimes.

Morpheus continuously observes and learns as periodic jobs (scheduled runs of the same job on newly arriving data) execute over time. The findings are used to reserve resources for the job ahead of job execution, and dynamically adapt to changing conditions at runtime. Periodic jobs are supported by recurring reservations, a scheduling construct that isolates jobs from the noisiness of sharing induced performance variability by assigning dedicated resources. Morpheus can only enforce container-level resources, but lacks control over globally-shared resources. When Morpheus needs to allocate resources to a new periodic job, it ignores most of the scheduled non-periodic jobs, and then attempts to reallocate resources for non-periodic jobs in case they need more resources. Morpheus assumes a homogeneous cluster. Extra resources are granted for up to T seconds and then are reevaluated. This allows an elastic job to use extra parallelism to make up for lost time. OpenCCS does not displace already planned jobs while planning new ones.

Mapping of containers is done by a cost-based approach that takes into account current cluster allocation and the resource demand of each job. Each time slot in the plan is associated with a cost and the mapper allocates incoming jobs in a way that is cost-efficient with respect to the overall costs. This is analogous to limits and FreePools in OpenCCS. However OpenCCS then reduces the number of available resources for the job in the related time slots.

8   Conclusion

We presented a data structure and a heuristic to plan and map arbitrary resources in complex combinations while applying time dependent constraints. We implemented the heuristic in the planning based WLM OpenCCS. Our approach has stand up to the reality check during four years of real operation on two heterogeneous HPC clusters (one of them with about 10,000 cores) and proved its stability, flexibility, and performance. Of course, there are drawbacks inherent to our approach and there are plenty of additional features to be added. Backfilling, for example, is a time consuming operation, especially if using a more complex policy than First-Fit. A planning horizon (e.g., 4 weeks) could reduce the amount of jobs to be planned. Fair share is part of our limit design, and we see a good and fair system utilization. However, we learned that this approach does not work sufficiently if the jobs do not fully utilize the system. Therefore, we will include dynamic soft limits which depend on the utilization of the system, allowing consumers to extend their hard limits. Additionally, we plan to extend the mapping layer to allow topology aware mapping (e.g., group chunks by switches). Also, releasing and requesting resources while a job is running is part of our future work. There is a reason why queueing based WLMs dominate the market. Queues are fast and very flexible. However, we think the planning based approach is advantageous if time dependent constraints have to be considered.

Acknowledgements. I would like to thank Christoph Kleineweber, Dr. Lars Schäfers, and Dr. Jörn Schumacher for their valuable contribution to the current OpenCCS release.

References

1. Battre, D., Hovestadt, M., Kao, O., Keller, A., Voss, K.: Planning-based scheduling for SLA-awareness and grid integration. In: Proceedings of the 26th Workshop of the UK Planning and Scheduling Special Interest Group (PlansSIG 2007) (2007)
2. Brune, M., Gehring, J., Keller, A., Reinefeld, A.: RSD - resource and service description. In: Schaeffer, J. (ed.) High Performance Computing Systems and Applications (HPCS 1998), pp. 193–206. Kluwer Academic Press, Dordrecht (1998)
3. OpenCCS Manual, July 2017. https://www.openccs.eu
4. Chlumský, V., Klusáček, D., Ruda, M.: The extension of torque scheduler allowing the use of planning and optimization in grids. Comput. Sci. **13**(2), 5–19 (2012). https://doi.org/10.7494/csci.2012.13.2.5
5. Curino, C., Difallah, D.E., Douglas, C., et al.: Reservation-based scheduling: if you're late don't blame us! Tech-report MSR-TR-2013-108, Microsoft (2013)
6. Hovestadt, M., Kao, O., Keller, A., Streit, A.: Scheduling in HPC resource management systems: queuing vs. planning. In: Feitelson, D., Rudolph, L., Schwiegelshohn, U. (eds.) JSSPP 2003. LNCS, vol. 2862, pp. 1–20. Springer, Heidelberg (2003). https://doi.org/10.1007/10968987_1
7. Jyothi, S.A., Curino, C., Menache, I., et al.: Morpheus: towards automated SLOs for enterprise clusters. In: Proceedings of the 12th USENIX Symposium on Operating Systems Design and Implementation (OSDI 2016), November 2016
8. Kay, J., Lauder, P.: A fair share scheduler. Commun. ACM **31**, 44–55 (1998)
9. Kleban, S.D., Clearwater, S.: Fair share on high performance computing systems: what does fair really mean? In: Proceedings of 3rd IEEE International Symposium on Cluster Computing and the Grid (CCGrid 2003), pp. 145–153. IEEE Computer Society (2003)
10. Lifka, D.A.: The ANL/IBM SP scheduling system. In: Feitelson, D.G., Rudolph, L. (eds.) JSSPP 1995. LNCS, vol. 949, pp. 295–303. Springer, Heidelberg (1995). https://doi.org/10.1007/3-540-60153-8_35
11. Mu'alem, A., Feitelson, D.G.: Utilization, predictability, workloads, and user run-time estimates in scheduling the IBM SP2 with backfilling. IEEE Trans. Parallel Distrib. Syst. **12**(6), 529–543 (2001)
12. PBSPro Open Source, January 2017. http://www.pbspro.org
13. PC^2: Paderborn Center for Parallel Computing, July 2017. https://pc2.uni-paderborn.de
14. Schneider, J., Linnert, B.: List-based data structures for efficient management of advance reservations. Int. J. Parallel Prog. **42**, 77–93 (2014). https://doi.org/10.1007/s10766-012-0219-4
15. Torque, January 2017. http://www.adaptivecomputing.com/products/open-source/torque/
16. Tumanov, A., Zhu, T., Park, J.W., et al.: TetriSched: global rescheduling with adaptive plan-ahead in dynamic heterogeneous clusters. In: Proceedings of the 11th European Conference on Computer Systems (EuroSys 2016), April 2016. https://doi.org/10.1145/2901318.2901355
17. Vavilapalli, V.K., Murthy, A.C., Douglas, C., et al.: Apache Hadoop YARN: yet another resource negotiator. In: Proceedings of the 4th Annual Symposium on Cloud Computing (SOCC 2013), October 2013. https://doi.org/10.1145/2523616.2523633

ScSF: A Scheduling Simulation Framework

Gonzalo P. Rodrigo[1(✉)], Erik Elmroth[1], Per-Olov Östberg[1],
and Lavanya Ramakrishnan[2]

[1] Department of Computing Science, Umeå University, 901 87 Umeå, Sweden
`{gonzalo,elmroth,p-o}@cs.umu.se`
[2] Lawrence Berkeley National Lab, Berkeley, CA 94720, USA
`lramakrishnan@lbl.gov`

Abstract. High-throughput and data-intensive applications are increasingly present, often composed as workflows, in the workloads of current HPC systems. At the same time, trends for future HPC systems point towards more heterogeneous systems with deeper I/O and memory hierarchies. However, current HPC schedulers are designed to support classical large tightly coupled parallel jobs over homogeneous systems. Therefore, there is an urgent need to investigate new scheduling algorithms that can manage the future workloads on HPC systems. However, there is a lack of appropriate models and frameworks to enable development, testing, and validation of new scheduling ideas.

In this paper, we present an open-source scheduler simulation framework (ScSF) that covers all the steps of scheduling research through simulation. ScSF provides capabilities for workload modeling, workload generation, system simulation, comparative workload analysis, and experiment orchestration. The simulator is designed to be run over a distributed computing infrastructure facilitating large-scale tests. We demonstrate ScSF through a case study to develop new techniques to manage scientific workflows in a batch scheduler. The evaluation consisted of 1728 experiments and equivalent to 33 years of simulated time, were run in a deployment of ScSF over a distributed infrastructure of 17 compute nodes over two months. Finally, the experimental results were analyzed using the ScSF framework to demonstrate that our technique minimizes workflow turnaround time without over-allocating resources. Finally, we discuss lessons learned from our experiences to inform future large-scale simulation studies using ScSF and other similar frameworks.

1 Introduction

In recent years, high-throughput and data-intensive applications are increasingly present in the workloads at HPC centers. Current trends to build larger HPC

Source code available to download at: http://frieda.lbl.gov/download.
G. P. Rodrigo—Work performed while working at the Lawrence Berkeley National Lab.

© Springer International Publishing AG, part of Springer Nature 2018
D. Klusáček et al. (Eds.): JSSPP 2017, LNCS 10773, pp. 152–173, 2018.
https://doi.org/10.1007/978-3-319-77398-8_9

systems point towards heterogeneous systems and deeper I/O and memory hierarchies. However, HPC systems and their schedulers were designed to support large communication-intensive MPI jobs run over uniform systems.

The changes in workloads and underlying hardware have resulted in an urgent need to investigate new scheduling algorithms and models. However, there is limited availability of tools to facilitate scheduling research. Currently available simulator frameworks do not capture the complexities of a production batch scheduler. Also, they are not powerful enough to simulate large experiment sets, or they do not cover all its relevant aspects, i.e., workload modeling and generation, scheduler simulation, and result analysis.

Schedulers are complex systems and their behavior is the result of the interaction of multiple mechanisms that rank and schedule jobs, while monitoring the system state. Many simulators, e.g., Alea [12], include state of art implementations of some of these mechanisms, but do not capture the interaction between the components. As a consequence, hypotheses tested on such simulators might not hold in real systems.

Scheduling behavior depends on the configurations of the scheduler and characteristics of the workload. As a consequence, the potential number of experiments needed to evaluate a scheduling improvement is high. Also, experiments have to be run for long time to be significant and have to be repeated to ensure representative results. Unfortunately, current simulation tools do not provide support to scale up and run large numbers of long experiments. Finally, workload analysis tools to correlate large scheduling result sets are not available.

In this paper, we present ScSF, a scheduling simulation framework that captures the scheduling research life-cycle. It includes a workload modeling engine, a synthetic workload generator, an instance of Slurm wrapped in a simulator, a results analyzer, and an orchestrator to coordinate experiments run over a distributed infrastructure. ScSF will be available as open source software[1], enabling community extensions and user customization of modules. We also present a use case that illustrates the use of the scheduling framework for evaluating a workflow-aware scheduling algorithm. Our case study demonstrates the modeling of the workload of a peta-scale system, Edison at the National Energy Research Scientific Computing Center (NERSC). We also describe the mechanics of implementing a new scheduling algorithm in Slurm and running experiments over distributed infrastructures.

Specifically, our contributions are:

- We describe the design and implementation of scalable scheduling simulator framework (ScSF) that supports and automates workload modeling and generation, Slurm simulation, and data analysis. ScSF will be available as open source.
- We detail a case study that works as a guideline to use the framework to evaluate a workflow-aware scheduling algorithm.
- We discuss the lessons learned from running scheduling experiments at scale that will inform future research in the field.

---

[1] Available at: http://frieda.lbl.gov/download.

The rest of the paper is organized as follows. In Sect. 2, we present the state of art of scheduling research tools and the previous work supporting the framework. The architecture of ScSF and the definition of its modules are presented in Sect. 3. In Sect. 4, we describe the steps to use the framework to evaluate a new scheduling algorithm. In Sect. 5, we present lessons learned while using ScSF at scale. We present our conclusions in Sect. 6.

2   Background

In this section, we describe the state of art and challenges in scheduling research.

2.1   HPC Schedulers and Slurm

ScSF support research on HPC scheduling. The framework incorporates a full production scheduler and is modified to include new scheduling algorithms to be evaluated.

Different options were considered for the framework scheduler. Moab (scheduler) plus Torque (resource manager) [5], LSF [9], and LoadLeveler [11] are popular in HPC centers. However, their source code is not easily available which makes extensibility difficult. The Maui cluster scheduler is an open-source precursor of Moab [10]. However it has not been kept up to date to support current system needs. Slurm is one of the most popular recent workload managers in HPC. It is currently used in 5 of top 10 HPC systems [2]. It was originally developed at Lawrence Livermore National Laboratory [20], now maintained by SchedMD [2], and it is available as open source. Also, there are publicly available projects that support simulation in it [19]. Hence, our simulator framework is based on Slurm.

As illustrated in Fig. 1, Slurm is structured as a set of daemons that communicate over RPC calls:

slurmctld is the scheduling daemon. It contains the scheduling calculation functions and the waiting queue. It receives batch job submissions from users and distributes work across the instances of slurmd.

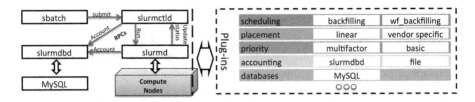

Fig. 1. Slurm is composed by three daemons: slurmctld (scheduler), slurmd (compute nodes management and supervision), and slurmdbd (accounting). A plug-in structure wraps the main functions in those daemons.

slurmd is the worker daemon. There can be one instance per compute node or a single instance (front-end mode) managing all nodes. It places and runs work in compute nodes and reports the resources status to slurmctld. The simulator uses front-end mode.

sbatch is a command that wraps the Slurm RPC API to submit jobs to slurm-ctld. Most commonly used by users.

Slurm has a plug-in architecture. Many of the internal functions are wrapped by C APIs loaded dynamically depending on the configuration files of Slurm (slurmctld.conf, slurmd.conf).

The Slurm simulator is a wrapper around Slurm to emulate HPC resources, emulate user's job submission, and speed up Slurm's execution. We extended previous work from the Swiss Supercomputing Center (CSCS, [19]) that is based on work by the Barcelona Supercomputing Center (BSC, [14]). Our contributions increase Slurm's speed up while maintaining determinism in the simulations, and adds workflow support.

2.2   HPC Workload Analysis and Generation

ScSF includes the capacity to model system workloads and generate synthetic ones accordingly. Workload modeling starts with elimination of flurries (i.e., events that are not representative and skew the model) [8]. The generator models each job variable with the empirical distribution [13], i.e., it recreates the shape of job variable distributions by constructing a histogram and CDF from the observed values.

2.3   Related Work

Previous work [18] proposes three main methods of scheduling algorithms research: theoretical analysis, execution on a real system, and simulation. The theoretical analysis is limited to produce boundary values on the algorithm, i.e. best and worst cases, but does not allow predicting regular performance. Also, since continuous testing of new algorithms on large real systems is not possible, simulation is the option chosen in our work.

Available simulation tools do not cover the full cycle of modeling, generation, simulation, and analysis. Also, public up-to-date simulators and workload generators are scarce. As an example, our work is based on the most recent peer reviewed work on Slurm Simulation (CSCS, [19]). We improve its synchronization to speed up its execution. For more grid-like workloads, Alea [12] is an example of a current HPC simulator. However, it does not include a production simulator in its core and does not generate workloads.

For workload modeling, function fitting and user modeling are recognized methods [7]. ScSF's workload model is based on empirical distributions [13], as it produces good enough models and does not require specific information about system users. Also, our work modeling methods are based on the experience of our previous work on understanding workload evolution of HPC systems life cycle [15] and job heterogeneity in HPC workloads [16].

In workload generation, previous work compares close and open loop approaches [21], i.e. taking into account or not the scheduling decisions to calculate the job arrival time. ScSF is used in environments with reduced user information, which is needed to create closed-loop models. Thus, ScSF uses an open-loop workload generation model to fill and load mechanisms (Sect. 3.4) to avoid under and over job submission.

Finally, other workloads and models [6] are available, but are less representative of current HPC systems. In our work, we use workloads from Edison, a Cray XC30 supercomputer, deployed in 2013 with 133,824 cores and 357 TB of RAM.

3   ScSF Architecture

Figure 2 shows ScSF's architecture. The core of ScSF is a MySQL database that stores the framework's data and meta-data. Running experiments based on a reference system requires modeling its workload first by processing the system's scheduling logs in the *workload model engine*. This model is used in the experiments to generate synthetic workloads with similar characteristics to the original ones.

In ScSF, the simulation process starts with the description of the experimental setup in an *experiment definition* provided by the user. The definition includes workload characteristics, scheduler configuration, and simulation time. The *experiment runner* processes experiment definitions and orchestrates experiments accordingly. First, it invokes the *workload generator* to produce a synthetic workload of similar job characteristics (size, inter arrival time) as the real ones in the reference system chosen. This workload may include specific jobs (e.g., workflows) according the experiment definition. Next, the runner invokes the simulator. The ScSF simulator is a wrapper around Slurm that increases the execution pace and emulates the HPC system and its users. The simulator sets Slurm's configuration according to the experiment definition and emulates

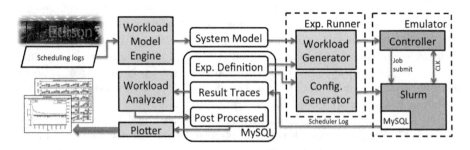

Fig. 2. ScSF schema with green color representing components developed in this work and purple representing modified and improved components. (Color figure online)

the submission of the synthetic workload jobs. Slurm schedules the jobs over the virtual resources until the last workload job is submitted. At that moment, the simulation is considered completed.

Completed simulations are processed by the *workload analyzer*. The analysis covers the characterization of jobs, workflows, and system. This module includes tools to compare experiments to differentiate the effects of scheduling behaviors on the workload.

3.1   Workload Model Engine

A workload model is composed of statistical data that is used to generate synthetic jobs that with characteristics similar to the original ones. The workload model engine extracts a job's characteristics from Slurm or Moab scheduling logs including wait time, allocated CPU cores, requested wall clock time, actual runtime, inter-arrival time, and runtime accuracy ($\frac{runtime}{requestedWallClockTime}$). Jobs with missing information (e.g. start time), or individual rare and very large jobs that would skew the model (e.g. system test jobs) are filtered out.

Next, the extracted values are used to produce the empirical distributions [13] of each job variable as illustrated in Fig. 3. A normalized histogram is calculated on the source values. Then, the histogram is transformed into a cumulative histogram, i.e., each bin represents the percentage of observed values that are less or equal to the upper boundary of the bin. Finally, the cumulative histogram is transformed into a table that maps probability ranges on a value. For example, in Fig. 3, bin $(10-20]$ has a $[0.3, 0.8)$ probability range as its value is 80% and its left neighboring bin's value is 30%. The probability ranges map to the mid value of the range that they correspond to, e.g., 15 is the mid value of $(10-20]$. This model is then ready to produce values, e.g., a random number (0.91) is mapped on the table to obtain 25.

Each variable's histogram is calculated with specific bin sizes adapted to its resolution. By default, the bin size for the request job's wall clock time is one minute (Slurm's resolution). The corresponding bin size for inter-arrival time is one second as that corresponds to the resolution of timestamps in the logs. Finally, for the job CPU core allocation, the bin size is the number of cores per node of the reference system, as in HPC systems node sharing is usually disabled.

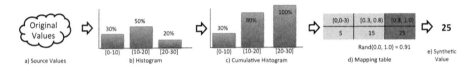

Fig. 3. Empirical distribution constructions for job variables: calculating a cumulative histogram and transforming it into a mapping table.

3.2   Experiment Definition

An experiment definition outlines the conditions in an experiment process, configuring the scheduler, workload characteristics, and experiment duration. A definition is composed of a scheduler configuration file and a database entry (Table 1) that includes:

trace_type and subtraces: The tag "single" identifies the experiments that are meant to be run in the simulator. A workload will be generated and run through the simulator for later analysis. The experiments with trace_type "grouped" are definitions that list the experiments that are the different repetitions of the same experimental conditions in the "subtraces" field.

system model: selects which system model is to be used to produce the workload in the experiment.

workflow_policy: controls presence of workflows in the workload. If set to "no", workflows are not present. If set to "period" a workflow is submitted periodically once every workflow_period_s seconds. If set to "percentage", workflows contribute workflow_share of the workload core hours.

Table 1. Experiment definition fields

trace_type	"single": regular experiment. "grouped": experiments aggregated
subtraces	list of single experiments related to this grouped one
system	name of system to model workload after
workflow_policy	"period": one workflow workflow_period_s. "percent": workflow_share core hours are workflows. "no": no workflows
manifest_list	list of workflows to appear in the workload
workflow_handling	workflows submission in workload. "single": pilot job. "multi": chained jobs". "manifest": workflow-aware job
start_date	submit time of first job valid for analysis
preload_time_s	time to prepend to the workload for stabilization
workload_duration_s	workload stops at start_date + workload_duration_s
seed	string to init random number generators

```
1  {"tasks": [
2    {"id":"SWide", "cmd":"./W.py", "cores":480, "rtime":360.0},
3    {"id":"SLong", "cmd":"./L.py", "cores":48, "rtime":1440.0,
4      "deps": ["SWide"]}]}
```

Fig. 4. WideLong workflow manifest in JSON format.

manifest_list: List of pairs (share, workflow) defining the workflows present in the workload: e.g., {(0.4 Montage.json), (0.6 Sipht.json)} indicates that 40% of the workflows will be Montage, and 60% Sipht. The workflow field points to a JSON file specifying the structure of the workflow (e.g., Fig. 4). It includes two tasks, the first running for 6 min, allocating 480 cores (wide task); and the second running for 24 min, allocating 48 cores (long task). The SLong task requires SWide to be completed before it starts.

workflow_handling: This parameter controls the method to submit workflows. The workload generator supports workflows submitted as chained jobs (*multi*), in which workflow tasks are submitted as independent jobs, expressing their relationship as job completion dependencies. Under this method, workflow tasks allocate exactly the resources they need, but intermediate job wait times might be long, increasing the turnaround time. Another approach supported is the pilot job (*single*), in which a workflow is submitted as a single job, allocating the maximum resource required within the workflow for its minimum possible runtime. The workflow tasks are run within the job, with no intermediate wait times, and thus, producing shorter turnaround times compared to chained jobs approach. However, it over-allocates resources, that are left idle at certain stages of the workflow.

start_date, preload_time_s, and workload_duration_s: defines the duration of the experiment workload. The variable start_date sets the submit time of the first job in the analyzed section of the workload, which will span until (start_date + workload_duration_s). Before the main section, a workload of preload_time_s seconds is prepended, to cover the cold start and stabilization of the system.

random seed: The random seed is an alphanumeric string that is used to initialize the random generator within the workload generator. If two experiments definitions have the same parameters, including the seed, their workloads will be identical. If two experiment definitions have the same parameters, but a different seed, their workloads will be similar in overall characteristics, but different as individual jobs (i.e. repetitions of the same experiment). In general, repetitions of the same experiment with different seeds are subtraces of a "grouped" experiment.

3.3 Experiment Runner

The experiment runner is an orchestration component that controls the workload generation and scheduling simulation. It invokes the workload generator and controls through SSH a virtual machine (VM) that contains a Slurm simulator instance. Figure 5 presents the experiment runner operations after being invoked with a hostname or IP of a Slurm simulator VM. First, the runner reboots the VM (step 0) to clear processes, memory, and reset the operative system state. Next, an experiment definition is retrieved from the database (step 1)

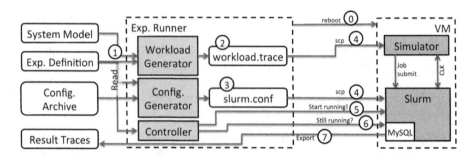

Fig. 5. Steps to run an experiment (numbers circled indicate order) taken by the experiment runner component. Once step seven is completed, the step sequence is re-started.

and the workload generator produces the corresponding experiment's workload file (step 2). This file is transferred to the VM (step 4) together with the corresponding Slurm configuration files (obtained in step 3). Then, the simulation inside the VM (step 5) is started. The main part of the simulation stops after the last job of the workload is submitted. Additionally, some extra time in included in the end to avoid abrupt system termination noises in the results. The experiment runner monitors Slurm (step 6), and when it terminates, the resulting scheduler logs are extracted and inserted in the central database (step 7).

Only one experiment runner can start per simulator VM. However, multiple runners manage multiple VMs in parallel, which enables scaling such that the experiments run concurrently.

3.4   Workload Generation

The workload generator in ScSF produces synthetic workloads representative of real system models. The workload structure is presented in Fig. 6. All workloads start with a *fill* phase, which includes a group of jobs meant to fill the system. The fill job phase is followed by the stabilization phase, which includes 24 h of regular jobs controlled by a job-pressure mechanism to ensure that there are enough jobs to keep the system utilized. The stabilization phase captures the cold start of the system, and it is ignored in later analysis. The next stage is the experiment phase, it runs for a fixed time (72 h in the figure) and includes regular batch jobs complemented by the experiment specific jobs (in this case workflows). After the workload is completely submitted, the simulation runs for extra time (drain period, configured in the simulator) to avoid the presence of noise from the system termination.

In the rest of this section, we present all the mechanisms involved in detail.

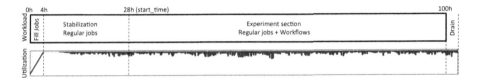

Fig. 6. Sections of a workload: fill, stabilization, experiment, and drain. Presented with an the associated utilization that this workload produced in the system.

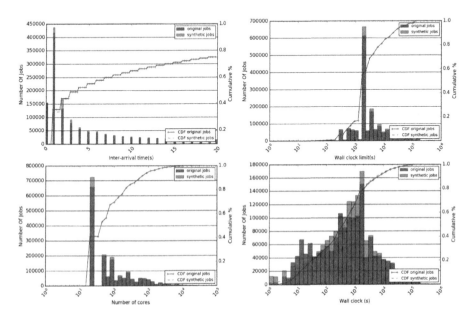

Fig. 7. Job characteristics in a year of Edison's real workload (darker) vs. a year of synthetic workload (lighter). Distributions are similar.

Job Generation: The workload generator produces synthetic workloads according to an experiment definition. The system model is chosen among those produced by the workload model engine (Sect. 3.1). Also, the random generator is initialized with the experiment definition's seed. The system model selected in the definition is combined with a random number generator to produce synthetic batch jobs. Finally, the workload generator also supports the inclusion of workflows according to the experiment definition (Sect. 3.2).

The workload generator fidelity is evaluated by modeling NERSC's Edison and comparing one year of synthetic workload with the system jobs in 2015. The characteristics of both workloads are presented in Fig. 7, where the histogram and Cumulative distribution functions (CDFs) for inter arrival time, wall clock limit and allocated number of cores are almost identical. For runtime, there are small differences in the histogram that barely impact the CDF.

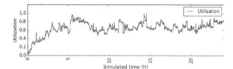

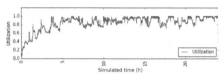

Fig. 8. No Job pressure mechanism, No Fill: Low utilization due not enough work.

Fig. 9. Job pressure 1.0, No Fill: Low utilization due to no initial filling jobs.

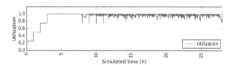

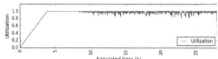

Fig. 10. Job pressure 1.0, Fill with large jobs: initial falling spikes.

Fig. 11. Job pressure 1.0, Fill with small jobs: Good utilization, more stable start.

Fill and Load Mechanisms: Users of HPC systems submit a job load that fills the systems and creates a backlog of jobs that induces an overall wait time. The fill and load mechanisms steer the job generation to reproduce this phenomenon.

The **load mechanism** ensures that the size of the backlog of jobs does not change significantly. It induces a job pressure (submitted over produced work) close to a configured value, usually 1.0. Every time a new job is added to the workload, the load mechanism calculates the current job pressure t as $P(t) = \frac{coreHoursSubmitted}{coreHoursProduced(t)}$ where $coreHoursProduced = t * coresInTheSystem$. If $P(t) < 1.0$ new jobs are generated and also inserted in the same submit time until $P(t) \geq 1.0$. If $P(t) \geq 1.1$, the submit time is maintained as reference, but the job is discarded, to avoid overflowing the system. The effect of the load mechanism is observed in Fig. 9, where the utilization raises to values close to one for the same workload parameters as in Fig. 8.

Increasing the job pressure raises system utilization but does not induce the backlog of jobs and associated overall wait time that is present in real systems. As an example, Fig. 12a presents the median wait time of the jobs submitted in every minute of the experiment using the load mechanism of Fig. 9. Here, the system is utilized but the job wait time is very short, only increasing to values of 15 min for larger jobs (over 96 core hours) at the end of the stabilization period (versus the four hours intended).

The **fill mechanism** inserts an initial job backlog equivalent to the experiment configured overall wait time. The job filling approach guarantees that they will not end at the same time or allocate too many cores. As a consequence, the scheduler is able to fill gaps left when they end. Figure 10 shows an experiment in which the fill job allocations are too big, their allocation is 33,516 cores (1/4 of the system CPU cores count). Every time a fill job ends ($t = 8, 9, 10$, and 11 h), a drop in the utilization is observed because the scheduler has to fill a large gap

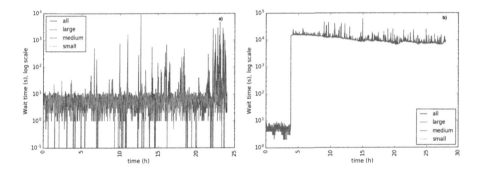

Fig. 12. Median wait time of job's submitted in each minute. a: Job pressure 1.0, not fill mechanism, and thus no wait time baseline is present. b: Job pressure 1.0, fill mechanism configured to induce four hours of wait time baseline.

with multiple small jobs. To avoid this, the filling mechanism calculates a fill job size that induces the desired overall wait time while not producing utilization drops. Fill job size calculation is based on a fixed inter-arrival time, the capacity of the system, and the desired wait time. Figure 11 shows the utilization of a workload where fill jobs are calculated following such a method. They are sub-mitted in 10 s intervals creating the soft slope in the figure. Figure 12b shows the wait time evolution for the same workload, sustained around four hours after the fill jobs are submitted.

Customization: The workload generator includes classes to define user job submission patterns. Trigger classes define mechanisms to decide the insertion times pattern, such as: periodic, alarm (at one or multiple time stamps), re-programmable alarm), or random. The job pattern is set as a fixed jobs sequence, or a weighted random selection between patterns. Once a generator is integrated it is selected by setting a special string in the workflow_policy field of the exper-iment definition.

3.5   Slurm and the Simulator

ScSF uses Slurm version 14.3.8. as the scheduler of the framework. Also, as a real scheduler, it includes the effect and interaction of mechanisms such as priority engines, scheduling algorithms, node placement algorithms, compute nodes management, job submissions system, and scheduling accounting. Finally, Slurm includes a simulator to use it on top of an emulated version of an HPC system, submitting a trace of jobs to it, and accelerating its execution. This tool enables experimentation without requiring the use of a real HPC system.

The architecture of Slurm and its simulator is presented in Fig. 13. The Slurm daemons (slurmctld and slurmd) are wrapped by the emulator. Both daemons are dynamically linked with the sim_func library that adds the required functions to

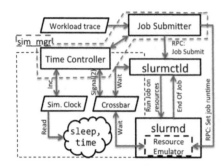
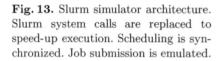

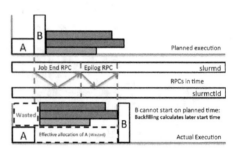

Fig. 13. Slurm simulator architecture. Slurm system calls are replaced to speed-up execution. Scheduling is synchronized. Job submission is emulated.

Fig. 14. Simulated time running during RPC communications delay resource deallocation compromising backfilling's job planning and Job B start.

support the acceleration of Slurm's execution. Also, slurmd is compiled including a resource and job emulator. On the simulator side, the sim_mgr controls the three core functions of the system: execution time acceleration, synchronization of the scheduling processes, and emulation of the job submission. These functions are described below.

Time acceleration: In order to accelerate the execution time, the simulator decouples the Slurm binaries from the real system time. Slurm binaries are dynamically linked with the *sim_func* library, replacing the *time*, *sleep*, and *wait* system calls. Replaced system calls use an epoch value controlled by the *time controller*. For example, if the time controller sets the simulated time to 1485551988, any calls to *time* will return 1485551988 regardless of the system time. This reduces the wait times within Slurm i.e., if the scheduling is configured to run once every 30 simulated second, it may run once every 300 ms in "real" time.

Scheduling and simulation synchronization: The original simulated time pace set by CSCS produces small speed ups for large simulated systems. However, increasing the simulated time pace triggers timing problems because of the Remote Procedure Calls (RPC) in Slurm daemon communications.

Increasing the simulation pace has different negative effects. First, timeouts occur triggering multiple RPC re-transmissions degrading the performance of Slurm and the simulator. Second, job timing determinism degrades. Each time a job ends, slurmd sends an RPC notification to slurmctld, and its arrival time is considered the job end time. This time is imprecise if the simulated time increases during the RPC notification propagation. As a consequence, low utilization and large job (e.g. allocating 30% of the resources) starvation occurs. Figure 14 details this effect - a large Job_B is to be executed after Job_A. However, Job_A resources are not considered free until two sequential RPC calls are completed (end of job and epilogue), lowering the utilization as they are not producing work. The later resource release also disables Job_B from starting but does not stop the jobs that programmed are to start after Job_B. As the process repeats, the utilization loss accumulates and Job_B is delayed indefinitely.

The *time_controller* component of the sim_mgr was modified to control a synchronization crossbar among the Slurm functions that are relevant to the scheduling timing. This solves the described synchronization problems by controlling the simulation time and avoiding its increase while RPC calls are traveling between the Slurm daemons.

Job submission and simulation: The job submission component of the sim_mgr emulates the submission of jobs to slurmctld following the workload trace of the simulation. Before submitting each job, it communicates the actual runtime (different from the requested one) to the resource emulator in slurmd.

The daemon, slurmctld, notifies slurmd of the scheduling of a job. The emulator uses the notification arrival time and job runtime (received from sim_mgr) to calculate the job end time. When the job end time is reached, the emulator forces slurmd to communicate that the job has ended to slurmctld. This process emulates the job execution and resource allocation.

3.6   Workload Analyzer

ScSF includes analysis tools to extract relevant information across repetitions of the same experiment or to plot and compare results from multiple experimental conditions.

Value Extraction and Analysis: Simulation results are processed by the workload analyzer. The jobs in the fill, stabilization, and drain phases (Fig. 6) are discarded to extract (1) for all jobs: wait time, runtime, requested runtime, user accuracy (estimating the runtime), allocated CPU cores, turnaround time, and slowdown grouped by jobs sizes. (2) for all and by type of workflow: wait time, runtime, turnaround time, and stretch factor. (3) overall: median job wait time and mean utilization for each minute of the experiment.

The module performs different analyses for different data types. Percentile and histograms analyze the distribution and trend of the jobs' and workflows' variables. Integrated utilization (i.e., coreHoursProduced/coreHoursExecuted) measures the impact of the scheduling behavior on the system usage.

Finally, customized analysis modules can be added to the analysis pipeline.

Repetitions and Comparisons: Experiments are repeated with different random seeds to ensure that observed phenomena are not isolated occurrences. The workload analysis module analyzes all the repetitions together, merging the results to ease later analysis. Also, experiments might be grouped if they differ only in one experimental condition. The analysis module studies these groups together to analyze the effect of that experimental condition on the system.

For instance, some experiments are identical except for the workflow submission method, which affects the number of workflows that get executed in each experiment. The module calculates compared workflow turnaround times correcting any possible results skew derived from the difference in the number of executed workflows.

Result Analysis and Plotting: Analysis results are stored in the database to allow review of visualization using the *plotter* component. This component includes tools to plot histograms (Fig. 7), box plots, and bar charts on the median of job's and workflow's variables for one or multiple experiments (Fig. 17). It also includes tools to plot the per minute utilization (Figs. 8, 9, 10 and 11) and per minute median job wait time in an experiment (Figs. 12a and b), which allows us to observe dynamic effects within the simulation. Finally, it also include tools to extract and compare utilization values from multiple experiments.

4   ScSF Case Study

In this section, we describe a case study that demonstrates the use of ScSF. The case study implements and evaluates a workflow-aware scheduling algorithm [17]. In particular, we model a real HPC system, and implement a new algorithm in the Slurm simulator. Also, we detail a distributed deployment of ScSF for our evaluation and present examples of the results to illustrate the scalability of the ScSF framework.

4.1   Tuning the Model

Experiments to evaluate a scheduling algorithm require workload and system models that are representative. NERSC's Edison is chosen as the reference system. Its workload is modeled by processing almost four years of its jobs. In ScSF, a Slurm configuration is defined to imitate Edison's scheduler behavior, including - Edison's resource definition (number of nodes and hardware configuration) FCFS, backfilling with a depth of 50 jobs once every 30s, and a multi-factor priority model that takes into account age (older-higher) and job geometry (smaller-higher). The workload tuning is completed by running a set of experiments to explore different job pressure and filling configurations to induce a stable four hour wait time baseline (observed in Edison).

4.2   Implementing a Workflow Scheduling Algorithm in Slurm

As presented in Sect. 3.2, workflows are run as pilot jobs (i.e., single job over-allocation resources) or chained jobs (i.e., task jobs linked by dependencies supporting long turnaround times). However, the workflow-aware scheduling [17] is a third method that enables per job task resource allocation, while minimizing the intermediate wait times.

The algorithm integration required us to modify Slurm's jobs submission system, and include some actions on the job queue before and after scheduling happens. First, sbatch, Slurm's job submission RPC, and the internal job_record data structure are extended to support the inclusion workflow manifests in jobs. This enables workflow-aware jobs to be present as pilot jobs attaching a workflow description (manifest).

Second, queue transformation actions are inserted before and after FCFS and backfilling act on it. Before they act, workflow jobs are transformed into task jobs but keeping the original job priority. When the scheduling is completed, original workflow jobs are restored. As a consequence, workflow task jobs are scheduled individually, but, as they share the same priority, the workflow intermediate wait times are minimized.

4.3   Experiment Setup

The workflow-aware scheduling approach is evaluated by comparing its effect on workflow turnaround time and system utilization with the pilot and chained job ones. Three versions (one per approach) of experiments are created to compare the performance of the three approaches under different conditions.

Table 2 shows the three sets the experiments created. Workflows in *set0*, exhibit different structures to study their interaction with different approaches. *Set1* studies the effect of the approaches on isolated workflows and includes four real (Montage, Sipht, Cybershake, FloodPlain [4]) and two synthetic workflows submitted with different intervals (0, 1/12h, 1/6h, 1/h, 2/h, 6/h). *Set2* studies the effect of the approaches on systems increasing dominated by workflows. It includes the same workflows as *set1* submitted with different workflow shares (1%, 5%, 10%, 25%, 50%, 75%, 100%). In total, they sum 1728 experiments equivalent to 33 years of simulated time.

Experiments are created and stored using a Python class that is initialized with all the experiment parameters. The manifest files for the synthetic workflows are created manually following the framework's manifest JSON format. Real workflow manifests are created using a workflow generator from the Pegasus project [4] that captures the characteristics of science workflows. ScSF includes a tool to transform the output of the workflow generator into the expected JSON format.

Table 2. Summary of experiments run in ScSF.

Set	Wf. Submit	#Wfs.	Wf. Pres.	#Pres.	Sim. t.	#Reps	#Exps	Agg. Sim. t.
Set0	aware/single/multi	18	Period	1 per wf.	7d	6	324	2268d
Set1	aware/single/multi	6	Period	6	7d	6	648	4536d
Set2	aware/single/multi	6	Share	7	7d	6	756	5292d

4.4   Running Experiments at Scale

We run 1728 individual experiments that sum 33 years of simulated time. Estimating an average speedup of 10×, experiment simulation would require more than three years of real time. In order to reduce the real time required to complete this work, simulation are parallelized to increase throughput.

As presented in Sect. 3, the minimum experiment worker unit is composed by an instance of the *experiment runner* component and a VM containing the Slurm simulator. As shown in Fig. 15, parallelization is achieved by running multiple worker units concurrently. To configure the infrastructure, Virtualbox's hypervisor is deployed on six compute nodes at the Lawrence Berkeley National Lab (LBNL) and 17 compute nodes at Umeå University (UMU). 161 Slurm Simulator VMs are deployed across the two sites. Each VM allocates two cores, four GB of RAM, and 20 GB of storage. Each compute node has different configurations and thus, the number of VMs per host and their performance is not uniform, e.g., some compute nodes only host two VMs, and some host 15.

All the experiment runners run in a single compute node at LBNL (Ubuntu, 12 cores × 2.8 GHz, 36 GB RAM). However, VMs are not exposed directly through their host NIC and required access from the control node over *sshuttle* [3], a VPN over ssh software that does not required installation on the destination host. Even if both sites are distant, the network is not a significant source of problem since the connection between UMU and LBNL traverses two high performance research networks, Nordunet (Sweden) and ESnet (EU and USA). Latency is relatively low (170–200 ms), data-rate is high (firewall capped ≈100 Mbits/s per TCP flow), and stability consistent.

4.5   Experiment Performance

The experiments wall clock time is characterized as a function of the experiment setup to understand the factors driving simulation speed-up. Figure 16 shows the experiments median runtime of one experiment set, grouped by scheduling method, workflow type, and workflow presence.

For the same simulated time, simulations run longer under the chained job and workflow-aware approaches compared to pilot job. Also, for the chained

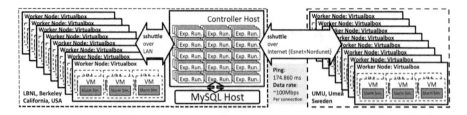

Fig. 15. Schema of the distributed execution environment: VMs containing the Slurm Simulator are distributed in hosts at LBNL and UMU. Each VM is controlled by an instance of the experiment runner in the controller host at LBNL.

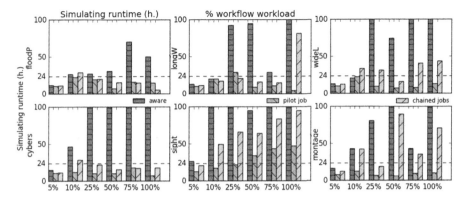

Fig. 16. Median wall clock time for a set of simulation. More complex workloads (more workflows, large workflows) present longer times. Pilot job approach presents shorter times. Simulation time is 168 h (7 days).

job and aware approaches, experiments run longer time if more workflows are present, or the workflows include more task jobs. As individual experiments are analyzed, longer runtimes, and thus smaller speed-ups, appear to be related to longer runtime of the scheduling passes because of higher numbers of jobs in the waiting queue.

In summary, simulations containing numbers of jobs similar to real system workloads present median runtimes between 10 to 12 h for 7 days (168 h) of simulated time, or 15× speedup. Speed-up degrades as experiments become more complex. Speed-ups under 1 are observed for experiments whose large job count would be hard to manage for a production scheduler (e.g., Montage-75%). The limiting factor of the simulations speed-up is the scheduling runtime, which, in this case study, depends on the number of jobs in the waiting queue.

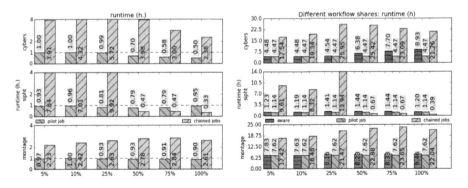

Fig. 17. Comparison of median workflow runtime on different experimental conditions as speed-up (left), and absolute numbers (right). Data of workflows in 108 experiments.

4.6   Analyzing at Scale

The analysis of the presented use case required synthesis of the results of 1278 experiments into meaningful, understandable metrics. The tools described in Sect. 3.6 supported this task.

As an example, Fig. 17 condenses the results of 324 experiments (six repetitions per experiment setting): median workflow runtime speed up (left) and value (right) observed for Cybershake, Sipht, and Montage, for different workflow shares and scheduling approaches. Results show that chained job workflows support much longer runtime in all cases, while aware and pilot jobs workflows show shorter (than chained job workflows) but similar runtimes to each other.

5   Discussion

The initial design goal of ScSF was functionality, not scale, and its first deployment included four worker VMs. As the number experiments and simulation time expanded for our case study (33 years), the resource pool size had to be increased (161 VMs and 24 physical hosts), even expanding to resources in distributed locations.

Loss-less experiment restart is needed: As the framework runs longer and on more nodes, the probability for node reboots becomes higher. In the months of experiments our resources required rebooting due to power cuts, hypervisor failures, VM freezes, and system updates (e.g. we had to update the whole cluster to patch the Dirty Cow exploit [1]).

Our goal in ScSF has been to keep the design light-weight and easily portable. Thus, rebooting a worker host means that work in the VMs are lost. Also, if the controller host is rebooted, all the experiment runners are stopped and the work in the entire cluster is lost. For some of the longest experiments, the amount of work lost accounts in days of real time. In the future, we need to consider the trade-offs and ScSF should include support graceful pause and restart so resource reboots do not imply loss of work. This would be provided by a control mechanism to pause-restart worker VMs. Also, the experiment runner functionality should be hosted in the worker VM to be paused with the VM, unaffected by any reboot.

Loaded systems network fail: In our experiments, surges of experiment failures appeared occasionally. Multiple VMs would become temporarily unresponsive to ssh connections when their hypervisor was heavily loaded. Subsequently, the experiment runner would fail to connect to the VM, and the experiment was considered failed. Thus, saturated resources are unreliable. All runner-VM communications were hardened, adding re-trials, which reduced the failure rate significantly.

Monitoring is important: Many types of failures impact experiments, such as simulator or Slurm bugs, communication problems, resource saturation in the VMs, or hypervisor configuration issues. Failures are expected, but early version of ScSF lacked the tools and information to quickly diagnose the cause of the problems. Monitoring should register metadata that allows quick diagnosis of problems. As a consequence, the logging levels were increased and a mechanism to retrieve Slurm crash debug files was added.

The system is as weak as its weakest link: All ScSF's data and metadata are stored in a MySQL database hosted in the controller host. In a first experiment run, at 80% of completed experiments the hard disk containing the database crashed, and all experiment data was lost that included two months of work. Currently, data is subject to periodic backups and the database is replicated.

6   Conclusions

We present ScSF, a scheduling simulation framework which provides tools to support all the steps of the scheduling research cycle - modeling, generation, simulation, and result analysis. ScSF is scalable, it is deployed over distributed resources to run and manage multiple concurrent simulations and provides tools to synthesize results over large experiment sets. The framework produces representative results by relying on Slurm, which captures the behavior of real system schedulers. ScSF is also modular and might be extended by the community to generate customized workloads or calculate new analyses metrics over the results. Finally, we improved the Slurm simulator which now achieves up to 15× simulation over real time speed-ups while preserving its determinism and experiment repeatability.

This work provides a foundation for future scheduling research. ScSF will be released as open source, enabling scheduling scientists to concentrate their effort on designing scheduling techniques and evaluating them in the framework. Also, we share our experience of using ScSF to design a workflow scheduling algorithm and evaluating it through the simulation of a large experiment set. Our case study demonstrates that the framework is capable of simulating 33 years of real system time in less than two months over a distributed infrastructure.

Acknowledgments. This material is based upon work supported by the U.S. Department of Energy, Office of Science, Office of Advanced Scientific Computing Research (ASCR) and uses resources at the National Energy Research Scientific Computing Center, a DOE Office of Science User Facility, supported by the Office of Science of the U.S. Department of Energy, both under Contract No. DE-AC02-05CH11231. Financial support has been provided in part by the Swedish Government's strategic effort eSSENCE and the Swedish Research Council (VR) under contract number C0590801 (Cloud Control). Special thanks to Stephen Trofinoff and Massimo Benini from the Swiss National Supercomputing Centre, who shared with us the code base of their Slurm Simulator. Also, we would like to thank the members of the DST department at LBNL and the distributed systems group at Umeå University who administrated and provided the compute nodes supporting our case study.

References

1. Dirty cow, January 2017. https://dirtycow.ninja/
2. SchedMD, January 2017. https://www.schedmd.com/
3. shuttle, January 2017. https://github.com/apenwarr/sshuttle
4. Workflowgenerator, January 2017. https://confluence.pegasus.isi.edu/display/pegasus/WorkflowGenerator
5. Declerck, T.M., Sakrejda, I.: External Torque/Moab on an XC30 and fairshare. Technical report, NERSC, Lawrence Berkeley National Lab (2013)
6. Feitelson, D.G.: Parallel workloads archive 71(86), 337–360 (2007). http://www.cs.huji.ac.il/labs/parallel/workload
7. Feitelson, D.G.: Workload Modeling for Computer Systems Performance Evaluation. Cambridge University Press, Cambridge (2015)
8. Feitelson, D.G., Tsafrir, D.: Workload sanitation for performance evaluation. In: 2006 IEEE International Symposium on Performance Analysis of Systems and Software, pp. 221–230. IEEE (2006)
9. IBM: Platform computing - lsf, January 2014. http://www-03.ibm.com/systems/technicalcomputing/platformcomputing/products/lsf/sessionscheduler.html
10. Jackson, D., Snell, Q., Clement, M.: Core algorithms of the Maui scheduler. In: Feitelson, D.G., Rudolph, L. (eds.) JSSPP 2001. LNCS, vol. 2221, pp. 87–102. Springer, Heidelberg (2001). https://doi.org/10.1007/3-540-45540-X_6
11. Kannan, S., Mayes, P., Roberts, M., Brelsford, D., Skovira, J.: Workload Management with LoadLeveler. IBM Corporation, Poughkeepsie (2001)
12. Klusáček, D., Rudová, H.: Alea 2 - job scheduling simulator. In: Proceedings of the 3rd International ICST Conference on Simulation Tools and Techniques (SIMU-Tools 2010). ICST (2010)
13. Lublin, U., Feitelson, D.G.: The workload on parallel supercomputers: modeling the characteristics of rigid jobs. J. Parallel Distrib. Comput. **63**(11), 1105–1122 (2003)
14. Lucero, A.: Simulation of batch scheduling using real production-ready software tools. In: Proceedings of the 5th IBERGRID (2011)
15. Rodrigo, G., Östberg, P.O., Elmroth, E., Antypass, K., Gerber, R., Ramakrishnan, L.: HPC system lifetime story: workload characterization and evolutionary analyses on NERSC systems. In: The 24th International ACM Symposium on High-Performance Distributed Computing (HPDC) (2015)
16. Rodrigo, G., Östberg, P.O., Elmroth, E., Antypas, K., Gerber, R., Ramakrishnan, L.: Towards understanding job heterogeneity in HPC: a NERSC case study. In: 2016 16th IEEE/ACM International Symposium on Cluster, Cloud and Grid Computing (CCGrid), pp. 521–526. IEEE (2016)
17. Rodrigo, G.P., Elmroth, E., Östberg, P.O., Ramakrishnan, L.: Enabling workflow-aware scheduling on HPC systems. In: Proceedings of the 26th International Symposium on High-Performance Parallel and Distributed Computing, pp. 3–14. ACM (2017)
18. Schwiegelshohn, U.: How to design a job scheduling algorithm. In: Cirne, W., Desai, N. (eds.) JSSPP 2014. LNCS, vol. 8828, pp. 147–167. Springer, Cham (2015). https://doi.org/10.1007/978-3-319-15789-4_9
19. Stephen Trofinoff, M.B.: Using and modifying the BSC Slurm workload simulator. In: Slurm User Group (2015)

20. Yoo, A.B., Jette, M.A., Grondona, M.: SLURM: simple Linux utility for resource management. In: Feitelson, D., Rudolph, L., Schwiegelshohn, U. (eds.) JSSPP 2003. LNCS, vol. 2862, pp. 44–60. Springer, Heidelberg (2003). https://doi.org/10.1007/10968987_3
21. Zakay, N., Feitelson, D.G.: Preserving user behavior characteristics in trace-based simulation of parallel job scheduling. In: IEEE 22nd International Symposium on Modelling, Analysis & Simulation of Computer and Telecommunication Systems (MASCOTS), pp. 51–60. IEEE (2014)

DJSB: Dynamic Job Scheduling Benchmark

Victor Lopez[1(✉)], Ana Jokanovic[1(✉)], Marco D'Amico[1(✉)], Marta Garcia[1(✉)], Raul Sirvent[1(✉)], and Julita Corbalan[2(✉)]

[1] Barcelona Supercomputing Center, Barcelona, Spain
{victor.lopez,ana.jokanovic,marco.damico,
marta.garcia,raul.sirvent}@bsc.es
[2] Universitat Politecnica de Catalunya, Barcelona, Spain
julita.corbalan@bsc.es

Abstract. High-performance computing (HPC) systems are very big and powerful systems, with the main goal of achieving maximum performance of parallel jobs. Many dynamic factors influence the performance which makes this goal a non-trivial task. According to our knowledge, there is no standard tool to automatize performance evaluation through comparing different configurations and helping system administrators to select the best scheduling policy or the best job scheduler. This paper presents the Dynamic Job Scheduler Benchmark (DJSB). It is a configurable tool that compares performance metrics for different scenarios. DJSB receives a workload description and some general arguments such as job submission commands and generates performance metrics and performance plots. To test and present DJSB, we have compared three different scenarios with dynamic resource management strategies using DJSB experiment-driven tool. Results show that just changing some DJSB arguments we can set up and execute quite different experiments, making easy the comparison. In this particular case, a cooperative-dynamic resource management is evaluated compared with other resource management approaches.

Keywords: Dynamic resource management · Job scheduling
Benchmark · Performance evaluation

1 Introduction and Motivation

HPC systems are big systems with very powerful computational and communication capacities, specially designed for parallel applications with high requirements in terms of computation and inter-process communication. This specific hardware makes HPC systems very expensive and complex, resulting in the necessity of expert software systems, i.e., *job schedulers* to deal with the job scheduling and resource allocation. Additionally, system administrators configure and control system behaviour. An example of job schedulers used in the top five HPC systems are SLURM [20], PBS [14], or Cobalt [9].

© Springer International Publishing AG, part of Springer Nature 2018
D. Klusáček et al. (Eds.): JSSPP 2017, LNCS 10773, pp. 174–188, 2018.
https://doi.org/10.1007/978-3-319-77398-8_10

The complexity of HPC systems has grown with their size, as well as with the jobs complexity. They are composed of nodes with many cores and GPUs. The resources are shared among jobs at different levels: memory, network, etc. being hierarchically organized. As a consequence, parallel jobs have also evolved to hybrid programming models to fit this configuration. Most of the jobs executed in these systems are programmed in pure MPI [4], OpenMP [8] or OmpSs [6], or hybrid models such as MPI+OmpSS.

Job schedulers allow system administrators to configure the machine with different partitions, policies, policy arguments, etc. Users can also configure their job submissions with as many requirements and details as needed for a *"perfect"* job execution. Job schedulers try to execute jobs as soon as possible based on the job requirements, priorities (e.g., arrival order), and resource availability. If resource requirements are very specific to improve execution time, that may increase wait time, resulting in a poor global performance, i.e., slowdown. If job requirements are flexible, jobs can start before but their execution time can suffer variations because of sharing of resources such as network bandwidth, for example.

Traditional approach in HPC systems is to statically allocate resources to jobs once they are started, i.e., they are not preempted and they own these resources until the end of their execution. This approach simplifies job management but reduces potential performance improvements that can be achieved with dynamic approaches. The deployment and evaluation of dynamic job scheduling strategies is complicated and it is a normal approach for system administrators when upgrading their systems, or starting new HPC centers, to select well known static approaches rather than evaluating different dynamic strategies and selecting the one with best performance. This evaluation must be based on center characteristics and specific workload.

The aim of this paper is to present the Dynamic Job Scheduler Benchmark (DJSB). DJSB is a tool that evaluates how fast and efficiently a full loaded system accommodate new resources requests, by submitting jobs that execute real or synthetic applications in a real HPC environment. We will refer to this ability as the "dynamicity" of an HPC system.

DJSB can be configured to deal with different job schedulers, as well as, interactive sessions that do not use job schedulers, different job submission frequencies and different application arguments such as number of tasks. Early prototype of the benchmark has already proven its usefulness and has been used by other research groups [7].

DJSB actual workload is based on a use case defined as a reference case in the Human Brain Project [2]. The use case consists in a situation where there is a big and long running job using all the resources, typically a scientific simulation, and a new, small and short job that arrives to the system requesting a percentage of these resources during a short period of time. In this use case, the second job does a partial analysis of results reported by the scientific simulation. Therefore, we will refer to the long running job as the "simulation" and to the new job as the "analytics".

To illustrate the potential of DJSB, we have performed three different sets of experiments, each one including many variations concerning system size, application size, number of applications, memory requirements, etc. We have compared a stop&continue approach with oversubscription and a cooperative-dynamic resource management.

To evaluate the benefits of such a dynamic environment we will present traditional performance metric slowdown but also a new synthesized metric that combines slowdown of both jobs and tries to summarize in a single value the *dynamicity* of a system. This metric is presented in Sects. 2 and 4.

The rest of the paper is organized as follows: Sect. 2 describes DJSB tool, experimental setup and the metrics reported. Section 3 describes our dynamic resource management execution environment. Section 4 presents evaluation results comparing among the different scenarios. Section 5 presents related work, from the point of view of benchmarks and dynamic scheduling evaluation. Finally, Sect. 6 presents conclusions and future work.

2   DJSB: Dynamic Job Scheduler Benchmark

The purpose of the dynamic scheduling benchmark is to do an automatic performance comparison of different solutions on pilot systems. It provides a synthetic model of a hypothetic interactive session workload. DJSB is implemented as a Python (configurable) script that drives application execution, monitoring, metric collection and generation of performance metrics and graphs. The benchmark is distributed under Free BSD license.

Some mock-up parallel applications are provided to represent two types of applications: a single long running simulation and a potential in situ analysis. The benchmark will measure the impact of one application on the other and the decrease of their performances. The focus will be on the ability to support dynamic scheduling policies, so I/O will be minimal.

DJSB behaviour is configured based on several configurable parts:

- **General options.** This component defines the global DJSB experiment. It includes arguments such as the number of samples of applications.
- **Job submission options.** DJSB can be executed in systems with different queueing systems. The basic job submission and monitoring commands can be specified.
- **Application options.** Specific details for the long running simulation and the analytics can be specified such as execution time or memory consumption.

DJSB assumes applications are previously compiled. Once it starts, it computes reference metrics, that is, execution time of each application when running alone based on Application options. This is the *reference stage*. Once references are available, it starts the job submission based on Job submission options and General options. This *execution stage* includes the re-execution of the experiment several times to provide statistically significant measurements. Once execution stage finishes, a performance metrics file is generated together with the plots to make easy performance evaluation.

2.1   General Options

Some of the most relevant general options are:

- **num_of_samples** Number of samples or repetitions. One repetition implies one execution of the whole benchmark (simulation + analysis).
- **sleep_min_time, sleep_max_time** Minimum/Maximum sleep time between each analysis in the execution stage sample.
- **num_of_ref_analysis** Number of total analytics to be executed per sample of the reference stage.
- **num_of_dyn_analysis** Number of total analytics to be executed per sample of the execution stage.

2.2   Job Submission Options

DJSB uses a job (Python) module where an API to deal with job submission and monitoring is specified. This API supports jobs executed in an interactive session, or submitted in a previously created reservation, together with the interaction with job schedulers such as SLURM or LSF [21]. Commands to be implemented in the job module are the next one (a job module template is provided):

- **get_submit_command(self)**: The method must return the shell command to submit a job. The command can be complemented by the class attributes from the constructor, such as the total number of tasks, etc.
- **get_poll_completion_command(self, submit_stdout, submit_stderr)**: The benchmark needs to poll the system until the job completion occurs. This command returns a shell command to test the condition.
- **get_{suspend, resume}_command**: To be executed when suspending or resuming a job.

2.3   Application Options

DJSB is developed to support different applications but the results presented in this paper are based on different configurations of the STREAM benchmark since it was a requirement of the Human Brain Project [2] in its previous stage.

- **A single, long running, simulation job.** The preferred mock-up application will be based on a version of the STREAM benchmark written in Fortran/C [16]. Parallel versions using MPI only and MPI plus OpenMP (based on parallel loop) are provided. The STREAM benchmark is a simple synthetic benchmark program that measures sustainable memory bandwidth (in MB/s) and the corresponding computation rate for simple vector kernels.
- **Application analytics.** For analytics we use the same approach and application. We use a small version of STREAM executed periodically in the middle of the big STREAM and requesting part of the resources used by the big one.

Arguments to provide detailed application descriptions are:

- **total_tasks** Number of tasks (MPI processes) for the specific application.
- **cpus_per_task** Number of CPUs per task for the application. Also, number of OpenMP threads per MPI process.
- **same_nodes_as_sim** Only valid for the analysis application. If true, the analysis will be submitted in the same nodes as the simulation, as long as the job interface allows it.
- **total_memory** Total amount of memory to be used for the application.
- **exec_time** Estimated execution time of each instance of the application.
- **node_host_names** List of nodes where the application is allowed to run. The list is forwarded to the job module. If the list is empty, the job scheduler should decide the allocation (default option).
- **command** Path to the application binary.

2.4 Application Performance Metrics

During reference stage, DJSB collects reference execution time per application, both simulation and analytics. This reference time is computed as the average of the several executions performed at the reference stage. During the execution stage, traditional scheduling metrics are computed such as wait time, response time, or slowdown.

1. Wait time - the time elapsed between the job submission and the start of the job.
2. Execution time - the time elapsed between the start of the application and its completion.
3. Response time - the time elapsed between the job submission and the job completion (wait time + execution time).
4. Slowdown - the ratio between the response time when the application is executed in a workload, i.e., sharing resources with other applications, $T^{sharing}$, and the execution time of the application executed alone on the exclusive resources, T^{alone}_{REF}, that is collected in reference stage.

$$slowdown = \frac{T^{sharing}}{T^{alone}_{REF}} \tag{1}$$

Along with these metrics, DJSB computes *application weights*, which are equal to the resources the application was occupying during its execution multiplied by the execution time of the application. The benchmark calculates the weights for each application and for each scenario. The formulae for calculating the weights for each specific scenario are given in the Sect. 4 along with the description of the scenarios.

2.5   Workload Metrics

Based on individual application metrics, traditional workload metrics are provided such as average wait time, average slowdown and average response time, along with specific DJSB metric such as the *dynamicity*. The dynamicity will greatly depend on the system capability to manage and run different jobs at the same time. For calculating dynamicity, DJSB uses weighted geometric mean, suggested in various works [13,15,17] to be used for comparing among the systems when using relative values such as slowdown. The more capable the system is to accommodate the applications without high performance penalty, the dynamicity should be higher. Therefore, we use inverse weighted geometric mean of the applications slowdowns. For a use case workload, consisting of a simulation and an analytics, calculating the dynamicity of a specific system, i.e., scenario reduces to calculating the formula 2. The weights w_s and w_a are for simulation and analytics, respectively, and are calculated for each scenario differently. The $slowdown_s$ and $slowdown_a$ are the slowdowns of simulation and analytics, respectively. Thus, we will get a dynamicity value for each scenario, which allows us to compare different scenarios.

$$dynamicity = e^{-\frac{w_s \cdot \ln slowdown_s + w_a \cdot \ln slowdown_a}{w_s + w_a}} \qquad (2)$$

3   Cooperative Dynamic Resource Management

Dynamic scheduling has been a research topic for many years. In this section we describe the execution environment used in this work, as well as, dynamic resource management scenario that we will use in the experiments.

Figure 1 shows the main components of our execution environment. The main characteristic of our execution environment is that the job scheduler and the resource manager, in this case SLURM, cooperate with an additional runtime library, Dynamic Load Balancer (DLB), that helps the system to exploit malleability in an efficient way. One of the main components of DLB is Dynamic Resource Ownership Manager (DROM).

The execution environment is composed by the following software components:

- **Job scheduler i.e., SLURM controller.** SLURM is composed of two components, the SLURM controller and a SLURM daemon per node. The job scheduler is implemented by SLURM controller, it is in charge of job submissions. It receives job requirements and it decides *when* and *where* a job can be started based on its requirements, scheduling policy and system status.
- **Node manager, i.e., SLURM daemon extended with DLB-DROM component.** Each Node manager is aware of the number of jobs and processes being executed in the node. The Node manager provides resource management services offered by SLURM extended with DLB-DROM API for process ownership management. DLB ownership mechanism gives a possibility

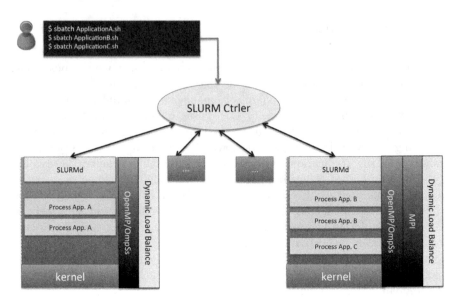

Fig. 1. Cooperative dynamic resource management

for a flexible resource allocation, where processing cores can be used by processes that do not own them during the cores' idle periods.

- **Programming model libraries, i.e., MPI/OpenMP/OmpSs.** These three programming models are transparently supported. Malleability is easily supported in OpenMP [8] and OmpSs [11]. Malleability has been also proposed for MPI in different contexts: Virtual malleability was proposed for MPI in [12,18] and it is also included MPI-3. However, even having these proposals, it is a normal practice to exploit the malleability by using a second level of parallelism and using OpenMP in it. DLB-DROM supports MPI+OpeMP/OmpSs or only OmpSs as indicated in Fig. 1.

Cooperative-dynamic resource management scenario in case of our simulation-analytics workload works as follows. When the analytics arrives to the system, the simulation resources are shrunk to accommodate the analytics on as much resources as it requests. The simulation resources are practically lent to analytics for some period of time. This dynamic redistribution of resources among simulation and analytics is done by our SLURM-DROM environment. As soon as analytics finishes its execution, the resources are returned to simulation, and the simulation is expanded, using all of its resources. The same scenario repeats when the new analytics arrives to the system. Section 4 presents the explained scenario along with the other evaluated scenarios and gives the graphical view in the Fig. 2.

4   Evaluation

4.1   Scenarios

Three different scenarios are used to evaluate the *dynamicity* of the system. Dynamicity is defined as the capacity to react to workload changes and reallocate resources to running jobs in order to minimize expected slowdown. Figure 2 shows these three scenarios.

– **Oversubscription.** This is a scenario where the simulation has been previously started by the scheduler and the analytics jobs are submitted to the same job reservation, thus positively reducing the wait time to zero, but sharing resources with the simulation. The sharing of resources is fully controlled

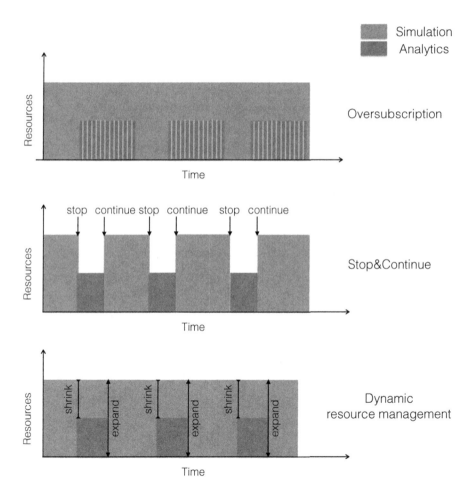

Fig. 2. Three scenarios: oversubscription, stop&continue, and dynamic resource management. A single execution of simulation is performed, while multiple instances of analytics are submitted to the same resources over time of simulation's execution.

by operating system. This is untypical scenario in HPC environment and it is enabled by configuring SLURM to force resource sharing. Typical scenario would be the one where each job waits in the queue until enough resources are available. Since analytics jobs need to be executed along with simulation, the typical scenario is not applicable in this use case.

- **Stop&Continue.** When the analytics job is submitted, the already running simulation job is stopped. The analytics job starts without waiting for resources. The old job remains in memory. This is not a problem in case the memory is not a critical resource. The overhead in this scenario comes from the time required to stop/resume processes and from the memory that may be overloaded. We have used SLURM's [20] suspend/resume mechanism for this scenario.
- **Cooperative-Dynamic Resource Management.** Scenario described in the previous section.

4.2 Configurations

Configuration parameters of DJSB benchmark are given in Table 1. Configuration parameters for simulation and analytics are given in Table 2.

Table 1. DJSB configuration parameters

Argument or module	Value
Number of samples	3
Number of simulation runs per sample	1
Number of analytics runs per sample (reference stage)	2
Number of analytics runs per sample (execution stage)	1, 2, 4, and 6

Table 2. Simulation and analytics configuration parameters

Argument	Simulation	Analytics
Duration	5 min	10 s
Job size	512 or 1024 CPUs	50% of simulation size
Tasks per node	4	2
Memory per task	1 GiB, 4 GiB and 5 GiB	50 MiB
OpenMP threads	4 per task	4 per task

4.3   Metrics

For evaluating the results we will use slowdown and dynamicity, already explained in the Sect. 2. Here we give the formulae for calculating weights for simulation and analytics for each of the scenarios. We use the following notation:

- N_{CPUS}^s - Number of CPUs used by simulation
- N_{CPUS}^a - Number of CPUs used by analytics
- $T_s^{scenario}$ - Execution time of simulation for a given scenario
- $T_a^{scenario}$ - Execution time of analytics for a given scenario
- n_a - Number of analytics runs during a single simulation execution

In case of Oversubscription scenario DJSB uses the following formulae:

$$w_s^{oversubs} = N_{CPUS}^s \cdot T_s^{oversubs} - \frac{1}{2} \cdot N_{CPUS}^a \cdot n_a \cdot T_a^{oversubs} \qquad (3)$$

$$w_a^{oversubs} = \frac{1}{2} \cdot N_{CPUS}^a \cdot T_a^{oversubs} \qquad (4)$$

In (3) and (4) the term $1/2$ means we assume CPU time is equally divided among simulation and analytics during oversubscription.

In case of Stop&Continue scenario DJSB uses the following formulae:

$$w_s^{stopcont} = N_{CPUS}^s \cdot (T_s^{stopcont} - n_a \cdot T_a^{stopcont}) \qquad (5)$$

$$w_a^{stopcont} = N_{CPUS}^a \cdot T_a^{stopcont} \qquad (6)$$

In case of Dynamic scenario DJSB uses the following formulae:

$$w_s^{dynamic} = N_{CPUS}^s \cdot T_s^{dynamic} - N_{CPUS}^a \cdot n_a \cdot T_a^{dynamic} \qquad (7)$$

$$w_a^{dynamic} = N_{CPUS}^a \cdot T_a^{dynamic} \qquad (8)$$

4.4   Results

In order to show the usefulness of DJSB, we have performed a set of real experiments on the local, MareNostrum supercomputer [3]. MareNostrum consists of 3098 computing nodes, with 16 processing cores per node. For our experiments we requested the computing nodes with 32 GB of main memory per node.

We have evaluated the impact of the following parameters on the performance of the simulation, the analytics and the system:

- The number of the analytics jobs
- Memory per task of simulation
- The size of the system

Figure 3(a) shows that slowdown of simulation increases as the number of analytics that it shares resources with increases. The least impact is in the case of dynamic scenario – at most 20% of performance loss. The highest impact on simulation's performance is in the case of oversubscription scenario, up to 20% worse than in the case of stop&continue, and up to 30% worse than in case of dynamic scenario. As Fig. 3(b) shows, the analytics job is the most impacted in the case of oversubscription up to 214%. It is the least impacted in the case of stop&continue scenario, as the simulation is stopped during its execution and the total request for memory per node by both applications is less than 15% of the total node memory. Dynamic scenario leads to up to 104% loss of analytics performance. We present analytics results for each of the experiments with different number of analytics (x-axis), but as expected, the analytics does not change performance depending on how much instances of analytics have been run. We present average of all the analytics run within a single experiment. Regarding the system dynamicity, Fig. 3(c) shows that as number of analytics increases in the workload in general the system is less capable to mange the load in an effective way. In particular, dynamicity in case of oversubscription goes as

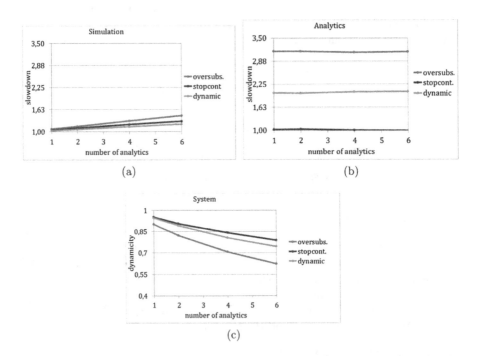

(a)

(b)

(c)

Fig. 3. Impact of number of analytics on: (a) slowdown of the simulation, (b) slowdown of the analytics, and (c) the dynamicity of the system. System size 1024 CPUs, i.e., 64 computing nodes. Total memory per node is 32 GB. Simulation job requests 1024 CPUs. Analytics job requests 50% of simulation size. Total memory per node requested by simulation is 4 GiB. Total memory per node requested by analytics is 100 MiB. Number of analytics per simulation run is indicated at x-axis.

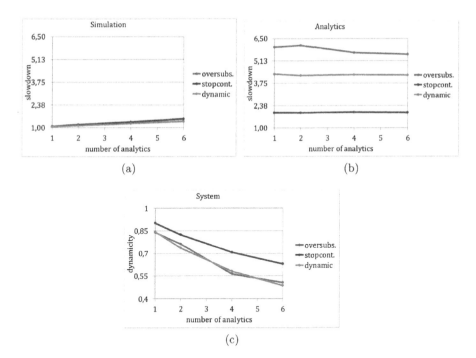

Fig. 4. Impact of number of analytics on: (a) slowdown of the simulation, (b) slowdown of the analytics, and (c) the dynamicity of the system. System size 1024 CPUs, i.e., 64 computing nodes. Total memory per node is 32 GB. Simulation job requests 1024 CPUs. Analytics job requests 50% of simulation size. Total memory per node requested by simulation is *16* GiB. Total memory per node requested by analytics is 100 MiB. Number of analytics per simulation run is indicated at x-axis.

low as 62%, the highest is in case of stop&continue – at least 79%, and in the case of dynamic, the dynamicity is at least 74%.

Further we configured the benchmark, i.e., the simulation options to request more memory. The total memory requested by simulation and analytics per node was more than 50% of total node memory. Figure 4 shows the same set of experiments in the case of higher memory demand. Regarding the slowdowns of the application, the simulation at most 20% more impacted when its demand for memory is higher, whereas, analytics suffers significant impact of almost a double performance loss comparing to the previous set of experiments. The dynamicity plot shows that the impact of increase in memory requirements by simulation makes system less capable to deal with the new coming applications. The dynamicity goes as low as 52%, 63% and 49%, for oversubscription, stop&continue and dynamic scenario, respectively. While dynamic scenario might be good for the system with computation-intensive applications, in case of dominantly memory-intensive applications, such as STREAM, the dynamic resource management does not bring better performance than oversubscription scenario.

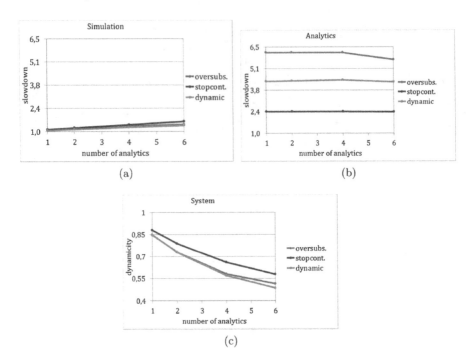

Fig. 5. Impact of number of analytics on: (a) slowdown of the simulation, (b) slowdown of the analytics, and (c) the dynamicity of the system. System size 512 CPUs, i.e., 32 computing nodes. Total memory per node is 32 GB. Simulation job requests 512 CPUs. Analytics job requests 50% of simulation size. Total memory per node requested by simulation is *16* GiB. Total memory per node requested by analytics is 100 MiB. Number of analytics per simulation run is indicated at x-axis.

Finally, we configured benchmark to test the smaller system size, i.e., 512 CPUS. Memory request is the same as in Fig. 4. The same set of experiments is performed in this case, as well. As we can see in the Fig. 5 with the change of system size, the behavior of the system with respect to slowdown of individual applications and dynamicity of the system remains the same.

5   Related Work

DJSB benchmark is a novel contribution in the literature, proposing a tool and new metrics for evaluating what we defined as the dynamicity of an HPC system.

Typical benchmarks tend to evaluate performance of a HPC systems by launching and measuring a set of applications' performance executed in isolation. Those performances are related to the application, that usually stresses only some component of the system, like processors, memory hierarchy and network. Some examples are the HPC Challenge Benchmark [1] or the benchmark used by Top500 [5], Linpack [10].

The ESP Benchmark [19] is an approach for evaluating HPC performance. It evaluates system utilization and effectiveness by executing a medium length workload of 82 jobs, that varies in type of applications and requested resources, from a small job to jobs that take all system resources. With this approach, ESP permits to measure the efficiency of the system evaluating scheduling, and the system utilization. Our approach, DJSB permits, not only running diverse applications, but configuring differently the same applications in terms of memory requirements, application size, duration, etc. It evaluates the impact of different dynamic resource management approaches on each application individually, as well as the overall dynamicity of the system.

6   Conclusions and Future Work

This paper presents DJSB, a tool targeted to evaluate HPC systems using different schedulers, applications characteristics and submission arguments. DJSB is an experiment-driven tool for HPC systems that, based on its configuration, executes a *reference stage* to collect reference performance metrics and later on executes the described workload. Workload description can be more or less specific, resulting in a fixed workload or something more variable. DJSB automatically collects performance metrics for applications and generates performance metric summaries and plots to make easy the comparison between scenarios. To illustrate the potential of DJSB, we have performed three different sets of experiments, each one including many variations concerning system size, application size, memory size, number of applications, etc. We have compared a stop&continue approach compared with oversubscription and a cooperative-dynamic resource management. Our experiments show that DJSB allows for an easy comparison of the systems that use different resource management approaches.

As future work, DJSB could be expanded to support other use cases, different from the scientific simulation and analysis scenario, for instance by accepting generic workloads.

Acknowledgments. This work is supported by the Spanish Government through Programa Severo Ochoa (SEV-2015-0493), by the Spanish Ministry of Science and Technology (project TIN2015-65316-P), by the Generalitat de Catalunya (grant 2014-SGR-1051), by the European Union's Horizon 2020 research and innovation program under grant agreement No. 720270 (HBP SGA1).

References

1. HPC Challenge Benchmark website. http://icl.cs.utk.edu/hpcc/
2. The Human Brain Project. https://www.humanbrainproject.eu/
3. MareNostrum   Supercomputer.   https://www.bsc.es/discover-bsc/the-centre/marenostrum
4. Message Passing Interface Forum. http://www.mpi-forum.org/

5. Top500 website. https://www.top500.org/
6. Barcelona Supercomputing Center: The OmpSs Programming Model. https://pm.bsc.es/ompss
7. Clauss, C., Moschny, T., Eicker, N.: Dynamic process management with allocation-internal co-scheduling towards interactive supercomputing. In: Proceedings of the 1st Workshop Co-Scheduling of HPC Applications, January 2016
8. Dagum, L., Enon, R.: OpenMP: an industry standard API for shared-memory programming. IEEE Comput. Sci. Eng. **5**(1), 46–55 (1998)
9. Desai, N.: Cobalt: an open source platform for HPC system software research. In: Edinburgh BG/L System Software Workshop (2005)
10. Dongarra, J.J., Luszczek, P., Petitet, A.: The LINPACK benchmark: past, present and future. Concurr. Comput. Pract. Exp. **15**(9), 803–820 (2003)
11. Duran, A., Ayguadé, E., Badia, R.M., Labarta, J., Martinell, L., Martorell, X., Planas, J.: OmpSs: a proposal for programming heterogeneous multi-core architectures. Parallel Process. Lett. **21**(02), 173–193 (2011)
12. El Maghraoui, K., Desell, T.J., Szymanski, B.K., Varela, C.A.: Malleable iterative MPI applications. Concurr. Comput. Pract. Exp. **21**(3), 393–413 (2009)
13. Fleming, P.J., Wallace, J.J.: How not to lie with statistics: the correct way to summarize benchmark results. Commun. ACM **29**(3), 218–221 (1986)
14. Henderson, R.L.: Job scheduling under the portable batch system. In: Feitelson, D.G., Rudolph, L. (eds.) JSSPP 1995. LNCS, vol. 949, pp. 279–294. Springer, Heidelberg (1995). https://doi.org/10.1007/3-540-60153-8_34
15. Hoefler, T., Belli, R.: Scientific benchmarking of parallel computing systems: twelve ways to tell the masses when reporting performance results. In: Proceedings of the International Conference for High Performance Computing, Networking, Storage and Analysis (2015)
16. McCalpin, J.D.: Memory bandwidth and machine balance in current high performance computers. In: IEEE Computer Society Technical Committee on Computer Architecture (TCCA) Newsletter, pp. 19–25, December 1995
17. Smith, J.E.: Characterizing computer performance with a single number. Commun. ACM **31**(3), 1202–1206 (1988)
18. Utrera, G., Tabik, S., Corbalan, J., Labarta, J.: A job scheduling approach for multi-core clusters based on virtual malleability. In: Kaklamanis, C., Papatheodorou, T., Spirakis, P.G. (eds.) Euro-Par 2012. LNCS, vol. 7484, pp. 191–203. Springer, Heidelberg (2012). https://doi.org/10.1007/978-3-642-32820-6_20
19. Wong, A.T., Oliker, L., Kramer, W.T., Kaltz, T.L., Bailey, D.H.: ESP: a system utilization benchmark. In: ACM/IEEE 2000 Conference on Supercomputing, p. 15. IEEE (2000)
20. Yoo, A.B., Jette, M.A., Grondona, M.: SLURM: simple Linux utility for resource management. In: Feitelson, D., Rudolph, L., Schwiegelshohn, U. (eds.) JSSPP 2003. LNCS, vol. 2862, pp. 44–60. Springer, Heidelberg (2003). https://doi.org/10.1007/10968987_3
21. Zhou, S., Zheng, X., Wang, J., Delisle, P.: Utopia: a load sharing facility for large, heterogeneous distributed computer systems. Softw. Pract. Exp. **23**(12), 1305–1336 (1993)

Author Index

Printed in the United States
By Bookmasters